The Gardens
of Emily Dickinson

*The immortality of Flowers must enrich our
own, and we certainly should resent a
Redemption that excluded them —*

*Emily Dickinson to
Mrs. Sarah Tuckerman,
1877*

THE GARDENS OF

Emily Dickinson

Judith Farr

with Louise Carter

HARVARD UNIVERSITY PRESS
CAMBRIDGE, MASSACHUSETTS
LONDON, ENGLAND
2004

For George and Ted

Preface

THIS BOOK IS WRITTEN for the general reader, for gardeners, and for scholars interested in Emily Dickinson's life and writing and in nineteenth-century gardening as depicted in American literature and painting. It offers a vision of the poet's life in relation to her avocation—in truth, a second vocation—as a gardener. Through close readings of her poems and letters, I explore how often and how frankly, specifically, and variously she expressed her love for plants and flowers and her conviction that their "world" and her own were one. Although Dickinson's fascination with botany has long been acknowledged, the extensive role played by flowers in her art as in her life has not been deeply considered. Whether she wrote about love or war, ugliness or beauty, vanity or virtue, heaven or hell, her flower garden often provided her with the narratives, tropes, and imagery she required. Occasionally, misreadings of Emily Dickinson's poems have occurred when the critic fails to recognize that her subject or governing metaphor is a plant, or mistakes the kind of flower, plant, or even climatic condition she envisions. This book attempts to provide a picture of her horticultural tastes and interests with an indication of their broad extent and application.

The book purposely adheres to no single contemporary scholarly methodology and eschews any but the most traditional and classic theoretical terminology. The common names of flowers are assigned their horticultural or botanical identifications; for example, the carnation grown by Emily Dickinson in her conservatory is *Dianthus caryophyllus,* while the cottage pink grown in her garden is *Dianthus plumarius.* Some names are assigned provisionally when the flower to which Dickinson alludes is without an obvious modern equivalent. A list of flowers and plants grown by Emily Dickinson is provided in the Appendix.

Quotations from and allusions to Dickinson's poems given within the body of the text are usually from R. W. Franklin's *The Poems of Emily Dickinson,* Reading Edition (Harvard University Press, 1999). Sometimes, when textual or circumstantial information is needed, Franklin's three-volume *Poems* is cited. This new variorum text, the work of forty years of arduous scholarship, now replaces Thomas H. Johnson's groundbreaking *Poems* (1955)—the first volumes to represent Dickinson's diction, orthography, and punctuation with (for the most part) accuracy. Occasionally a poem will be reproduced here in accordance with its appearance in Emily Dickinson's manuscript books or "fascicles." In her manuscripts, the lineations of her poems often differ—sometimes with exciting aesthetic effects—from those found in the Franklin text, whether by Dickinson's design or from other causes like an indifference on her part to keeping strict quatrain formation or margins in the copies she made for her personal use, or even from poor peripheral vision. The embattled textual controversies that now rage among Dickinson scholars are not addressed at length here because they are not central to the matter of this book. Interested readers may consult R. W. Franklin's *Manuscript Books of Emily Dickinson* to see facsimiles of the poems as Dickinson entered them into her private worksheets. The poet's letters are quoted from Thomas H. Johnson's *The Letters of Emily Dickinson* (Harvard University Press, 1958).

The parts of the book that I have written—the Introduction, Chapters 1 through 4, and the Epilogue—attempt to place Emily Dickinson's love for gardens in the cultural context of her day; to describe its origin, development, and relation to her family's interests; and to consider the architecture and contents of her planted garden as a kind of analogue to those hundreds of poems and poetic letters about crocuses, daisies, daffodils, gentians, trillium, mayflowers, hyacinths, lilies, roses, jasmine, and other flowers that compose the landscape of her art. Her real garden served as an index to Dickinson's conception of "that garden *unseen*"—the inner plot she called the soul, with all its needs of cultivation and improvement, and beyond it, in a continually interrogated, distrusted, but yearned-for distance, the garden of Heaven or "Paradise" to which she frequently alludes (L 92).

Chapter 5, "Gardening with Emily Dickinson," was prepared by Louise Carter, whose professional knowledge of flowers and landscape gardening has been a valuable resource for this book. From memoirs of the Dickinson family and friends, from the poet's own testimony, and from modern analyses of the Dickinson grounds, this chapter hypothesizes the contents of Emily Dickinson's garden and conservatory. It also describes the steps one might take to reproduce and maintain them. Those who love Dickinson's poems, those who love gardens may want to grow the flowers *she* did. Therefore, each of the flowers she is known to have cultivated is described, and the best conditions for its growth and care are laid out.

Readers less interested in gardening may still be glad to read descriptions of Dickinson's flowers and their requirements—to learn, for instance, that Emily's "Sweet Sultans," to which she alluded on several occasions with punning delight, were not oriental monarchs but thistle-like blooms from the Levant and, like most of her favorite flowers, heavily scented. Such knowledge clarifies her language in poems and letters and helps to explain tastes that were often confidently paradoxical: Dickinson's passion for the romantic and unknown inhabited a consciousness that saw "New Englandly" and chose to write in both astringent and voluptuous cadences (F 256).

In the Epilogue I address a topic of importance: the seasons as they appear in Dickinson's natural garden and in the garden of her art. While it is true that Emily Dickinson's garden was surrounded by her father's land, it was also in its way a *hortus conclusus,* a private domain like the conservatory or her unpublished manuscripts. The actual garden she gazed at in various seasons helped to inspire the garden of the poems. There, summer and fall, springtime and winter had differing powers that moved her to envision a mythic universe.

Judith Farr

Contents

Illustrations

There is no conceivable

beauty of blossom

so beautiful as words—

none so graceful,

none so perfumed.

Thomas Wentworth Higginson

Introduction

If we love Flowers, are we not "born again" every Day . . .

Emily Dickinson to Mrs. George S. Dickerman, 1886

THIS BOOK IS ABOUT THE SEVERAL gardens of the great American poet Emily Dickinson, who lived from 1830 to 1886 in Amherst, Massachusetts, during that period in American history when nature was most enjoyed and celebrated. It explores her sensibility, art, and vision of life in relation to her knowledge and practices as a gardener. The phrase "several gardens" alludes to the actual spaces where Dickinson cultivated her plants and flowers, the imaginative realm of her poems and letters wherein flowers were often emblems of actions and emotions, and the ideal Garden of Paradise, which—in earnest, incandescent language—she sought to envision beyond the limits of her own grounds.

Emily Dickinson was born in the village of Amherst, Massachusetts, on December 10, 1830, and died there at age fifty-five on May 16, 1886. The indisputable facts of her life are few. Her schooling—first at Amherst Academy and then at Mary Lyon's Female Seminary (now Mount Holyoke College)—was ambitiously classical for a Victorian girl, including Latin, botany, chemistry, and readings in Milton and Pope as well as drawing and singing. It was subsequently enriched through deep intellectual attunements: to literature, art, music, and botany in particular. After age thirty, her days were almost entirely spent on her father's 14-acre property, in the Federal Revival mansion that allowed her a large bedroom overlooking Amherst's Main Street. There, at a table under a window, she wrote most of her almost two thousand poems, watched the coming of dawn and of circuses that visited the village, recorded the meandering steps of the local drunkard, the swaying of a pine nearby, the clamor of the jays, the poignance of memory, the pangs of love and grief, the climbing of the moon up the sky.

She was reproached during her lifetime for her shy avoidance, at first, of unfamiliar company and, at last, of almost everyone but her brother Austin and sister Lavinia. Yet her correspondence was brilliant, intense, and considerable, and included neighbors, old friends, and the relatively new friends she made and deeply cherished. She was called "the Myth of Amherst" by villagers,[1] and one myth attended Emily Dickinson in particular: that she had withdrawn from society out of secret love for a married man, later identified as a Philadelphia minister, Charles Wadsworth. This story was repeated by her sister-in-law, Susan Gilbert Dickinson, and published by Susan's daughter Martha.[2] It was denounced as a lie by Lavinia, who called Emily's withdrawal "only a happen."[3] It may have been invented both to make Emily's "story" fit the well-known mid-Victorian trope of the sublimating spinster and to divert suspicion from another, famous man whom Emily Dickinson clearly cared for: Samuel Bowles, editor of *The Springfield Republican* and a friend of the Dickinson family. When a small collection of Emily Dickinson's poems was finally published in 1890, reviewers remarked (as readers have since) that her understanding of the sufferings provoked by passion was acute and her knowledge of the human heart, vast.

At her funeral, held privately in the Dickinson parlor, it was recalled that birds sang full-throated outside the windows and butterflies flitted among her richly colored flowers. Flowers were of rare importance on that day, May 19, for Dickinson had asked to have her coffin not driven but carried through fields of buttercups to the West cemetery, always in sight of the house. Moreover, Lavinia's placement of heliotrope in her sister's hand and violets and pink cypripedium at her throat had a symbolic significance that Emily would have understood. While some who attended the funeral knew she had been a poet, all knew that Emily Dickinson was a gardener.

Indeed, during her lifetime, Emily Dickinson was known more widely as a gardener, perhaps, than as a poet. Susan Dickinson's unfulfilled plan for a memoir of her sister-in-law listed "Love of flowers" as Emily's first attribute. Her poetry, for the most part privately "published," was often enclosed in letters pinned together by flowers, or in bouquets that made the poem concealed at the flowers' center and the flowers themselves one message. His father said of John Ruskin, whose *Modern Painters* deeply influenced Emily Dickinson, that he was a geologist first and an artist later. Even before she wrote poems, Dickinson was engaged in gathering, tending, categorizing, and pressing flowers. After writing poetry became her central preoccupation, cultivating bulbs, plants, and flowers within a portion of her father's land and in the glass enclosure of a conservatory, built just for her, remained a favorite occupation.

Not only Emily Dickinson but her mother and sister Lavinia tended the gardens of the mansion called the "Homestead."[4] In 1881, Emily speaks with frank possessiveness of "my Puritan Garden," yet in 1877 she describes "Vinnie's Garden [that] from the Door looks like a Pond, with Sunset on it" and deplores the heat, writing, "Vinnie rocks her Garden and moans" (L 685, 521, 502). Martha Dickinson Bianchi suggests that Lavinia's garden was a "riot[ous]" "blur of confusion" with "nasturtiums [running] wild over defenceless peony bushes"—a typical "cottage garden." Emily's sections remained the more disciplined descendants of Mrs. Dickinson's, composing a "mixed border" garden or orderly mix of flowering shrubs, perennials, and bulbs.

Emily had assisted her mother in the garden since she was twelve: first, at a house on West (now North Pleasant) Street, then in the mansion on Main Street. During the 1860s and 1870s, her years of greatest artistic productivity, she was also developing skills at growing gardenias, jasmine, sweet peas, camellias, Gallica roses, oleander, lilies, heliotrope, and many other naturalized and native flowers. Just as her poems were uncommon, some of the flowers she chose to grow are unusual, gorgeous and complex, requiring the grower's knowledge, prudence, and insight. Others like gentians and anemones were wildflowers, associated for her with simplicity of mind and heart, with youth and humility, fresh imagination, and the possibility of everlasting life. All were indices of her own spiritual and emotional state, while in her letters and poems, she continually associates flowers with herself and making gardens with making poems.

It has been argued that Emily Dickinson's devotion to gardening was determined largely by her membership in the upper class of New England, and her "floral preferences . . . [were] saturated with the language and supposition of class distinctions."[5] That her father built a conservatory especially for her use has been interpreted as a snobbish effort to distinguish her from rural or lower-class Amherst women who kept gardens. But Dickinson's passion for gardening was more intrinsic both to her personality and to a much larger movement in American culture—especially in American literature and painting—than this supposition suggests. Moreover, her conservatory reflected her *need* to have flowers to look at and tend, even in winter.

Mid-Victorians liked to pun on the aesthetic associations between "posies" and "poesie." Her flowers were Emily Dickinson's other "poems," which the conservatory could safely enshrine in an age when what Hawthorne contemptuously called women "scribblers" were not always received in society. Indeed, to be a notable gardener was a much more acceptable avocation for mid-Victorian women (meant to be the angel of their house) than to be a poet. Edward Dickinson, who was prouder of his only son's letters than of his brilliant daughter's poems, may have given Emily a conservatory not only because he wished to please her but because growing flowers was, to him, a more suitable occupation for a woman than writing verse.

Emily Dickinson's obituary, written by her sister-in-law Susan and published in *The Springfield Republican* on May 18, 1886, made as much—even more—of her housekeeping arts and horticultural skills as her genius for poetry. In fact, Susan Dickinson—perhaps anxious after the poet's death to make a final apology for Emily's reclusiveness—emphasizes her eagerness to send gifts of flowers to neighbors. If Emily was considered difficult to understand in some ways, her love for gardening was not:

> The death of Miss Emily Dickinson, daughter of the late Edward Dickinson, at Amherst on Saturday, makes another sad inroad on the small circle so long occupying the family mansion. . . . Very few in the village, except among the older inhabitants, knew Miss Emily personally, although the facts of her seclusion and intellectual brilliancy were familiar Amherst traditions. There are many houses among all classes into which treasures of fruit and flowers were constantly sent, that will forever miss those evidences of her unselfish consideration. . . . One can only speak of 'duties beautifully done'; of her gentle tillage of the rare flowers filling her conservatory, into which, as into the heavenly Paradise, entered nothing that could defile, and which was ever abloom in frost or sunshine, so well she knew her chemistries.[6]

Although Susan writes admiringly (if impressionistically) of Emily's poems—her "swift poetic rapture [that] was like the long glistening note of a bird . . . in the June woods at high noon," it is to her gardening that she attributes technical, virtuosic knowledge. The poems, over two hundred and fifty of which were sent to Susan to read over the years, are described as "*tossed* in startling picturesqueness" on the page (emphasis mine)—a remark that is itself startling, coming from one who had constant evidence over four decades of how ardently Dickinson strove for the right word and image. Herself an amateur journalist and an aspiring if incompetent verse writer, Susan tries to explain Emily Dickinson as a sort of female prophet or "magician" "with no creed, no formulated faith, hardly knowing the names of dogmas" (unlike Susan herself, who was a Sunday school teacher, interested in ecclesiology, and a near-convert both to the Episcopal and Roman Catholic faiths). Dickinson's poems are mentioned in the obituary, as might be expected; Susan had once called Emily's poetic project important to her. But the first of Emily's talents that Susan praises is her gift for growing flowers, as if her girlhood friend and sister-in-law had a holy touch that originated in her goodness and sympathy with nature. Thus, in the very first published piece of biographical criticism that exists on Emily Dickinson, her gardening and her poetry are mentioned together. Her artistry in "till[ing]" flowers and her "intimate and passionate love of Nature" are correctly related to Dickinson's poems.

The Dickinson property during the poet's lifetime was in effect a small farm with a barn, a fruit orchard (the plum trees were Mrs. Dickinson's special care), a vegetable garden, and a meadow across the road.[7] Because Dickinson's poems and letters almost wholly concern flowers, chief "Products of [her] Farm," however, this book does not give space to the pear and apple trees, the asparagus and potatoes that her niece remembers (F 1036). It focuses on the premise that an understanding of the importance to her of flowers in general and specific flowers in particular enriches the understanding of Emily Dickinson's life and art. She herself defined her flowers and her poems as related gifts of the Muse.[8] One of her early lyrics, written around 1859, appears to conflate her poetry itself with the posies or "nosegays"—small ornamental bouquets—that she so often sent to friends, neighbors, shut-ins, and the sick:

> My nosegays are for Captives –
> Dim – long expectant eyes –
> Fingers denied the plucking,
> Patient till Paradise –

> To such, if they sh'd whisper
> Of morning and the moor —
> They bear no other errand,
> And I, no other prayer. (F 74)

It is striking that an artist as independent and original in vision and technique as was Dickinson in her mature oeuvre should associate the writing of poems with the cultivation and presentation of flowers in this way. As the elder daughter of the house and especially after her mother was paralyzed, Emily Dickinson was accustomed to assuming social obligations such as the writing of condolences or congratulations, often accompanied by flowers from her garden or fruit from her mother's orchard. In "My nosegays are for Captives —," she is the fastidious gentlewoman who (with apparent sincerity) called "Publication . . . the Auction / Of the Mind of Man —" (F 788); she presents her activity as both poet and gardener in the guise of corporeal acts of mercy, good deeds designed to relieve both aesthetic yearning and physical debility. There was no "moor" in Amherst, but her father's meadows lay opposite her house. Her poem suggests that, if the reader/recipient of her nosegays/poems is perceptive, the meadows (and the morning) will be made plain by her hand.

Several important lyrics imagine Dickinson's garden as a theater in which the conclusive events of her life take place.[9] Thus, in an early, apparently allegorical poem that begins "Baffled for just a day or two —," Dickinson's speaker encounters what she calls an "unexpected Maid." The maid is not met in the bedroom where Emily composed, bound, and hid her poems; the strange maid is discovered in her garden. At the age of twenty-eight, beginning to compose constantly, she wrote:

> Baffled for just a day or two —
> Embarrassed — not afraid —
> Encounter in my garden
> An unexpected Maid.

> She beckons, and the woods start —
> She nods, and all begin —
> Surely — such a country
> I was never in! (F 66)

This poem was sent by Dickinson to her friend Elizabeth Chapin Holland in the spring of 1859 "with a rosebud attached."[10] Joanna Yin, commenting that "the Dickinsonian garden is a place of possibilities," wonders whether the Maid is "nature, poetry, and the speaker herself."[11] The last lines of the poem might be puzzling if one accepted Yin's reading, for the speaker has certainly been "in" the "country" of her own self for twenty-eight years, has lived in Amherst all her life, and has tended her own garden at the Dickinson mansion since she was twenty-five. The poem might simply be a hyperbolic description of the early coming of spring: the unexpected maid, Flora, who "beckons, and the woods start." "Such a country" would then be a tribute to this spring's loveliness, evident in the budding rose.

But the first lines of Emily Dickinson's poem may invite a different reading. The poem may be describing that moment when a woman who has been writing poetry since she was a girl suddenly realizes that she is meant to be a true poet. She has been "baffled" for some time, apparently by a problem intimately concerned with her own life. Not afraid of the prospect of being called to the artistic vocation, she is nevertheless "embarrassed"—perhaps by her own hubris in conceiving it. The "country" she "was never in" is the Elysium or Eden of poets, rooted in her own garden, where the Muse (a maid like herself) beckons, "the woods start," and "all begins"—that is, where Nature offers herself as the poet's subject. Elizabeth Holland may have been expected to understand only the superficial meaning of this poem: how beautiful is spring, when all bloom recommences. But gardens and spring provoke other births in Emily Dickinson's poetry: the birth of artistic expression and of the emotion requisite to it.

So important were flowers to Emily Dickinson, so knowledgeable was she about botany, that the key to a successful reading of an individual Dickinson lyric can depend on one's knowledge of the background and identity of a plant or flower or of weather and climatic conditions to which the poet may familiarly allude. As an example of the latter, to misrepresent "A Visitor in Marl" (F 558) as dew rather than frost drastically distorts the poem's meaning. Dickinson herself observes that "Frost is different from Dew — / Like Element — are they — / Yet one — rejoices Flowers — / And one — the Flowers abhor —" (F 885). Nevertheless, two critics at least declare that Dickinson's "Visitor in Marl" is dew, and one, engaged in feminist criticism, extends that image to mean a man's kisses that leave the poem's speaker "suspended in desire."[12] But here is the poem itself:

> A Visitor in Marl —
> Who influences Flowers —
> Till they are orderly as Busts —
> And Elegant — as Glass —
>
> Who visits in the Night —
> And just before the Sun —
> Concludes his glistening interview —
> Caresses — and is gone —
>
> But whom his fingers touched —
> And where his feet have run —
> And whatsoever Mouth he kissed —
> Is as it had not been — (F 558)

Dickinson is being supremely clear in this poem. Dew is condensed moisture that actually revivifies ("rejoices") flowers; frost, on the other hand, as Webster tells us, is "a covering of minute ice crystals on a cold surface." Both occur at night, but morning sun dissipates dew, leaving flowers sparkling yet alive and soft to the touch. It is frost, however, especially what is called a "killing frost," that stiffens flowers till they are "orderly" as stone busts and coldly glistening as wet marble—but dead. Dickinson's poem describes the killing of her flowers, an event that always seemed to her like murder. There is no "suspended desire" here, just devastation: "whatsoever Mouth he kissed — / *Is as it had not been —*" (emphasis mine). Finally, Dickinson's use of the word "marl" ought to excite attention as well as delight. Marl can be a white chalky deposit employed for fertilizer. But "marl" is also a contraction of "marble"; the Oxford English Dictionary notes George Eliot's use of the word in *The Mill on the Floss* (1860), a novel Dickinson loved. To Elizabeth Holland in January 1875, Dickinson wrote, "Mother is asleep in the Library – Vinnie – in the Dining Room – Father – in the Masked Bed – in the Marl House" (L 432). The masked bed was the coffin, whose interior might be covered in silk or satin; the marble house was the grave with its headstone. The marble visitor of poem 558 is obviously not dew but death in the guise of frost, and the poem's eroticism is not merely ominous but deadly.

When it comes to horticultural allusion, of course, Dickinson presents (often willful?) challenges to her reader. Sometimes, as in the case of "She dwelleth in the ground," the subject of an untitled poem was originally proclaimed by an attached flower. Keeping the 1863 manuscript of "She dwelleth," her cousin Frances Norcross noted that Emily had sent it to her "With a Crocus" (F 744). One *might* infer that the poem's subject is a crocus, since it most certainly is not about daffodils but about a bulb that dwells "Where Daffodils – abide –." Dickinson places great emphasis on the flower's smallness and "Fairness" of "Grace" and "Hue," all of which suggest the radiant purple-blue or pearly white or golden crocus, the spring flower she so loved. Nevertheless, one cannot be sure. These are among the perils of encounter with a poet who did not write for publication.

Sometimes Dickinson's floral poems seem to be quizzes, a witty game played with her reader with a flower's name the object and answer. Thus, she describes the tulip (and its responsiveness to her affection) in a few lines. But she includes no helpful title, though her first editors provided it in *Poems* (1896):

> She slept beneath a tree –
> Remembered but by me.
> I touched her Cradle mute –
> She recognized the foot –
> Put on her Carmine suit
> And see! (F 15)

Often she spoke of the written word as a flower, telling Emily Fowler Ford, for example, "thank you for writing me, one precious little 'forget-me-not' to bloom along my way" (L 161). She often spoke of a flower when she meant herself: "You failed to keep your appointment with the apple-blossoms," she reproached her friend Maria Whitney in June 1883, meaning that Maria had not visited her in May, as she had promised (L 830). Sometimes she marked the day or season by alluding to flowers that had or had not bloomed: "I said I should send some flowers this week . . . [but] My Vale Lily asked me to wait for her" (L 163). To Samuel Bowles, possibly the "Master" for whom Dickinson wrote passionate letters and poems, she wrote in April 1862, "The flowers waited – in the Vase – and love got peevish, watching." At first using her flowers as a mask for herself, waiting eagerly for Bowles to call upon her, she abruptly drops the mask and *becomes* her flower: "My Hope put out a petal –" (L 259). Just as her garden and conservatory were refuges for a shy poet who was unafraid to write with brave imagination about this world and the next but shunned most people, words were her primary refuge. Her poems, like her flower garden, were a means of creating order and beauty. Far more private than the flowers, the poems were gathered in her manuscript books as acts of self-expression related to her symbolic bouquets. Like her flowers, they were also protection against the blighting disorders of life. With the possible exception of a few narcissi, the flowers of Dickinson's Amherst garden and "the garden off the dining room," as she called her conservatory (torn down in 1915), are long dead (L 279). Yet they live in her poems and letters as one of her primary subjects, chief sources of themes and imagery, and foremost means of exploring her vision of reality.

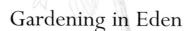

CHAPTER ONE

Gardening in Eden

Every bird that sings, and every bud that blooms, does but remind me more of that garden <u>unseen,</u> awaiting the hand that tills it.

Emily Dickinson to Susan Gilbert (Dickinson), 1852

As a young girl, Emily Dickinson described Heaven to one of her friends as the "garden we have not seen" (L 119). As a mature poet, in a striking group of love poems, she chose "Eden," the lost garden of pure natural delight, as a symbol for romantic ecstasy. Her own home and two-acre garden were "a little bit of Eden" where she herself was "Eve" (L 59, 9). When she died, her neighbors in Amherst mourned the passing of a "rare and strange" woman who seemed like "a flower herself,"[1] an aristocratic recluse who was known to them as much—perhaps more—for her exquisite garden and conservatory as for poems of challenging beauty and complexity.

To Thomas Wentworth Higginson, the Unitarian minister, social reformer, and genial man of letters who would become one of her posthumous editors, the poems Emily Dickinson sent him during a correspondence of more than twenty years resembled exotic "blossoms."[2] In April 1862, in her thirty-second year, Dickinson had first written to him, enclosing four poems in an envelope, inquiring whether he thought her "Verse [was] alive" (L 260). He quickly learned that Dickinson's desire in composing poems resembled that of a scrupulous gardener cultivating new plants: she wanted them to be vital, symmetrical, well-established, and likely to survive. Although the subjects of her poems (as he later classified them) were typical of Victorian poetry and aspired to lasting significance—Life, Love, Nature, Time, and Eternity—they seemed to Higginson daringly unusual in form, dangerously eccentric in tone. Emily Fowler Ford, one of Dickinson's school friends and a disastrously poor but nevertheless published "poet," said that they were "beautiful, so concentrated";[3] yet they reminded her of the curious flowers Emily tended behind the glass walls of her conservatory, her winter garden: "orchids, airplants that have no root in earth."[4] Higginson agreed. To him, the poems were like "skeleton leaves, so pretty but *too delicate*—not strong enough to publish."[5] He told his sister Anna in November 1875 that when he read "some of E. Dickinson's [poems]" "at the Women's Club" he sponsored, without giving the author's name, "their weird & strange power excited much interest."[6] Yet so different did Emily Dickinson's poems seem from the writings of his protégées Helen Hunt Jackson and Elizabeth Stuart Phelps (author of *The Madonna of the Tubs*) that he counseled her never to publish them.

A few years after her death in May 1886, however, Dickinson's energetic and faithful sister Lavinia (failing to coax "Sister Sue" to the task) implored Higginson and her friend Mabel Loomis Todd to edit and sponsor a selection of the more than seven hundred poems which she discovered in a locked chest not long after the poet's funeral. Orchids appear delicate; yet they are celebrated for hardy endurance. Leafing through the poems that Mrs. Todd had copied from Dickinson's manuscripts—Todd called the manuscripts "fascicles," a nineteenth-century synonym for bunches of flowers—Higginson came to recognize their tough earthiness and brilliant intensity. When Roberts Brothers of Boston brought out the slender silver-gilt volume of

Emily Dickinson's *Poems* (1890), it became, to everyone's amazement, an immediate and beloved best-seller. Two later collections in 1891 and 1896 were designed to please a delighted public. Reviewers especially noted the "wondrous ghost of a flower [*Monotropa uniflora,* or Indian pipe] which appears on the cover of [Miss Dickinson's] volumes" and associated it with the poet herself,[7] whose reputation for leading a life of fastidious withdrawal, limited (as Higginson put it) by her "friends and flowers,"[8] was assuming prominence. The Indian pipe, a white woodland flower that grows in hidden places, had been a favorite of Emily Dickinson from childhood. Indeed, the image on the cover of *Poems* was copied from a watercolor that Mrs. Todd had painted for Dickinson before she died [Fig. 1]. The poet had thanked her with rapture: "That without suspecting it you should send me the preferred flower of life, seems almost supernatural, and the sweet glee that I felt at meeting it, I could confide to none" (L 769).

Emily Dickinson had mysteriously worn the white hue of the Indian pipe since her early thirties. She was born in 1830 to Edward and Emily Norcross Dickinson in a wing of her grandfather Samuel Fowler Dickinson's house. It was the same Federal Revival mansion, called the Homestead and now a national shrine, in which she would live most of her life and die. Her grandfather (who helped to found Amherst College), her father (a lawyer and later a member of the House of Representatives), and her brother Austin (also a lawyer and a civic leader) were devoted to politics and public affairs. Different in temperament—Samuel's imprudent philanthropy cost him his fortune; Edward's prudence was proverbial; Austin was canny, but with a vulnerable, impulsive side—they shared a commitment to social improvements that included gardening and horticulture. The "simple wreath of white daisies from his own meadows opposite" that was placed on Edward's coffin (tender, small flowers for a stern, imperious man),[9] the floral tributes brought annually to Samuel Fowler Dickinson's grave, and the brilliant rhododendrons on Austin Dickinson's grounds—all commemorated the Dickinson interest in planting.

1. Panel of Indian pipes painted by Mabel Loomis Todd for Emily Dickinson in 1882.
Amherst College Archives and Special Collections.

In 1874, while planning the Amherst village common, Frederick Law Olmsted visited Austin Dickinson's property, on which some of the flora had been culled during Austin's excursions to outlying valleys and meadows. The great designer of Central Park wished, he said, "to examine the shrubs and trees, the plants and flowers." Eventually, Olmsted would plan the grounds of the George Biltmore estate in Asheville, North Carolina: forest, park, agricultural bottomlands, esplanade, south terrace, bowling green, ramble, and walled garden. "The scale of [that] operation" would be "worthy of a pharaoh,"[10] with Olmsted conveying two or more specimens of 4,200 varieties of trees and shrubs to the site. Close to three million plants were in place there by 1893. That so experienced and clever a gardening engineer as Olmsted would have taken an interest in an Amherst lawyer's grounds is therefore surprising (despite Austin's probable support for him as designer of the Amherst common). Olmsted was said to have been especially interested in how the Dickinsons set out their roses. Did he mean the Austin Dickinsons or their sisters next door, whose trellised roses might easily be seen after a short walk east? Although there are more than four hundred references to flowers in Dickinson's oeuvre, although her allusions to lilies are the most loving and sensuous, the rose appears most often in her poems and letters. Like Emily, Susan Dickinson grew, sent, and "revelled" in flowers;[11] in August 1870 she managed an Amherst flower show. But while Susan's pronounced cultural interests—in books, cuisine, art, décor—were popularly acknowledged, she was not an obsessive gardener. Her chief passion was entertaining—what Emily called "scintillation" (L 491). If Olmsted examined a garden (as opposed to studying plant or tree specimens) in Amherst, it may well have been Emily's garden he visited.

This garden, later considered Emily's, had first been envisioned by *Mrs.* Emily Dickinson, the mother who loved Paris gowns but was said by her poet daughter not to "care for thought" (L 261). A graduate of a Connecticut finishing school, Emily Norcross had been persuaded after years of courtship to marry and lead a "life of rational happiness"[12] (as he put it) with that earnest and upstanding Yale graduate, Edward Dickinson. But she declared that she could not survive housekeeping without a splendid garden. In a popular nineteenth-century guide to gardening and good manners, *Every Woman Her Own Flower Gardener* (1871), Mrs. S. O. Johnson ordained that gardening was an index of gentility because "a beautiful garden, tastefully laid out and well-kept, is a certain evidence of taste, refinement, and culture" to which all women might aspire.[13] Mrs. Johnson summed up beliefs inculcated in American women since the early 1820s, when not mere gentility but knowledge, piety, and good health were thought to be promoted by gardening. In Dickinson's mother, these ideas found a welcome reception.

The poet is said to have told her Norcross cousins, "I was reared in the garden."[14] If poetry made Emily Dickinson exult as "if the top of [her] head were taken off," old-fashioned Bourbon roses with French names thrilled Mrs. Dickinson (L 342a). Emily's mother may have been unintellectual when it came to her family's interests—government, politics, and (in Emily's case) literature—but she was an aesthete about roses. The climbing roses intertwined with honeysuckle in two arbors of Emily's garden at the Homestead were probably inspired in part by her mother's fondness for them. Martha Dickinson Bianchi recalled in the 1930s that "the tiny Greville rose with its clustering buds, each stem a complete little bouquet in itself, . . . was brought by my grandmother from Munson when she came to Amherst as a bride in 1828; and . . . is still cherished."[15]

If that was so, Mrs. Dickinson must have transplanted her Greville roses, at least, when the family moved from the Homestead to a house on West (then North Pleasant) Street when Emily was ten. In 1830, Samuel Fowler Dickinson had been forced to sell the Homestead to a cousin. His son Edward bought the west wing of the mansion; there, the poet was born. Then, when David Mack, a hat manufacturer, purchased the house in 1833, Edward bought the east wing, living there with both his own family and the Macks until 1840. Requiring more space and privacy for his family of five, however, he purchased what Joseph Lyman recalled as a "charming" house on North Pleasant Street in 1840.[16] In this house, Emily Dickinson grew up and lived until she was twenty-five. The house possessed not only a spacious garden but a fruit orchard and a stand of pines. Yet at the rear it overlooked the town cemetery. (Like her adored Charlotte and Emily Brontë, who looked out upon seven-foot gravestones from the windows of their father's parsonage, Emily Dickinson was accustomed to the idea and appurtenances of death from childhood. Indeed, the garden and the cemetery were more than vaguely related in her mind, the dead being described in her mature poems as flowers or bulbs that would arise at a brighter time and season.) In 1855, Edward Dickinson—now a successful attorney—fulfilled his own failed father's dream and managed to repurchase the Homestead.

The Homestead garden, then, remembered for its "long beds" of roses and flourishing seasonal plantings, was not the only garden that Emily Dickinson and her mother knew and tended. It had been preceded by the "beautiful flower-garden" of the earlier house, which Emily rhapsodizes upon in a letter written to a school chum when she was fifteen: "I would love to send you a bouquet if I had an opportunity, and you could press it & write under it, The last flowers of summer. Wouldn't it be poetical, and you know that is what young ladies aim to be now-a-days" (L 8). Although her final phrase smiles at an aspiration to be "poetical," this letter shows that from her earliest years the poet associated flowers with both poetry and affection. In 1842, at the age of twelve, Emily had observed to Austin that it was May and the trees were abloom, yet "our garden is not made yet" (L 2)— probably a reference to the vegetable garden, whose establishment was a criterion of stability. But the care and state of the entire Dickinson garden were always of importance to her. Thus, grieving for her father immediately after his death, she told Fanny and Louisa Norcross with characteristically metaphysical absolutism, "Father does not live with us now—he lives in a new house. Though it was built in an hour it is better than this. He hasn't any garden because he moved after gardens were made, so we take him the best flowers, and if we only knew he knew, perhaps we could stop crying" (L 414).

As a girl, Emily Dickinson was vivacious and as tenderhearted and sociable as her letters quoted above suggest. Yet her profound sensitivity was also apparent. It manifested itself in keen sympathies: Sophia Holland's death when both girls were fifteen, for example, plunged her into deepest mourning. It kindled a lively responsiveness to nature, growth, and change that was dramatically thoughtful and sometimes almost comically grave. If at twenty-three, she wrote, "The ceaseless flight of the seasons is to me a very solemn thought," at only sixteen she confided to a friend, "it is my nature always to anticipate more than I realize" and "I feel that I have not yet made my peace with God" (L 13, 12, 13). Educated first at Amherst Academy and later at Mary Lyon's Female Seminary (now Mount Holyoke College), she was remembered for the enviable precocity of her essays and the pleasure she took in reading, writing, playing the piano, and gathering wildflowers in the woods beyond the seminary. Collecting and preserving woodland flowers was the habit of many girls at Mary Lyon's, for the headmistress was an enthusiastic and avid botanist, having been trained by Dr. Edward Hitchcock, the famous educator, horticulturalist, and author of the *Catalogue of Plants Growing without Cultivation in the Vicinity of Amherst College*. Emily Dickinson was probably alluding to this book (under a made-up title) in telling T. W. Higginson in 1877, "When Flowers annually died and I was a child, I used to read Dr Hitchcock's Book on the Flowers of North America. This comforted their Absence – assuring me they lived" (L 488). Hitchcock encouraged students to make herbariums, collections of pressed flowers that recorded the typical flora of the Northampton and East and South Hadley regions.

Emily Dickinson's passion for wildflowers was singularly intense, even in that era when the common flowers of the field were especially prized, painted, sung about, and studied by scientists like Hitchcock. Her herbarium, moreover, completed at Amherst Academy, included meadow blooms and sophisticated garden varieties, sometimes existing side by side on the same page. At the seminary, she took classes in botany and joined the other girls in combing the woods for plant specimens. Unlike other boarders, she cautiously left her own plants at home, writing her brother Austin, "Some of the girls here, have plants, but it is a cold place & I am very glad that I did not bring any, as I thought of doing" (L 17). Her plants were even then dear charges that called up in her a nearly maternal sympathy.

At Mary Lyon's, Emily Dickinson was regarded as a wit, a mimic, a brilliant essayist and dutiful student, but a girl who, surprisingly, felt no need to "declare for Christ" under the pressure of the Second Great Awakening in New England. Singled out as someone who liked her own company, she was once left behind by other students enjoying a circus event, and later reported, "I enjoyed the solitude finely" (L 16). That Emily was one of the few students who found themselves unable to respond to the coercive evangelical fervor at the Seminary in 1847, and thus unable to join the (Congregational) Church, is evidence of the honesty that characterized her life.

In 1873, Lavinia Dickinson's one-time beau, Joseph Lyman, recorded his memories of Emily and Lavinia and the Dickinson mansion in the 1860s. Lyman was a vain cad who called well-raised girls who would not "pet"—for Victorians, extensive (forbidden) caressing and some undress—"morbid."[17] To his mother, he wrote of Lavinia: "She is a Christian girl and begs me to be very good," but after wooing and then jilting her, he condescended to Lavinia as "poor little soft-lipped Vinnie." Lyman managed to forget his self-obsession sufficiently to be fascinated by Emily Dickinson, however. His description of her, composed when Emily was a woman in her thirties and had given up brown silk for starched white piqué dresses with a pocket in them to hold paper and pencil, recalls her home and books, first, and then her flowers:

A library dimly lighted, three mignonettes on a little stand. Enter a spirit clad in white, figure so draped as to be misty[,] face moist, translucent alabaster, forehead firmer as of statuary marble. Eyes once bright hazel now melted & fused so as to be two dreamy, wondering wells of expression, eyes that see no forms but gla[n]ce swiftly to the core of all thi[n]gs—hands small, firm, deft but utterly emancipated from all claspings of perishable things, very firm strong little hands absolutely under control of the brain, types of quite rugged health[,] mouth made for nothing & used for nothing but uttering choice speech, rare thoughts, glittering, starry misty figures, winged words.[18]

Although Joseph Lyman's sensuality was so cherished that calling Dickinson "a spirit" might have been, for him, no compliment, his remembrance of Emily Dickinson *is* complimentary in its effort to distinguish her from the ordinary run of girls. It provides a marvelously acute insight into a nature and bearing which Clara Newman Turner thought an "angel['s]" but which were "absolutely under control of [her] brain."[19] This was not the case of most girls Lyman tried to seduce. His preoccupation with women's mouths and kisses in other parts of his memoir makes his judgment that Emily's "mouth [was] made for nothing & used for nothing but uttering choice speech . . . winged words" a tribute to her imagination and her power to charm and transport. It is also expressed in a manner foreign to Lyman's usual style, which was florid with cliché. "Choice speech" and "winged words" might serve as a perceptive judgment upon Dickinson's published poems. On the other hand, Lyman denies Emily Dickinson that propensity for passion and susceptibility to love that engendered such poems as "Love – thou art high –" (452), "He touched me" (349), "I gave Myself to Him –" (426), or, indeed, "Wild nights – Wild nights!" (269). To him, her manner and conversation implied austerity.

Nevertheless, one of Lyman's recollections is important. Emily's "very firm, strong little hands" are the hands of a gardener, surely. His confession that, to him, they seemed "emancipated from all claspings of perishable things" is, in retrospect, ironic since she herself made clear that her hands were frequently occupied with helping the servants pick fruit and with planting seeds and tending flowers. Fruits and flowers are eminently perishable; yet by the 1860s, Emily Dickinson, whose chief artistic theme in the poems is "Eternity" and whose quest was always for Immortality, was spending long hours "train[ing]" the ephemeral flowers of her garden, always showing them a more intimate concern than she did her father's favorites: shrubs and trees, a garden's more architectural and ideally permanent features (L 102). The trees of her father's orchard were handsome; she noted the times when "the pines lift their light leaves and make sweet music" (L 129). The pine at her bedroom window was "Just a Sea – with a Stem" (F 849) and, like the other trees, inspired poems that coupled the near with the far—Amherst and the South Seas, the forests of the present with the Bible's oaks and cedars. But flowers seemed to her the best emblems of the eternal. So radiantly did they prefigure the heavenly Paradise that, when she needed a metaphor for something lasting, she saw no reason not to choose them: "Memory is the Sherry Flower not allowed to wilt —" (L 764).

For Dickinson, to whom a garden was a refuge, a sanctuary, and a studio of sorts in which artistic as well as practical decisions were made, flowers were metaphors, of both her own self and others. Flowers were her children, friends, and counterparts. They had souls and played a role in the Christian mystery of death and resurrection. Thus, when a neighbor, Mrs. Adelaide Hills, sent her hyacinth bulbs during a dark February when her own plants were dead or dormant, Emily envisioned the "sleeping" Dickinson garden as the scriptural kingdom of the dead, arisen and transfigured on the Last Day. "The Snow will guide the Hyacinths to where their Mates are sleeping, in Vinnie's sainted Garden," she wrote (L 885). Though she was accustomed to Emily Dickinson's way of writing, this sentence might well have mystified Mrs. Hills. Emily herself had what she called "my Puritan Garden" (L 685). Was she saying that she intended to give Mrs. Hills's bulbs to Lavinia? Was Vinnie to plant them in a snowstorm? Martha Dickinson Bianchi recalled her Aunt Emily sitting near the Franklin stove in her bedroom every winter, hyacinth bulbs surrounding her, her eye quick to mark the slightest green they put forth. Emily's conservatory contained the vanilla-scented heliotrope, sweet alyssum, buttercups, and daffodils, even in February.[20] "Forcing" bulbs was, in fact, one of Dickinson's stratagems against winter gloom. Lavinia had apparently planted *her* bulbs outdoors, where they awaited spring. Snow was regarded in the nineteenth century, as it is now, as protective insulation, an atmospheric incentive for bulbs. Is this what Dickinson meant by saying "The Snow will guide . . ."? Or was snow, in her view, one of the many spirits of nature that order, dispose, and "guide" the landscape in its alterations and changes?

In her next line to Mrs. Hills, she quotes Saint Paul's First Epistle to the Corinthians—a favorite text of Emily Dickinson, who yearned to believe in eternal life: "'We shall not sleep, but we shall all be changed.'" In that age in which the Bible was read daily and committed to memory, Mrs. Hills would certainly have recognized the context of Dickinson's famous quotation: Paul's prophecy about the translation of "this corruptible" into "incorruption," the moment when "this mortal shall have put on immortality":

> As we have borne the image of the earthy, we shall also bear the image of the heavenly. . . .
> Behold, I shew you a mystery; We shall not all sleep, but we shall all be changed,
> In a moment, in the twinkling of an eye, at the last trump.

Paul's passage depends for its power, first, on the antithesis between earth and spirit, then, on the conceit of the earth *as* spirit; devoted gardeners like Emily Dickinson and Adelaide Hills would appreciate both. Bulbs are indeed transfigured when they bring forth bloom from their overlapping membranous tubers that resemble shrouds. To Dickinson, bulbs in particular were emblems of the beauty of the risen body. Not entirely orthodox in her Christian faith, disliking (though not ignorant of) fixed dogmas, she held certain doctrines to be precious, especially that of the Resurrection and the union of body and soul after death. Thus she wrote to Abiah Root when she was twenty-two, "Did you ever know that a flower, once withered & freshened again, became an immortal flower,—that is, that it rises again? I think resurrections here [in my garden] are sweeter, it may be, than the longer and lasting one – for you expect the one, & only hope for the other" (L 91). Still, since her tulips and hyacinths "rose" each spring, the Resurrection itself began to appear to the skeptical Dickinson more likely.

Summing up her life, Dickinson would write three months before her death: "In Childhood I never sowed a Seed unless it was perennial – and that is why my Garden lasts" (L 989). She may have been speaking metaphorically, as she often did, meaning that she never had a strong affection that did not endure. But it was also true that she loved the "Siren Circuit" of perennials, especially woodland flowers (L 983). Some bulbs like the narcissus survive for years in a garden, proof against disappearance and decay. Dickinson's fondness for bulbs probably stems in part from this hardiness and in part from their complexity, their essential richness: they require little to sustain them. About the bulbs of lilies in particular, she was, she said, "a Lunatic" (L 823). Translating her own living but ephemeral flowers into poems about the idea of gardens and the fact of flowers, she could be assured that her art would make nature "perennial."

In 1860, when Lyman was studying her face to make his analysis, Emily Dickinson had developed both a more pronounced shyness and that dislike of social pretension which caused her—who had, she said, a "Heart, which is barefoot always"—to prefer fields to drawing rooms (L 966). After her formal schooling ended in 1847, she returned to what she always called "my Father's ground," baking for her family, helping the servants with canning fruit, paying formal visits, and for a while entertaining and being entertained by the young people of Amherst (L 330). Increasingly, however, she began to dedicate herself (without most people realizing it at first) to an intense and private life as a poet. The artfulness of her letters to friends was scarcely less important to her than the art of her verse. Indeed, it was often in receiving bouquets containing them that friends and neighbors read and came to value Dickinson's poems.

Thus, when she sent "a basket of rare geraniums" to a neighbor,[21] for instance, it was often with a lyric under the leaves. Frances Hodgson Burnett recalled "a strange, wonderful little poem lying on a bed of exquisite heartsease"—pansies—"in a bow," a greeting from Emily Dickinson.[22] In the edition she compiled of Dickinson's letters, Mabel Todd recounted that "in the dim and early dawn of a fragrant summer morning . . . Emily caused a large cluster of sweet-peas to be gathered from her dewy, old-fashioned garden, that they might be put on the very first train to Springfield, taking the freshness of summer to her friends." This note accompanied them:[23]

> Dawn and Dew my Bearers be —
>   Ever,
>   Butterfly (L 1013)

Her sweet peas (wrapped in soaked paper, perhaps) might have survived in an unrefrigerated car; a letter of Emily's written in 1853 observed that the train trip from Amherst to Springfield took only three hours. But perhaps the remains of bright flowers sufficed. She once included the corpse of a cricket in the copy of "Further in Summer than the Birds" (F 895) that she sent to Mabel, entitling the poem "My Cricket."

Dickinson herself called her poems "Blossoms of the Brain" (F 1112). A letter sent to her mysterious lover called "Master" tells him she has given her "flowers" "messages," but whether she means

real flowers or love poems (or both) is unclear (L 187). Making po-
ems, like cultivating gardens, required time, skill, industry, love. In
her large bedroom facing Main Street, she often wrote before dawn,
hearing the birds awake, watching the meadows fill with light. If she
went to the back windows of the mansion, she could measure the
fences that all but ran, she thought, in the morning's brilliance, the
spring daffodils and, later, the dahlias, lilies, and sweet peas of her
summer garden. "I measure every Grief I meet," she wrote of her ana-
lytic mind and meticulous but spacious imagination (F 550). Of land-
scape, she was equally observant. One of Emily Dickinson's most mas-
terly letters describes the career of a fire, like "an awful sun," in the
town of Amherst on the fourth of July, 1879. To her cousins, Louisa
and Fanny Norcross of Boston, she sent a lively account, in which the
presence of the orchard that inspired poems like "A Solemn thing
within the Soul / To feel itself get ripe" enriches the scene:

> *Did you know there had been a fire here, and that but for a whim of
> the wind Austin and Vinnie and Emily would all have been homeless?
> But perhaps you saw* The Republican.
>   *We were waked by the ticking of the bells,—the bells tick in
> Amherst for a fire, to tell the firemen.*
>   *I sprang to the window, and each side of the curtain saw that awful
> sun. The moon was shining high at the time, and the birds singing like
> trumpets. . . .*
>   *And so much lighter than day was it, that I saw a caterpillar mea-
> sure a leaf far down in the orchard . . .* (L 610)

Could she really have seen a caterpillar at the end of her father's
orchard? Hardly. Her vision of the small caterpillar continuing its me-
thodical existence amid the terrifying illumination caused by the
blaze was a painterly conception; like the mid-Victorian landscapes of
Frederic Edwin Church or Martin Johnson Heade, in which a minute
object is distinguished more sharply by being contrasted with a river
torrent or canyon in the distance, Dickinson's painting of "Orchard

with Caterpillar" creates pity, awe, and that "terribilità" which art
critics associate with nature's sublime revelations. Dickinson's rever-
ence for specific detail, carefully observed, was one she shared with
many painters of her day. Evidence shows that she was acquainted
with the style of the Hudson River painters, of whom Thomas Cole
was among the first to interest her and whose *Voyage of Life* series, in
particular, is probably referred to in her poems; she chose Cole's
name as a pseudonym in a letter of 1859.[24] Dickinson shared the re-
spect for detail of American Pre-Raphaelites such as William Trost
Richards, John Henry Hill, and especially Fidelia Bridges, a woman
painter/gardener whose landscapes of finely rendered flowers most
closely evoke Dickinson's precision in her mature floral portrait-
poems.

Most of these painters, like many literary figures of the age, were
botanists, gardeners, and students of nature following the precepts
of John Ruskin, the English artist-critic whose essays on nature and
art shaped the aesthetic of the nineteenth century. The "exuberant
cottage garden" of Thomas Cole, popularly celebrated as the father
of American landscape painting and a poet besides, was a "place of
pilgrimage for the next generation."[25] Celia Thaxter, the poet and
china painter, was as famous for her garden at Appledore on the Isle
of Shoals, Maine, as for her verses; she was painted there by the great
Impressionist Childe Hassam, poised in meditation among her holly-
hocks. The still-life painter George Cochran Lambdin was a skill-
ful gardener who, as an artist, drew roses in particular. Cultivating
roses—an avocation—he regarded as seriously as painting them.
Henry Wadsworth Longfellow had rescued his gardens in Cambridge
from a Mrs. Craigie who would not kill the cankerworms and other
pests that afflicted her elms and roses, telling the poet, "Why, Sir,
[worms] have as good a right to live as we; they are our fellow
worms."[26] By 1870 after he had labored long on his grounds, first
making a flower garden in the shape of a lyre and later like a Persian
rug, Longfellow's plantings were famous. His grounds full of "old-

fashioned pinks, heliotropes, Solomon's seal, spiderwort, bachelor's buttons, and dicentra,"[27] his lilacs and lilies, were the poet's great joy. He kept a conservatory to sustain him when winter came, and like Emily Dickinson, he loved buttercups. The extent to which gardening was honored among nineteenth-century creative artists is illustrated by the fact that a distraught, impoverished, but flower-loving Edgar A. Poe regularly weeded the cramped grounds of his Fordham cottage—his only wholesome entertainment while his teenage wife Virginia lay dying. To Bronson Alcott, gardens were prayers.

In that Wordsworthian age of devout nature worship, poets and painters alike praised floral and plant forms by regarding them closely. Men as well as women artists made thousands of careful studies of both tiny and large plants and flowers, attempting to discover in the intricacy of their forms and the cycle of their lives some link between creation and the Creator. Hill's *Fringed Gentians* (1867), for example, praises a favorite of nineteenth-century gardeners, the gentian now classified as *Gentianopsis crinita,* then identified as *Gentiana crinita* and misspelled by the young Emily in her herbarium as *"crenita."* He observes it closely in a group, its whorls of blue contrasting with red leaves. Dickinson's experimental quatrain of 1858, "The Gentian weaves her fringes –" (F 21), similarly seeks to comment on the textural appearance of the small herbal with its showy blue flowers by distinguishing its "fringes." It was a technique of reverent study of singular details that she began to perfect in her later poetry wherein, as in "The Lilac is an ancient Shrub" (F 1261), the "Corolla," "Calyx," and "burnished Seeds" of a flower become indices of a grander phenomenon. In that ardent, aspirational lyric, the lilac flower is regarded as a sunset in miniature; the sunset, a "Flora unimpeachable / To Time's Analysis –," becomes an emblem of St. John's apocalyptic dream, in Dickinson's favorite Book of Revelation.

The Hudson River painter and essayist Asher Brown Durand had written in his important second letter "On Landscape Painting" that nature was "fraught with lessons of high and holy meaning, only surpassed by the light of Revelation."[28] It was, he taught, the task of both poet and painter to reveal the "meaning" of nature by realistically depicting its forms. The Austin Dickinson household was absorbed by painting; Austin was a passionate collector, first of Hudson River landscapes by Arthur Parton and Sanford Gifford and then of the Barbizon School. Readers of art critics like James Jackson Jarves (an acquaintance of their friend Samuel Bowles), the Dickinsons probably received the *Crayon,* the influential magazine of art criticism which published Durand's nine formative "Letters on Landscape Painting." Since books and magazines passed continually from Austin and Susan to Emily, it is likely that she, too, encountered the new theories of Durand, Thomas Cole, and Frederic Church, which resulted in *plein air* painting, with the artist drawing directly from—and in—nature so as to observe its appearances most intimately, immediately, and reverently, without the sterilizing intervention of the studio. In his canvas *View from Mount Holyoke (The Ox-bow),* Thomas Cole represented himself as a small figure seated in the landscape of that very picture, painting it. The implication of such works, in which the artist is part of his picture—or of poems like Dickinson's "A narrow Fellow in the Grass" wherein seer and seen, the poet and the snake, are composed in one purview—was of a rare and special communion between the artist/poet and God's creation (F 1096). It was the kind of communion that could lead to the exultation Emerson describes in a well-known passage of his seminal book *Nature* (1836), a document of great importance for American writers:

> In the woods we return to reason and faith. There I feel that nothing can befall me in life—no disgrace, no calamity (leaving me my eyes), which nature cannot repair. Standing on the bare ground—my head bathed by the blithe air and uplifted into infinite space—all mean egotism vanishes. I become a transparent eyeball; I am nothing; I see all; the currents of the Universal Being circulate through me; I am part or parcel of God.

Nineteenth-century American poets and painters regarded Emerson's lines as fundamental to artistic aspiration and performance. That Emerson locates the sanctuary of moral and aesthetic stability "in the woods," moreover, is especially significant with respect to Emily Dickinson. Profoundly influenced by *Nature* as well as by Emerson's *Poems* (1847) and *Essays, First Series* (1841), Dickinson had also been an instinctive walker in the woods from childhood. For the cultivated lily and rose, she reserved a passionate attraction, founded on their literary significance as well as their beauty. But woodland flowers pleased her preference for the unsung and unexpected, for hidden loveliness that triumphs over mud, rocks, and thorny places. The plucky triumph of these small, seemingly weak posies over the vast and dangerous woods amused her. She always sought her favorites: the Indian pipe, violet, gentian, fritillaria, anemone, orchis, and lady's slipper.

Emerson's definition of "calamity" as being deprived of eyesight would have heightened Emily Dickinson's anxieties in the late 1850s, when her own sight became impaired. For both Emerson and Ruskin, clear sight (metaphoric and actual) was the primary requirement of aesthetic understanding. The American Ruskinian painter Charles Herbert Moore, for instance, observed, "the truly imaginative mind is a *deep seer*"—that is, one whose inspiration is fed by careful looking. In Dickinson's early poem "The Gentian weaves her fringes," the observed flower is not scrupulously detailed as are flowers in her later poetry. But it does become an index of what she construed as the heavenly garden, in which the humble dandelion (a meadow weed on which she especially doted) adorns God's throne. She loves and "mind[s]," or notices, the gentian because, though apparently insignificant, when it blooms in the autumn it calls to mind the prospect and glamour of the lost summer of carnations and bees. Nature could inspire faith, as it did in Emerson. Then one might divine in the lineaments of "so small a flower" the beauties that are permanent in Paradise. Typical of Emily Dickinson's favorites, they, too, will be simple—bobolinks and dandelions which were golden here and will be golden hereafter:

> We should not mind so small a flower
> Except it quiet bring
> Our little garden that we lost
> Back to the Lawn again.
>
> So spicy her Carnations nod —
> So drunken, reel her Bees —
> So silver steal a hundred flutes
> From out a hundred trees —
>
> That whoso sees this little flower
> By faith may clear behold
> The Bobolinks around the throne
> And Dandelions gold (F 82b)

Emily Dickinson's trouble with her eyes in the late 1850s[29] caused her skill at brilliant description—the lightning's "yellow Beak" and "livid Claw," the moon's "Chin of Gold," the "Purple Ribaldry — of Morning" (F 796, 735, 624)—to be temporarily imperiled. Her malady has been variously defined, either as "exotropia/strabismus," an imbalance of the muscles of the eyeballs that makes steady binocular vision very difficult, or (more probably) "anterior uveitis" or (as it was sometimes called then) rheumatic iritis, an extraordinarily painful disease that causes intolerance of light. Her Boston physician, Dr. Henry Williams, prescribed exercises and forbade her to read, which terrified her. (She told Higginson, however, "When I lost the use of my Eyes it was a comfort to think there were so few real *books* that I could easily find some one to read me all of them" [L 342a]. It was reading Shakespeare that she most missed; as soon as her doctor's ban was lifted, she opened *Antony and Cleopatra*.)

Later, in one of her first letters to Higginson in April 1862, Dickinson confided to him, "I had a terror – since September – I could tell to none – and so I sing, as the Boy does by the Burying Ground – because I am afraid" (L 261). Not entirely cured, her eyes were so irritated by daylight that she had begun to garden in the very early morning, at twilight, or even at night, a lamp beside her. Her neighbors recalled glimpsing a white figure, slightly illumined by lantern light, kneeling in the darkness above her lobelia and sweet sultans. Even in 1865, she wrote the Norcross cousins of her difficulty in looking at bright snow or tolerating daylight indoors: "For the first few weeks [after returning from the doctor's care] I did nothing but comfort my plants, till now their small green cheeks are covered with smiles" (L 302). When the condition improved later in 1865, she kept her habit of gardening at night or in diminished light; strangers thought it an oddity quite suited to "the Myth of Amherst."

Dickinson might have feared a number of things in 1862; but fear of blindness may have been the "terror" that made her "sing" by the burial ground, that is, write poetry—over three hundred poems in 1862 alone—before her ability to survey her lines on the page might be "buried." (The arrangement of her verses was especially important to Emily Dickinson. Dictating her poems might have been awkward. One of the prominent scholarly concerns of our own time, ever since the facsimile publication of her fascicles or "manuscript books," is how actually to print her poems—in hierarchical arrangements such as the quatrain or triplet that she adopted publicly, or in the apparently free-form style she sometimes set down privately in the later fascicles. Because she herself remained what Higginson described as a "Poet of the Portfolio,"[30] never preparing her own verse for publication, Dickinson's artistic intentions, like her life, have been regarded as mysterious and subjected to varied interpretations.)

To her unmarried, sociable Norcross cousins, women who loved literature, the theater, and horticulture, Emily Dickinson always showed an especially tender kindness. It was to Frances (Fanny) and

Louisa that she sent her last letter, a message comprising two words that were the title of a mystery novel by Hugh Conway, popular during her last illness. "Little Cousins," she wrote prophetically, "Called back" (L 1046). Although she was eminently capable of deep love and the manifest affection she showed her Norcross cousins, Emily Dickinson never married. She had at least two (unconsummated) love affairs with men: the married Samuel Bowles, whom her brother Austin claimed Emily loved "beyond sentimentality," and the widower Judge Otis Lord of Salem, who unsuccessfully sought to marry her when she was a recluse of forty-eight.[31] A Congregationalist minister, Charles Wadsworth, was her "closest earthly friend" (L 765). In the course of her life, she also had several intense friendships with women: her schoolmates (of five intimates whom she addressed with extreme sentimentality, pretty Abiah Root, first seen wearing a crown of Emily's loved dandelions, was the favorite); "Sister Golconda," the winsome and maternal Mrs. Elizabeth Holland, "doll-wife" of the editor of *Scribner's Monthly*, Dr. Josiah Holland; handsome Kate Scott Anthon, for a brief period marked by sensuous letters; and, for forty years, with her powerful sister-in-law Susan, to whom she wrote so passionately in youth that some scholars now seek to name Susan as the unidentified "Master" of three of Dickinson's love letters (L 734).

The metaphoric symmetry of her "Master" letters and poems makes it likely, however, that "Master" was a man, whether imaginary—a kind of Apollo or inspirational muse of her art—or actual, or a composite of real and ideal. In *The Passion of Emily Dickinson,* I argue at some length that Samuel Bowles [Fig. 2] may have been her inspiration for the figure called "Master," thus agreeing for additional reasons with several scholars, especially Richard Sewall in his *Life of Emily Dickinson.* Her relationship with Bowles produced letters replete with images and situations identical to those of the "Master" letters and poems. Many of her letters to Bowles are love letters. Certainly she gave him marks of extraordinary favor. In 1874, he was the only person invited to sit apart with the by-then almost apparitional Emily during her father's funeral. Earlier, in 1860, it was to him that she confided the emotions that were causing her to alter the pattern of her life and to confine her days thereafter to her father's grounds. When Bowles died in 1878, worn out by his extraordinary exertions as a crusading editor and philanthropist, she spoke of him as a god: "what he moved, he made" (L 536). She was probably the woman who was known to

2.
Samuel Bowles.
"The past is not
a package one
can lay away. I
see my father's
eyes, and those
of Mr. Bowles —
those isolated
comets" (L 830,
June 1883).

call his death an "eclipse"[32] since Bowles, with his eyes like "comets" and his "graphic countenance," was her personal "Sun" (L 830, 567). In 1884, as George S. Merriam's *Life of Samuel Bowles* was being prepared for publication, she imagined that biography as "a Memoir of the Sun, when the Noon is gone —" (L 908).

A famous, dynamic, even glamorous man, the friend of Emerson and Charles Dickens and, like T. W. Higginson, an abolitionist and supporter of women's rights, Bowles was editor of *The Springfield Republican,* a newspaper read daily by the Dickinson family. He was married to the plain Mary Schermerhorn Bowles, who, disliking Susan Dickinson (said by Amherst gossips to flirt shamelessly with Sam), rarely accompanied her husband on his visits to Austin's home adjoining the Homestead. It was at Austin's house, named (for its many firs) the "Evergreens," that Bowles played shuttlecock with Emily during what Kate Anthon called "celestial evenings" in 1859. During that period, Emily wrote letters that address Bowles and "Master" with extraordinary similarity. Indeed, so precise is the complicity of metaphor used for both men that it is eminently possible to construe them as one and the same. Within Dickinson's prevailing imagery of redemptive light, "Master" is the "Sun" his "Daisy" follows (F 161), just as Bowles himself, who called Emily "Daisy," was given the title of the luminous celestial body that makes daisies grow (L 908).

The actual identity of "Master" is important, of course, only insofar as it may shed light on Emily Dickinson's character and personality and how they are poetically represented. While I am not especially concerned with debating the identity of a real "Master" at length here, having devoted pages to that old *mysterium* elsewhere, still it appears to me reasonable—especially recalling the flower poems consecrated to Bowles, a gardener who sent Dickinson flowers—to defend him as the likeliest candidate. The recent dictum of Alfred Habegger, formed after reading an unfinished essay of Susan Dickinson's entitled "Annals of the Evergreens," seems unpersuasive. Susan describes

Bowles as "the first important visitor to our newly married home." Habegger hypothesizes that Bowles—rather than a stringer for the *Republican*—first went to Amherst to report the result of some agricultural experiments on the farm of Levi D. Cowles on June 30, 1858, was subsequently entertained by Sue and Austin, and may have met Emily.[33] He reasons that Bowles "entered the poet's life after the generally received date of her first 'Master' letter" and therefore could not have been the dazzling personage she associates with flowers, the tropics, brilliance of visage and accomplishment.

According to Thomas H. Johnson (and R. W. Franklin), the first "Master" letter was written "about 1858." Emily herself says in the first Master letter that she is writing while "Spring" is "going by the door"—that is, probably, while Spring is taking her leave and Summer is at hand: some time around June twentieth (L 187). Habegger concludes that since Emily had not met Bowles by then, "Master" was probably either her "Dusk Gem," the "Man of sorrow," Charles Wadsworth (L 1040, 776), or another minister as yet unknown. His revisionist position has been welcomed by a few as sound.

Caveats propose themselves, however. First, the dating of all the "Master" letters is hypothetical. It is entirely possible that this one could have been composed earlier or later than 1858, despite a few minor characteristics of the poet's penmanship (her *d*'s and *t*'s, for example) provisionally attributed to that year. Susan and Austin might have met Bowles and introduced him to Emily earlier than Sue—often wrong in recalling dates, as Habegger admits—remembered. Dickinson used "Spring" and springtime allusions very loosely. Although Susan married Austin on July 1, for example, Emily always thought of theirs as a spring wedding. Most important: If "Master" was addressed first in 1858, another letter *written about June 1858,* Johnson relates, speaks to Samuel and Mary Bowles as if Emily has known and cared deeply for Sam for some time. Following the lead of two earlier critics, Habegger reassigns this letter to June 1859 but provides no reasons for doing so. In the letter, Mary is politely included on this single occasion in the Bowles-Dickinson correspondence. Dickinson writes:

> *Dear Friends,*
>
> *I am sorry you came, because you went away. Hereafter, I will pick no Rose, lest it fade or prick me. I would like to have you dwell here. . . . Tonight looks like 'Jerusalem.' I think Jerusalem must be like Sue's Drawing Room, when we are talking and laughing there, and you and Mrs. Bowles are by. . . . How are your Hearts today? Ours are pretty well. I hope your tour was bright, and gladdened Mrs Bowles. Perhaps the Retrospect will call you back some morning. . . .*

The letter ends "Take Emilie" in those accents of daring tenderness especially reserved for Bowles (L 189). The "tour" mentioned in the letter followed the birth of a stillborn child to Mary Bowles in 1858.

Dickinson's letter to Sam and Mary was followed by another, written in "early summer 1858" to her uncle Joseph Sweetser. Habegger considers this letter "a performance" prompted by recent events concerning her father's business and her mother's illness,[34] but it sounds like the words of an imaginative woman who is amazed by a new personal enchantment: "Much has occurred, dear Uncle, since my writing you – so much – that I stagger as I write" (L 190). What occurred was perhaps an extraordinarily heightened sense of engagement in living or even a sexual awakening that resulted in the increased poetic activity of 1858–59. Emily tells her uncle (who was literary, wrote occasional verse, and could tolerate a metaphor): "Strange blooms arise on many stalks" (L 190). It is unlikely that the Dickinsons had suddenly introduced many foreign floral species to their garden. Instead, Emily appears to be declaring that her world has altered dramatically. As she frequently does, she expresses her feelings in terms of flowers and gardening. Being attracted to Bowles is compared to picking a rose—later she will say he has "plucked" *her*—and the experiences of a summer in which they walked together in her garden mark her life's redesign, as if she herself were her flowers. The tone and content of these letters suggest that Emily Dickinson had already been enjoying those "blissful evenings at Austin's" which Kate Anthon described to Martha Bianchi in 1917.

Whether or not he was "Master," it is obvious from her actions and language that Emily Dickinson's need of Samuel Bowles's attentions resembled that of her self-image, the daisy, for Apollo, the sun god (L 272). That Emily played a less than central role in Bowles's life (which she knew) is true. It is only appropriate to his godhead that Apollo maintains some indifference to the worshipful daisy. Dickinson writes in 1860:

> The Daisy follows soft the Sun —
> And when his golden walk is done —
> Sits shily at his feet —
> He — waking — finds the flower there —
> Wherefore — Marauder — art thou here?
> Because, Sir, love is sweet!
>
> We are the Flower — Thou the Sun!
> Forgive us, if as days decline —
> We nearer steal to Thee!
> Enamored of the parting West —
> The peace — the flight — the amethyst —
> Night's possibility! (F 161)

Samuel Bowles chose two nicknames for Emily Dickinson: if she was his "Daisy," she was also his "Queen." In the Victorian language of flowers typified by Catherine Harbeson Waterman's influential *Flora's Lexicon: An Interpretation of the Language and Sentiment of Flowers* (first published in Philadelphia in 1839, later in Boston in 1852, and popular in New England), the daisy invariably connotes innocence. (This meaning was extant in England, too: Dickens's sophisticated Steerforth calls the guileless David Copperfield "Daisy.") But the Dickinson daisy can be a coy "Marauder," a demure yet crafty tease. In 1863, Dickinson sent a pencil stub across the lawn to Samuel Bowles while he was visiting Susan and Austin, urging him to draw her a picture of a daisy

> Most as big as I was —
> When it [you] plucked me (F 184)[35]

A poet like Dickinson, steeped in the Shakespearean/Elizabethan mode, surely knew how sexually bold these lines are. To be "plucked" is to be "taken," and such a symbol as a pencil "stub" is inherently phallic. Dickinson was continually to play this game of little girl vs. grown man in mutual flirtatious banter that seems to have been actual as well as literary. "Mr. Bowles," as she called him in a parody of naïveté, may have chosen to partner her in the game. In "The Daisy follows soft the Sun —," Dickinson the gardener-poet describes the botanical phenomenon whereby heliotropic plants like the daisy always turn their faces to the sun as an orienting stimulus. Even as she follows her "Master"—here the Christian, biblical overtones come into play—the daisy faithfully gazes at the sun while it sets. "Night's possibility" suggests the boldness of her sexual imagination but also comprehends the fact that night provides a period of rest and renewal for flowers. If "The Daisy follows soft the Sun" was shown to Samuel Bowles, he might have been amused by his "Queen"'s use of the royal "We" in the seventh line.

Unlike Joseph Lyman, Bowles seems to have perceived the tremulous vulnerability and delicate appeal of Emily Dickinson's nature, but he also relished her sense of humor and the freedom and richness of her sensibility. He could sometimes be more hearty than sensitive, however, and blunderingly dismissive of her poems: "Tell Emily to give me one of her little Gems [for the *Republican*]," he wrote Austin and Susan. Bowles candidly admitted to a young poet, Colette Loomis, of West Springfield, "my 'weakness' is not poetry [but] I am always charmed with your little compact . . . poems." "Little Gems" was an accolade with Bowles; still, for his friend, Emily Dickinson, so eager for his approval, it would have been inadequate praise. (Alfred Habegger, among the valuable facts presented by his biography, reveals that the minister Charles Wadsworth considered the steam engine "'a mightier epic than the Paradise Lost,' the telegraph 'a lovelier and loftier creation of true poetry than . . . Shakespeare's Tempest.'"[36] Of the men who attracted Emily in her maturity, only Judge Otis Lord loved poetry.) What struck Bowles about Dickinson's snake poem was not its suspenseful audacity but Dickinson's knowledge that snakes prefer a "boggy acre."

It is significant, however, that Bowles shared several of Emily Dickinson's floral tastes, especially her attraction to wildflowers. In a letter to Austin, written in 1863 when the turmoil of the Civil War was burdening his life and temper, he confessed, "I have been in a savage, turbulent state for some time—indulging in a sort of [illegible] disgust at everything & everybody—I guess a good deal as Emily feels,—I have been trying to garden, too. But I tire out so soon, it is of small use,—& then I am gone for the day. I have to wait for the morning to come again."[37] He was gardening "too"—that is, like Emily—as a remedy for distress. What *her* distress in 1863 might have been is a still vexing question. Probably it was caused by multiple factors. Despite current revisionist critiques to the contrary, long-standing evidence shows that, though loyal, she was increasingly disenchanted and disappointed with her best friend Susan, her brother's gifted but temperamental wife. Higginson's tepid reception of her poems and total misunderstanding of her aesthetic intentions were a severe disappointment, masked by such brilliant disavowals of her own ambition as "Publication – is the Auction / Of the Mind of Man –" (F 788). Though she could write, "I love silence so," the constraints of her life that provided freedom to write—celibacy, semi-isolation, anxiety— gave pain to others, who showed her their resentment (L 843). "Master," described in her poems and letters as godlike but forbidden, had awakened both passion and frustration. Then there was her troubled eyesight.

In his book *The Far Western Frontier* (1869), Bowles enthusiastically described a flower called "the painter's brush" as "a beacon" that "would make a room glow." So burdened by many duties that his doctors claimed he died "worn out" by them—a prostrate Emily said "he found out too late, that Vitality costs itself" (L 542)—Bowles never failed to send Dickinson flowers on the anniversary of her father's death. It was a delicate attention, revealing that he understood her complex anguish for a father she said she never knew in life and who, she said bleakly, became after his death "that Pause of Space which I call 'Father'" (L 418). This attention was paid, moreover, by a vigorous, busy, and public man to a febrile if captivating woman of whose elected reclusion and seemingly neurotic behaviors he was too extroverted and commonsensical to approve. Most Victorians were aware of what was known as "the language of flowers"—indeed, few educated persons could avoid encountering it. Therefore, it is significant that at Christmas 1864, Bowles sent Emily Dickinson what she liked to call a "jasmine Tree" (L 935). A gardener like Emily, he might have known that the fragrant white flowers of *Jasminum officinale* had been given the nickname "poet's jessamine."

The jasmine [Fig. 3] "spoke" a specific language, depending on which of two American floral dictionaries one consulted. In Mrs. Thayer's *Flora's Gems* (1847), for example, the white jasmine connoted passion. To present another with a jasmine plant was to say, "You are the soul of my soul." In the popular *Flora's Lexicon* (1852), composed by Catherine Harbeson Waterman and likely to have been the dictionary Dickinson used if she had one, jasmine connoted separation. Either of these meanings would have been suitable to Emily Dickinson's experience with Bowles. She had told him outright that he was "the soul of [her] soul" in a letter of August 1862, sent to him in Europe: "it is a Suffering, to have a sea – no care how Blue – between your Soul, and you" (L 272). As for separation, Bowles was a frequent traveler—to Europe, New York City, California—whose absences intensified the longing she expressed for him in poems and let-

3. Jasmine *(Jasminum officinale)*. From *Curtis's Botanical Magazine*, 1787.

ters. If Samuel Bowles returned or understood the complexion of her love, the gift of a jasmine plant could have told her so.

Since silence was the "language" spoken by Victorian men and women who loved where they could or should not, communicating by means of flowers had become so unexceptional in the eastern United States by the 1860s as to be portrayed graphically in the paintings of the day. The author of *Flora's Lexicon* declared, "The language of flowers has recently attracted so much attention, that an acquaintance with it seems to be deemed, if not an essential part of a polite education, at least a graceful and elegant accomplishment . . . a desirable, if not an essential part of a Gentleman's or Lady's library." It is possible, though unlikely, that Samuel Bowles had no "meaning" at all in mind when he gave Emily Dickinson "poet's jessamine." Perhaps, in accord with the pronounced contemporary interest in the tropics, he merely wanted to add to the tropical flowers of her conservatory. As a man whose ambition was to be considered literary, however; as a newspaperman in love with the current and timely; as "a practical man, a product of the worldly, workaday side of the Connecticut Valley culture"[38] who was attracted to the Dickinsons for their gentility, he was likely to have understood the fashionable "language of flowers," and that his gift of "poet's" jasmine was a compliment—either to Emily Dickinson's verse or to herself. Whether it was a declaration of love remains a mystery.

Even though Dickinson's letters to Bowles imply his interest in her, and despite his known behavior, often teasing yet solicitous, we cannot know for certain (especially since the Bowles family destroyed his copies of letters to Emily and her letters to him) whether his feeling for her was romantic or brotherly. He had a pronounced reputation for attracting intellectual women like Emily and Susan Dickinson. It was manifest to gossips that he was amorously drawn to Maria Whitney, his wife's cousin and a Smith College language professor. Therefore, perhaps, Dr. Holland made a point of saying at Bowles's memorial service that "his unswerving and undiminished loyalty to the wife of his youth was known to none better than to those noble women [of the highest intellectual grade] who became the devoted and cherished friends of his later years."[39] Bowles—always busy, always pressed— could be remiss in the conduct of his friendships, however. In June 1870, for example, after he and Mary had stayed overnight with the Dickinsons, Emily presented him with the worshipful poem "He is alive, this morning –," a picture of all spring adorning herself to please Bowles while she alone stood "dumb"—a judgment the very fact of her poem belies (F1173). Yet R. W. Franklin reports that Bowles—carelessly? prudently?—"appears not [to] have taken the [poem's] manuscript with him."[40] Whether he chose "poet's jessamine" to indicate romantic attraction or friendship, as a tribute to Emily Dickinson as a maker of both gardens and poems, or in place of an emotion he could not reciprocate, we cannot know. But his gift was among the most cherished she ever received.[41]

To the hanging jasmine was assigned the place of prominence in Dickinson's conservatory. It constituted one of the "rare flowers" under her "gentle tillage," described by Susan Dickinson in her obituary. That Emily Dickinson chose to grow jasmine and did so successfully reveals much about her character. As Louise Carter makes clear in Chapter 5 of this book, both white (*Jasminum officinale*) and yellow jasmine (*Jasminum nudiflorum*) are difficult to grow and bring to bloom. As one who tries to perpetuate her jasmine plants indoors, I can attest to the *Jasminum*'s demanding nature. Emily Dickinson probably spent much effort situating her jasmine properly in the garden where it could profitably summer, bringing it into the conservatory where it wintered, making certain the temperature indoors never went below forty degrees or above sixty, feeding the plant at one stage, withholding nourishment at another, misting and grooming and shrouding it with canvas protection until at last—if only for about one week—she *might* be rewarded with that cloud of brilliant star-like bloom, that incredibly paradisal perfume that make such effort and self-discipline worthwhile. It is not surprising that jasmine was successfully grown by the author of "For each extatic instant / We must an anguish pay / In keen and quivering ratio / To the extasy —" (F 109). Such a spirit would be willing to "pay" some trouble for such loveliness.

Still grieving for him in 1882, six years after Bowles's death, Dickinson sent his son, Samuel Jr., a blossom from the same jasmine plant his father had once given her. Her note of enclosure included a poem:

> Dear friend,
> A Tree your Father gave me, bore this priceless flower.
> Would you accept it because of him
>
> Who abdicated Ambush
> And went the way of Dusk,
> And now against his subtle Name
> There stands an Asterisk
> As confident of him as we —
> Impregnable we are —
> The whole of Immortality
> Secreted in a Star.   E.Dickinson (L 935)

Dickinson's description of the jasmine as a "Tree" probably reflected her astonishment at its vivacity and size. The *Jasminum officinale* is in fact a vine, though lax in form. "Tree" suggests, as well, the size to which it must have grown since the senior Bowles had brought it to her years earlier, while the very word *tree* has a biblical ring: Genesis speaks of "every tree that is pleasant to the sight" being established by the Lord God in Eden (2:9).

Samuel Bowles Jr. invited Emily Dickinson to his wedding. Aware that by the 1880s, only a few years from her death in 1886, she had almost completely espoused solitude, he was probably honoring his father's friendship with her (and his own). He could not really have supposed that she would accept his invitation. Dickinson's letter-poem—now she was signing herself with the solitary letter "E," like her father—was both an elegy and an interpretation of Bowles's life. He had resigned the ways of "Ambush," of lying in wait for the sublime experience of death. Instead, he took "the way of Dusk": his illness was long and his energies slowly drained so that, like a precious day, he sank into evening. For her, Bowles had constituted "the whole of Immortality / Secreted in a Star." A "Star" or "Asterisk" now stood "against his subtle name." Thus, she distinguishes an urbane, highly talented man—by 1850, a gifted member of society was called a "star," and she incorporates the meaning—from everyone else who has lived. But her metaphors are richly complicated, for the five- or six-pointed flower of the white jasmine resembles an asterisk or star, while Dickinson may be calling Bowles's name "subtle" to draw upon Webster's primary meanings of the word: elusive or fragrant. Here, the man she loves is set apart from all others by the flower he gave; his name, like the jasmine, is fragrant of romance.

The long symbolic life led by Bowles's jasmine plant, both in Emily Dickinson's conservatory and in her imagination, suggests how closely flowers were interwoven with the pattern of her days and the progress of her thoughts. In the summer of 1883, she sent Cornelia Sweetser "My first Jasmin" (L 839) [Fig. 4], demonstrating how deeply she still loved that flower which had attained a second blooming under her careful hand. Another gift of the Bowles family illustrates the prominence of the language of flowers and the likelihood, as well, that Dickinson's circle understood and used it. In 1879, not long after Bowles died, Mary Bowles sent Emily Dickinson a cutting from an ivy plant. Thomas H. Johnson says blandly that it "had some association" with her husband.[42] But in *Flora's Lexicon,* as in most Victorian floral dictionaries, ivy meant "devoted friendship." In Elizabeth Wirt's *Flora's Dictionary,* it meant "matrimony," and in Sarah Edgarton's *The Flower Vase,* "I have found one true love." In 1911, Cecilia Beaux painted a moving portrait of the grieving widow Helena deKay, attired in black and clutching a strand of ivy geranium *(Geranium*

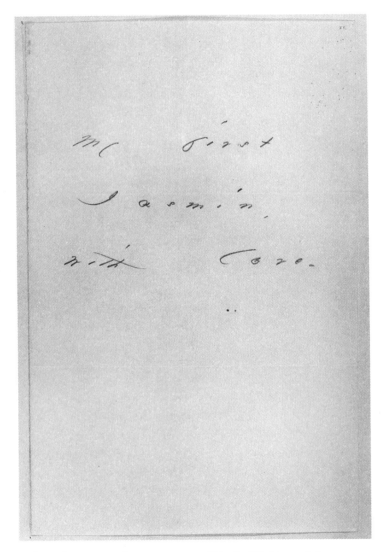

4. "My first Jasmin": manuscript of Emily Dickinson's letter to Cornelia (Nellie) Sweetser, summer 1883.

peltatum). Not only in America but in France and England, ivy was interpreted then—and indeed is now—as the symbol of attachments to which one clings fast despite tribulation.

Evidence shows that Mary Bowles was both angered and hurt by her cousin Maria Whitney's reciprocated devotion to her husband. Emily Dickinson's fervent, if often masked, letters to him might have irritated her as well. Therefore, Dickinson may have tried to forestall resentment by expressing her own feelings during an earlier separation from Bowles as if they were Mary's: "When the Best [Bowles himself] is gone . . . other things are not of consequence – The Heart wants what it wants" (L 262). When Bowles died, his wife apparently accepted this eloquent if strangely reclusive friend as a companion in sorrow. To Victorian readers, the ivy could signify Mary's love for Bowles and Emily's too. In her carefully modulated note of thanks, Emily Dickinson acknowledges Mary's tactful kindness: "How lovely to remember! How tenderly they told of you! Sweet toil for smitten hands to console the smitten!" (L 609). Whether Mary inferred a pun on *smitten*—to be smited by grief or smited by love—we do not know.

❧

Just as Emily Dickinson's letters continually allude to flowers and her poems consider their attributes, few of her personal relationships lack association with them. With the significant exception of the minister Charles Wadsworth, there are revealing connections between most persons she cared for and selected plants: Bowles's linkage with the white jasmine is the most poignant of these, perhaps, given the probable reliance of both giver and receiver on the tacit (yet highly vocative) language of flowers. But other people were also associated with flowers in Dickinson's letters. One may only wonder whether, and how deeply, Dickinson drew on the established language of flowers in making her associations.

Thus, her loyal, brisk, homemaking sister Lavinia is mentioned in Dickinson's letters in concert with sweet apple blossoms and sturdy chrysanthemums. The connotation of the apple-blossom in *Flora's Lexicon* is "my preference"; that Vinnie was Emily's preferred sibling and by way of being her "parents," the poet often made clear (L 391). The chrysanthemum meant "cheerfulness" and "truth": both words are suited to the sprightly younger sister who was Emily's protector and companion, a woman known for bustling good will and the pungency of her talk and opinions. Emily's vivid, ambitious sister-in-law Susan Dickinson [Fig. 5] (called by Bowles the "Queen of Pelham"— Western Massachusetts—because, as a striking hostess, she seemed to hold court at the Evergreens) is mentioned in the company of cardinal flowers and of that grand member of the fritillaria family, the "Crown Imperial." In floral dictionaries, both *Lobelia cardinalis* and *Fritillaria imperialis* signify power, disdain, and mercurial temper, but the Crown Imperial [Fig. 6] is particularly associated with conceit.[43] On one occasion, Emily reports herself deeply moved when Susan,

5.
Susan Gilbert Dickinson ("Sister Sue") as a young woman.

6. Crown Imperial *(Fritillaria imperialis)*. From *Curtis's Botanical Magazine,* 1796.

her chief or cardinal friend, sends her a cardinal flower. As early as 1852, she writes Susan comically, "I have got to go out in the garden now, and whip a Crown-Imperial for presuming to hold it's head up, until you have come home" (L 92). Richard Sewall remarks that most of Dickinson's allusions to Susan acknowledge her powerful personality. As I have pointed out, Susan assumes the code name and characteristics of Shakespeare's Cleopatra in Dickinson's letters and poems because she is clever and handsome yet also untrustworthy and capable of spite.[44] Emily wrote of her—sharply, realistically, perhaps sadly—"those who know [Susan] know her less / The nearer her they get" (F 1433). The Crown Imperial, with its crown-like whorl of orange, red, or yellow blossoms under a tiara of green leaves, is a spring flower that stands sometimes four feet tall. The young Emily's selection of this brilliant flower as a foil to her brilliant friend, her wry image of herself beating down this tall flower rather than another—the daffodils, tulips, or hyacinths that bloom at the same time—suggest (like her less trivial actions: wearing white, hiding behind doors) how metaphoric was her sensibility and how symbolically she lived. The Crown Imperial is a bold, stately flower, even as Susan's fine carriage and dark good looks were themes of Emily's praise. But *Fritillaria imperialis* is also strangely formed, with a repellent scent—like the fox, reported *Curtis's Botanical Magazine* (1796)—that compromises its usefulness in most gardens. Ironically, Susan as Emily's "Queen" was to disappoint and even repel.

Similarly, Susan's gift of the purple-red cardinal flower, a tall midsummer-blooming wildflower, suggests how fully Emily's intimates were encouraged by their culture to live on emblematic terms. *Lobelia cardinalis* is a wildflower especially loved in New England. Its one- to two-inch crimson flowers bloom in late summer, attracting hummingbirds. In 1882, Emily Dickinson composed a sorrowful reminiscence of her childhood by picturing her quest for *Lobelia cardinalis:* "Two things I have lost with Childhood — the rapture of losing my shoe in the Mud and going Home barefoot, wading for

Cardinal flowers and the mothers reproof which was more for my sake than her weary own for she frowned with a smile." She added, "now mother and Cardinal flower are parts of a closed world —."[45] (Dickinson's affection for her mother, which in its full power came late, is nowhere shown so clearly as in this linkage of lobelia with the gracious maternal figure who loved and cultivated it.)

Susan Dickinson's friendship with her sister-in-law would have taught her Emily's passion for wildflowers. Her fondness for hummingbirds, Susan must also have known. The poem "Within my Garden, rides a Bird / Opon a single Wheel —" (F 370) bespeaks Dickinson's lifelong affection for the iridescent bird frequently painted by landscape painters like Martin Johnson Heade. The women's exchange of flowers often had this quality of aptness; their letters acknowledge it. When around 1870 Emily sends Susan "Sweet Sultans"—with phlox and larkspur, the staple of an old-fashioned garden—she writes, "My Turks will feel at Home in her familiar East —" (L 345). Thus she acknowledges the exotic symbolism she chose for her sister-in-law, for Susan's home was west of the Homestead; she was "east" only in Emily's imagination. In 1878, at forty-eight, Dickinson writes to Sue again: "Susan — I dreamed of you, last night, and send a Carnation to indorse it —." The message ends in a poem:

> Sister of Ophir —
> Ah Peru —
> Subtle the Sum
> That purchase you — (L 585)

In the flower dictionaries, a carnation signified several qualities that Susan had shown, as Dickinson's quatrain about pricelessness and exoticism implies. In Hale's *Flora's Interpreter,* it meant "pride and beauty." In Mrs. Thayer's *Flora's Gems,* as in *Flora's Lexicon,* it connoted "disdain." Thomas H. Johnson dates this message to Susan in the winter of 1878; Emily had thus picked a flower from her conservatory to send to her. The carnation, or *Dianthus caryophyllus,* is greenhouse-grown because of the coldness of New England winters; unlike *Dianthus plumarius,* the cottage pink, it cannot be grown in the garden. "Ophir" in the Old Testament was that seaport or region from which Solomon bought gold, ivory, and peacocks. Emily's gift— a poem with a flower—is a tribute, then, to Susan's importance: she is richly endowed with brilliance, like the proud peacock, and she is precious, like the greenhouse carnation.

Susan Dickinson herself prized gifts of flowers if they came from special friends. In a Christmas letter that she wrote to Samuel Bowles, she thanks him for sending her flowers in words of a vaguely amorous complexion. They remind us that Susan engaged in a certain competition with both Austin and Emily for Bowles's attention and affection, and that she made him a confidant about her troubled marriage. (Her letter makes clear that of the two gifts she mentions, Bowles's and Austin's, it is Austin's that surprises her: it is unexpected and it is beautiful despite the fact that it comes from him.) Susan's language—her last line in particular—aspires to the customary *altitudo* of Emily's floral descriptions:

> I was most unexpectedly charmed by [your] flowers – they were perfect and fill the house with their unearthly fragrance – they are on the Library table . . . as I [stroll?] through the halls . . . their odor steals to me[.] [T]here is a suggestion in it . . . [too] subtle for worlds [*sic*] – half memory – half sadness – half hope – Bless you for them. I have planned a similar surprise of flowers for you, and Mary, but I did not carry it out so filled was I with the feeling that you would be loaded with them probably from your numerous city friends . . . Austin surprised me with an exquisite ivory comb, as an ornament for my hair – I hardly know when I have been so pleased with a gift. The thing itself is beautiful, even tho it was from Austin. I'll put it on when you come. Think of [illegible] Austin paying $13.50 for a trinket for his wife . . . I write with the flowers almost touching my hand . . . Sue.[46]

The entire Dickinson circle seems to have expressed itself by means of flowers. As we have seen, Emily Dickinson customarily gave metaphorically suitable flowers to their recipients. Her unassuming friend Sarah Tuckerman was sent a pressed dandelion tied with scarlet ribbon. The dandelion, a simple wildflower, was interpreted by both Waterman and Osgood to signify "a rustic oracle"; Sarah Cushing Tuckerman, wife of an Amherst College professor of botany and respected for her sensitivity and thoughtfulness, was among Dickinson's more pensive and earnest correspondents. Emily's providential aunt, Catherine Sweetser, reminded the poet of Easter lilies, which all the floral dictionaries associate with sweetness. (That *sweetness* puns on *Sweetser* is typically Dickinsonian.) To Mary Bowles, Dickinson wrote often about flowers, often in tones of quiet yearning as though she envies her correspondent her "bright fires" and family life (L 212). In 1859, before the Bowles-Dickinson friendship was far advanced, Mary received thanks on December tenth, Emily's birthday, for the "bright boquet, and afterwards Verbena" that she sent to Amherst. "I made a plant of a little bough of yellow Heliotrope which the boquet bore me," Emily confides, "and call it 'Mary Bowles'"; then she immediately recalls how long it is since the past summer when she walked with Mary and Sam in her garden, now "a little knoll with faces under it" (L 212). (Dickinson's association of heliotrope with Mary Bowles was nonce and fleeting, but the subject of gardens was always a safe one on which to address her: "How is your garden — Mary? Are the Pinks true –?" [L 235].) Emily's brother Austin was linked with the trillium or wood lily: "The Woods lend Austin Trilliums" (L 823). This plant has three leaves (even as there were three Dickinson children), and it signified rank and authority in most floral dictionaries. Austin, an only son and his father's heir, could be imagined as the trillium's single large flower, standing solitary among the low-lying greens.

Emily Dickinson's letters to her brother—much loved but envied, too, for his masculine advantages and their father's preference for him, his law partner and heir—make clear that they were competitors. She saw herself as no apparent match for him, a man in an age when women were subservient. When Edward Dickinson praised

Austin's compositions as being better than Shakespeare, she was especially, if guiltily, dismayed. On the other hand, in one of Dickinson's earliest poems which concludes a letter to her brother, she invites him to leave the dour workaday world of "faded forests" and "silent fields," and enter a more vivid and lasting garden:

> Here is a brighter garden,
> Where not a frost has been;
> In its unfading flowers
> I hear the bright bee hum;
> Prithee, my brother,
> Into *my* garden come! (J 2)

Her letter was sent because Emily wanted her brother to come home. The poem that ends the letter, however, introduces a different thought. Although she always saw their ancestral home as an Eden and refuge, although it is to the Dickinson land that, in sympathy with the body of her letter, she bids Austin return from afar, Emily's poem describes "a brighter garden" of "unfading flowers" to which frost has never come. Such a garden could never exist, except in metaphor. "My garden" is the garden of herself: her imagination, her love, each of which, she says, will outlast time. As well as any other in the Dickinson canon, this early poem, probably written when Dickinson was twenty-one, discloses the rapt identification she made between herself, her creativity, and her flowers. While she characterizes herself elsewhere as the retiring but perennial anemone or Indian pipe or arbutus, or the "modest," "low," "small" daisy—one of the favorite flowers of the Pre-Raphaelite and Aesthetic movements, and a flower continually celebrated in the drawings and poems of her day—"Here is a brighter garden" instinctively focuses on the garden of her mind, with its loving thoughts that transcend the "frost" of death. She thus invites her brother to give up the city life and return to nature and the life of the affections.

Judge Otis Phillips Lord of Salem [Fig. 7], eighteen years older

7.
Judge Otis Phillips Lord,
Emily Dickinson's suitor,
at age forty-eight.

than she and her father's best friend, asked Emily Dickinson to marry him after his wife died in 1877. By that time she was confirmed in reclusion, although Lord's visits to her (like Bowles's in the 1860s) were attempts to woo her to a wider sphere. Lord may have loved Dickinson as a child or young woman; certainly he was "the last great love of her life."[47] Probably because most of her important love poems had been written by the time she and Judge Lord were seriously considering marriage, too little has been made of their friendship.[48] Unlike her attraction to Susan Gilbert and her infatuation with Samuel Bowles, we *know* that Emily Dickinson's love for Otis Lord was reciprocated. Therefore, the letters they exchanged for seven years before he unexpectedly died of a stroke in 1884 provide a glimpse of the poet as a woman, profoundly attractive to a famous man who was "cast," his colleagues agreed, "in a large and heroic mould."[49]

Lord once wrote, "He that becomes master of the human mind and human passions has achieved a greater triumph than he who has discovered a planet." His respect for poets and poetry was complete. Shakespeare was for him, as for Emily Dickinson, the great experience; one of Lord's gifts to the poet was a Shakespeare Concordance. Reading Dickinson's eloquent, profoundly sensuous letters to Lord, written in her late forties, is, as Millicent Todd Bingham claimed, a "Revelation" of her ability to voice passionate yearning. In thoughtful, mellifluous, witty passages charged with Shakespearean allusion—especially to *Romeo and Juliet,* the sonnets, and *Othello*—she writes more directly and confidently than she did in her anxious letters to "Master." Certainly she writes with explicit sexual daring, and with innuendo equal to any in the letters to Susan Gilbert that persuade some writers to confine her as a lesbian poet. Especially remarkable in these letters is Dickinson's emphasis on envisioning the act of love, the "chapter . . . in the night," as she calls it, which she regards with a mixture of delight, curiosity, awe, longing, roguishness, and professional enterprise—a challenge to her powers of celebratory description:

I have a strong surmise that moments we have <u>not</u> known are tenderest to you.

It is strange that I miss you at night so much when I was never with you — but the punctual love invokes you soon as my eyes are shut — and I wake warm with the want sleep had almost filled —

I kissed the little blank — you made it on the second page you may have forgotten. I will not wash my arm — the one you gave the scarf to — 'twill take your touch away

. . . to lie so near your longing — to touch it as I passed, for I am but a restive sleeper and often should journey from your Arms through the happy night, but you will lift me back, wont you, for only there I ask to be —

(L 645, 562)

Emily Dickinson's indifferent health as well as Lord's conspired with the long-established pattern of her life to prevent their marriage; indeed, Dickinson wrote her ardent lover tellingly that in asking for her "Crust," he doomed the "Bread": that is, by inviting her to surrender her social self to him by moving to Salem and taking up a wife's duties, he was requiring her to sacrifice her inner, artist's self, the self that was her staff of life, the self that wrote poems (L 562). Lord died while they were still faithful correspondents. And though he was neither gardener nor sentimentalist, Lord, too, is associated for Emily Dickinson with flowers. When he was dying, she yearned to "fill his hand with love as sweet as Orchard Blossoms" (L 751). Affianced to him only in words and dreams, she chose a flower that New England brides often wore: apple in lieu of orange blossoms. After he died, she remembered that in Lord's last letter he had told her of spying "a crocus and a snowdrop in my yesterday's walk"—news that would have pleased his wildflower-loving correspondent far more than any tidings of civic significance. She added sadly, "the sweet Beings outlived him" (L 892). Since the crocus is notoriously short-lived, she may have been emphasizing how swiftly the judge succumbed to death.

T. W. ("Wentworth") Higginson recorded in his diary that at Emily Dickinson's funeral, Lavinia "put in two heliotropes by her hand [in the casket] 'to take to Judge Lord.'"[50] The significance of the heliotrope in *Flora's Dictionary* and *Flora's Interpreter* was "devotion." In *Flora's Lexicon,* however—most likely to have met Dickinson's eye and containing meanings identical to those listed in her old botany textbook—heliotropes "say," "I have been intoxicated with pleasure." Surprisingly enough, this is the more accurate connotation for this symbol of romance between the illustrious judge and the poet. Even as she liked to envision humble yellow dandelions—in etymology, the *dent de lion,* or "lion's tooth," for its jagged leaves—surrounding the throne of God, Emily Dickinson might have imagined the purple heliotrope as a worthy emblem of Judge Lord's greatness. Purple connotes royalty and triumph in her poetic vocabulary; thus, in "Success is counted sweetest," a victorious army is described as "the purple Host / Who took the Flag," while, for her, Death's "retinue" is "Full royal" and "Full purple is his state!" (F 112, 169). When Lavinia tucked purple heliotropes into Emily's casket, conceiving of a reunion between Emily and her lover in Paradise, she was fully participating in the symbolic rituals of her sister. It had been Emily's custom to greet people by offering them flowers.

Indeed, in one of her possibly autobiographical poems, she describes the visit of a man who has much moved the poem's narrator but whom she has never actually seen. (Seeing and being seen for the sensitive Dickinson, who wrote at twenty-three, "I . . . ran home . . . for fear somebody would see me, or ask me how I did," was almost always a fraught experience [L 127].) Timid but eager to please or placate—she had apparently refused to receive this visitor on an earlier occasion—the speaker carries a flower to him:

> Again – his voice is at the door –
> I feel the old *Degree* –
> I hear him ask the servant
> For such an one – as me –
>
> I take a *flower* – as I go –
> My face to *justify* –
> He never *saw* me – in *this life* –
> I might *surprise* his eye! (F 274)

In her poem, Dickinson's speaker offers flowers to the important caller to "justify" her "face": that is, probably to offer him a lovely appearance that she could count upon—the flower's—to atone for whatever he might find unattractive, be "surprise[d]" by, in her own countenance. In her manuscript, the alternate phrase for "surprise" is "not please," supporting this assumption. Emily Dickinson once called herself "the only Kangaroo among the Beauty" (L 268). In maturity, she never regarded herself as attractive, although as an exuberant fifteen-year-old she bragged to Abiah Root, "I am growing handsome very fast indeed! I expect I shall be the belle of Amherst when I reach my seventeenth year. I don't doubt that I shall have perfect crowds of admirers at that age." Then she added, "But away with my nonsense" (L 6). In some of the "Master" poems, *he* perceives in her face or even bosom a prettiness no one else has noticed.

Austin Dickinson once claimed that Emily retired from society because she knew that she was plain. However, his diagnosis finds no contemporary support.[51] Her dressmaker remembered Emily Dickinson as "handsome."[52] Her schoolmate Emily Ford wrote in 1894, "Emily was not beautiful yet she had great beauties. Her eyes were lovely auburn, soft and warm, and her hair lay in rings of the same color all over her head."[53] As Joseph Lyman's memoir (quoted earlier) records, her eyes—Emily herself described them to an inquisitive Higginson as "like the Sherry in the Glass, that the Guest leaves"—were entrancing, together with her porcelain-white skin, so translucent as to freckle easily; she complained of it good-naturedly in summer (L 268). Some friends, like Lyman, found her shy bearing intriguing. (The mignonette flowers that Lyman juxtaposes to Emily in his memoir, by the way, meant either "you possess moral beauty" or "your qualities surpass your charms"—certainly his estimate of her.) But although Higginson would recall her "beautiful brow" as she lay in her coffin, his first vivid impression was that Emily Dickinson's face had "no good feature."[54]

It was in motion that her niece Martha found her loveliest: gesturing extravagantly as she recited Browning's line "Who knows but the world may end tonight!"[55] Neighborhood children and young relatives remembered her as seeming like themselves—little and fleet, "a tiny figure in white" with "a little body, quaint, simple as a child and wholly unaffected."[56] Yet Emily Dickinson was not tiny—probably she was about five feet four inches tall, not small for a Victorian woman. Her coffin measured five feet six, two extra inches being usually allowed by Victorian undertakers. Her corpulent friend, Helen Hunt

Jackson, poet and author of *Ramona,* remarked that the poet near death reminded her of a dainty moth. Dickinson's preserved white dress, with its fine pleatings and its pocket to store scraps of paper and pencil, suggests that she was probably a modern size six or eight "Petite."

In writing to his wife on August 16, 1870, of a first meeting with his correspondent Emily Dickinson, Thomas Wentworth Higginson provided a sketch that attempted a quick insight into her character. Although he was genuinely fond of Dickinson, benevolent in offering her literary companionship, and faithful in seeking to protect her interests after she died, Higginson, like Bowles, was too vividly at ease in the world not to find what her sister-in-law called "Emily's peculiarities" anything but odd. At Dickinson's funeral he paid her a sensitive tribute, reading Emily Brontë's poem on immortality and remarking that the spiritual Dickinson had never "put it off." Yet she remained his "eccentric poetess," and he was capable of repeating his wife's remark of her, "Oh why do the insane so cling to you?"

The sketch he made of Emily Dickinson for Mrs. Mary Elizabeth Channing Higginson, his invalid and beloved first wife, must have illumined for her an existence not so remote from her own, which was necessarily circumscribed by her illness yet cheered by what Dickinson called Mrs. Higginson's "'Books and Pictures.'" The woman-in-white whose company Higginson described was the same who would write Mrs. Higginson six years later, "I bring you a Fern from my own Forest – where I play every Day. You perhaps sleep as I write, for it is now late, and I give you Good Night with fictitious lips, for to me you have no Face" (L 472). Even as Helen Hunt Jackson, congratulated upon her wedding by Dickinson's picture of her flung to "Dooms of Balm," was piqued to inquire what her friend could mean by "Dooms," Mrs. Higginson was probably startled by the poet's allusion to the fact that they had never met by saying that *she* had no face while Emily herself was "fictitious," her "lips"—her words—reaching Mrs.

Higginson as if in a story told by her husband (L 444, 472). The full richness of that story, epitomized in the figure of its heroine, began in the letter Higginson wrote his wife on that August evening:

> I shan't sit up tonight to write you all about E.D., dearest, but if you had read Mrs. Stoddard's novels you could understand a house where each member runs his or her own selves. Yet I only saw her.
>
> A large country lawyer's house, brown brick, with great trees & a garden – I sent up my card. A parlor dark & cool & stiffish, a few books & engravings & an open piano – Malbone & O[ut] D[oor] Papers among other books.
>
> A step like a pattering child's in entry & in glided a little plain woman with two smooth bands of reddish hair & a face a little like Belle Dove's; not plainer – with no good feature – in a very plain & exquisitely clean white pique & a blue net worsted shawl. She came to me with two day lilies which she put in a sort of childlike way into my hand & said, 'These are my introduction' in a soft frightened breathless childlike voice – & added under her breath, Forgive me if I am frightened; I never see strangers & hardly know what I say – but she talked soon & thenceforward continuously – & deferentially – sometimes stopping to ask me to talk instead of her – but readily recommencing. Manner between Angie Tilton & Mr. Alcott – but thoroughly ingenuous & simple which they are not & saying many things which you would have thought foolish & I wise – & some things you wd. have liked. (L 342a)

On August seventeenth, Higginson added, "I never was with any one who drained my nerve power so much. Without touching her, she drew from me. I am glad not to live near her. She often thought me *tired* & seemed very thoughtful of others" (L 342b).

It would be amusing to know how Emily Dickinson judged Higginson's conversation and appearance. He was bearded, pleasant-faced, and dapper [Fig. 8], though without Samuel Bowles's "triumphant" dark good looks or the "beautiful" Byronic eyes so lavishly praised in Dickinson's recollections of Bowles (L 489, 536). Immensely generous in her comments about Higginson's published poems, meek in receiving (if not following) his advice on her poetic technique, she nevertheless did, on one occasion, send him a strong, terse quatrain that summed up his genteel, leisurely, and torpid six-stanza lyric, "Decoration." It showed how great a gulf was fixed between his schooled poetic fancy and the originality of Emily Dickinson's imagination, although the affectionate letter in which the poet includes her poem gives no tonal indication that on *this* occasion his "Scholar" was teach-

8.
Thomas
Wentworth
Higginson,
c. 1860.

ing her teacher. Was she merely rendering his theme in her own characteristic accents? Or was she giving him an aesthetic lesson, illustrating (among other principles) that less is more?

Higginson's second, third, and fourth quatrains in "Decoration" declare that the real victor of the Civil War lies in an unmarked grave, which he cannot decorate with flowers:

> One low grave, yon tree beneath,
> Wears no roses, wears no wreath;
> Yet no heart more high and warm
> Ever dared the battle-storm,
>
> Never gleamed a prouder eye
> In the front of victory
> Never foot had firmer tread
> On the field where hope lay dead,
>
> Than are hid within this tomb . . .

Dickinson's quatrain, "Lay this Laurel"—as Higginson generously told Mabel Todd later (having sent it to her "for the pleasure of copying it")—was "the condensed essence of [his own poem] and so much finer." "Lay this Laurel," with its subtle and packed second line "Too intrinsic for renown" and its admirable metrical variation in line three, may have been, in the context of her letter, a symbolic *apologia* for a writing style that Higginson found graceless, spasmodic, and abstruse. Dickinson's quatrain—although it concerns the Civil War, death, memory, and valor, all emblematized by the laurel, fondly associated with art and myth—eschews the "flowery" sentimentality produced by Higginson's predictable substantives, relentless trochees, inversions, and archaisms. Hers is a rigorous poem, brilliant for its paradoxical avowal that the bravery of the dead transcends the capacity of the laurel to commemorate it. The laurel, in fact, cannot "chasten" the brave soldier by its "deathless" presence (as would normally

be the case) because he is "too intrinsic," too much part of the experi-
ence of deathlessness—too immortal—to require decoration:

> Lay this Laurel on the One
> Too intrinsic for Renown —
> Laurel — vail your deathless tree —
> Him you chasten, that is He! (F 1428c)

Perhaps because she had never been the "pupil" he might have un-
derstood, Emily Dickinson was at great pains to be welcoming when
Higginson visited her on that afternoon in 1870. That Dickinson
brought him two daylilies as a first offering has sometimes been
cited as proof of her eccentric, even self-advertising or theatrical
ways. I once imagined her gesture as (in part) an instinctive quotation
of late medieval and Renaissance cultural traditions, vibrantly contin-
ued in Pre-Raphaelite painting. In hundreds of paintings that Emily
Dickinson probably knew through reproductions (see Fra Filippo
Lippi's *Annunciation* [Fig. 9]), the Angel Gabriel extends lilies to
the Virgin Mary; it was his salute to her as a pure maiden, a lily
among women-flowers, and the metaphor of his good news. So estab-
lished was the convention of the Virgin receiving or carrying lilies
that Dickinson's contemporary, the aristocratic Massachusetts water-
colorist-photographer Sarah Choate Sears (1858–1935), made a plat-
inum print of a girl in a white veil clutching white flowers—possi-
bly hosta or freesia—as a seeming metaphor of innocence [Fig. 10].
Carrying flowers to her guest was a gesture that echoes this iconic
image. Dickinson compliments Higginson: his long-awaited advent is
cause for joy.

But the floral dictionaries of Dickinson's era often recommended
conveying messages by means of flowers. "How much easier is it,"
writes Elizabeth Washington Gamble Wirt in *Flora's Dictionary,* "to
present a flower than make a speech!" Wirt's book was published in
Baltimore in 1829 and steadily reprinted into the 1860s. Many of her
lines evoke Emily Dickinson's. "Flowers . . . without lips, have lan-

guage –," Dickinson told Eugenia Hall in 1885 (L 1002). "One may be worse employed than in conversing with flowers," Wirt says,[57] while Dickinson tells "Master" in her first letter to him, "You ask me what my flowers said – then they were disobedient – I gave them messages" (L 187). ("Master" has not understood the meaning of the flowers—or poems?—she sent him; he asks for enlightenment. Wittily, Dickinson's remark conflates posies with poems, the language of flowers with that of poetry, demonstrating that both were equally available to her.)

Her own flowers "spoke" to her; indeed, most flowers did. She reminds Susan Gilbert whom she misses that "your little flowers of moss opened their lips and spoke to me, so I was not alone" (L 88).

9. Fra Filippo Lippi, *The Annunciation.*
Samuel H. Kress Collection, image © 2003 Board of Trustees, National Gallery of Art, Washington.

10. Sarah Choate Sears (1858–1935), platinum print (untitled), young woman holding what is probably either hosta or freesia. Courtesy of the Fogg Art Museum, Harvard University Art Museums, gift of Montgomery S. Bradley and Cameron Bradley, image © 2003 President and Fellows of Harvard College.

Even decayed flowers had voices: "The Stem of a departed Flower / Has still a silent rank —" (F 1543). That is, though "silent," and so no longer capable of conveying its particular floral message, the stem maintains the dignity of its appointed place in "the Emerald Court" of the garden: an echo of its former, speaking self. Dickinson is, of course, being playful and sometimes witty in imagining the voices of her flowers. Yet she does so within a lively, accepted tradition. When flowers "spoke," mid-Victorians understood them to "say" what their forms and colors dictated.[58] Was her gesture of extending daylilies to Higginson also a message? "A Blossom," she wrote, "perhaps is an introduction, to whom — none can infer —" (L 803). A flower was *always* an introduction or passport, and perfect as it was, it might be proffered to anyone.

In the 1840s, '50s, and '60s, there were scores of decorative books which Dickinson might have seen that listed the feelings emblematized by certain flowers. Thus Waterman's popular *Flora's Lexicon* specifically bore as its subtitle, "An interpretation of the language and sentiment of flowers, with an outline of botany, and a poetical introduction," and Dickinson's school text, Almira H. Lincoln's *Familiar Lectures on Botany* (1815), included a floral dictionary that served as Waterman's source. In addition, other dictionaries mentioned earlier—*The Flower Vase* (Boston, 1843) and *Flora's Album* (New York, 1848), as well as Sarah Josepha Hale's *Flora's Interpreter; or, The American Book of Flowers and Sentiments* (Boston, 1832)—contrived to list the botanical names of the flowers and their commonplace meanings as usually established in American (as opposed to European) society, often including poems that celebrated the flowers themselves. While the books agreed that "flowers have . . . been symbols of the affections, probably since our first parents tended theirs in the garden of God's own planting,"[59] they did not, as we have seen, interpret the symbolism of the flowers identically at all times. The daylily, however, was almost universally understood to signify "secret sighs," ever since Erasmus Darwin had established that meaning in *The Botanic Garden*

(1798). In *Flora's Lexicon,* Emily Dickinson would have read that the daylily means "coquette."

Although she claims that Higginson understood the language of flowers, Elizabeth Petrino also infers that "he was unaware that [Dickinson's] offering him 'two day lilies' as her 'introduction' was a calculated act, since according to the language of flowers, daylilies signify, among other meanings, 'Coquetry.'"[60] Yet Higginson wrote later, in a memoir of Emily Dickinson, that on that August afternoon when they met, the decorous spinster entertained him with a charm and "skill such as the most experienced and worldly coquette might envy."[61] As an essayist whose frequent subject was flowers, as one often in the company of women poets acquainted with their language, it seems probable that Higginson could indeed pierce the code that Dickinson's daylilies represented. His subsequent choice of *"coquette"* (emphasis mine) in the Dickinson memoir is striking. But he may merely have "read" the lilies to mean "secret sighs,"[62] the yearning to please and be pleased.

Distinguishing the precise species of flowers associated with Emily Dickinson is worth the effort: such distinctions yield riches in parsing the symbolism of her poems and letters. For instance, which "daylily" did Higginson have in mind when he used the word? The famous Massachusetts horticulturalist and seedsman Joseph Breck, very possibly the Dickinsons' guide in growing flowers, wrote enthusiastically of the "Japan lily," "gorgeous," "hardy," and expensive, in vibrant shades of crimson, pink, white, and gold-and-white. In 1865, Emily wrote Lavinia that the pink lily she had given to the Norcross sisters now had five bell-flowers. Red Oriental lilies were introduced to the United States only in the past seventy years, yet we know that the Dickinson garden included some kind of crimson lily in May 1885 since Lavinia Dickinson invited Mabel Todd to view one in bloom. In November 1884, Emily thanked her aunt Katie Sweetser for a gift of "beloved lilies," saying, "my heart is so high it overflows . . . Easter in November" (L 952). Here she may be alluding to the white "Easter lily" *(Lilium longiflorum)* which she admired greatly and which may have been the kind of lily that inspired her allusions to Matthew 6:28, "the only Commandment that [she] ever obeyed, Consider the lilies" (L 904). Breck used that text in his first edition of *The Flower Garden* (1851) to defend flowers against the charge that they were useless.

In Emily Dickinson's amusedly contemplative, even fond poem "Through the Dark Sod — as Education —," in which a lily's development becomes prototypical of the soul's, the lily has a "Beryl Bell" and a "white foot." That combination suggests the Calla lily, *Zantedeschia aethiopica,* which commonly has only one funnel or bell and is white. Knowing that the bulbs of lilies often attract a greenish mold, gardeners will especially appreciate what is probably Dickinson's pun on "mold" and "mould," or "form," in the final quatrain of this poem. The lily forgets its humble earlier state when it was a bulb covered with mold, Dickinson declares, as soon as its formation in the ground is complete. Then, with its bell, it "swing[s]" like a bell in the meadow, ecstatic as a mystic who has been formed by the spiritual life. Indeed, the Calla lily's "cowl" recalls a monk's:

> Through the Dark Sod — as Education —
> The Lily passes sure —
> Feels her white foot — no trepidation —
> Her faith — no fear —
> Afterward — in the Meadow —
> Swinging her Beryl Bell —
> The Mold-life — all forgotten — now —
> In Extasy — and Dell — (F 559)

It seems likely, however, that the daylilies Emily Dickinson offered Higginson were more closely associated with herself than the white Calla lily. Emily Ford recalled, "When we girls named each other flowers, and I called [Lavinia] the pond lily, [Emily] answered so quickly ['and I am the Cow Lily['], referring to the orange lights in her hair and eyes."[63] Her cow lily was what today we call the common orange *Hemerocallis fulva* or daylily [Fig. 11]. In *The New Book of Flowers* (1866), Breck speaks of several lilies: the *Lilium Canadense* or Canada lily, the *Lilium Philadelphicum,* the wood-lily or "Common Red Lily of our pastures," and various Oriental lilies *(Lilium orientalis)* that were probably the colored ones grown chiefly by Lavinia. But the poet always acknowledged a symbolic identity between herself and her flowers, in this case not even the pond lily she said she "tilled" for years on their grounds (L 760) but the common daylily:

> Where I am not afraid to go
> I may confide my Flower –
> Who was not Enemy of Me
> Will gentle be, to Her –
>
> Nor separate, Herself and Me
> By Distances become –
> A single Bloom we constitute
> Departed, or at Home – (F 986)

In offering T. W. Higginson two daylilies, Emily Dickinson was probably offering her thoughts, friendship, loyalty, and artistry for his pleasure and acknowledgment. Since it was her habit, she wrote, to "pay – in Satin Cash / A Petal, for a Paragraph" (F 526)—that is, to re-quite her debts to correspondents with flowers—the lilies were her thanks, as well, for his letters and concern. Perhaps they were also a plea made by an unknown writer to a famous man; perhaps her gesture was an entreaty:

> The Grace – Myself – might not obtain –
> Confer upon My flower (F 779)

Like others permitted to call upon Emily Dickinson, Higginson kept an image of her that was ever thereafter colored by flowers. When he visited her next a few years later, she offered him a Daphne *(Daphne odora),* which signified "glory": perhaps her own, for by then

11. Daylily *(Hemerocallis fulva)*. From *Curtis's Botanical Magazine*, 1788.

she knew she was a poet; or perhaps it alluded to his own eminence as colonel of a black regiment, Unitarian minister, poet, horticultur-alist, journalist, and sage. To her correspondents, Dickinson contin-ued to send floral self-portraits. Although no painter ever captured her, as Childe Hassam did the poet Celia Thaxter,[64] standing among her beloved lilies and heliotrope, Dickinson encouraged her friends to imagine her thus. She was Eve in her own garden, where "Expulsion from Eden grows indistinct in the presence of flowers so blissful." In fact, she was a new Eve, for whom "Paradise remains" (L 552).

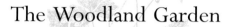

CHAPTER TWO

The Woodland Garden

When much in the Woods as a little Girl, I was told that the Snake would bite me, that I might pick a poisonous flower, or Goblins kidnap me, but I went along and met no one but Angels.

Emily Dickinson to T. W. Higginson, 1862

POSTERITY HAS BEEN PERMITTED only one photograph of Emily Dickinson: a solemn yet revealing daguerreotype, probably taken of her in Amherst in 1847 when she was seventeen [Fig. 12]. Now thought to be the work of an itinerant "Daguerrian Artist" named William C. North,[1] it was immediately disliked by the Dickinson family. Consequently, Emily's severe expression was softened and her prim dress embellished by a romantic white ruff when her niece Martha Dickinson Bianchi included the image in *The Life and Letters* (1924). Emily herself, apparently asked by Thomas Wentworth Higginson at the beginning of their correspondence to send him her photograph, observed, "Could you believe me – without? I had no portrait, now." This was in July 1862. She went on to give him a verbal portrait, possibly inspired by Dante Gabriel Rossetti's tremulously lyrical images of fair women which were reaching the United States in books and magazines: "[I] am small, like the Wren, and my Hair is bold, like the Chestnut Bur — and my eyes, like the Sherry in the Glass, that the Guest leaves —" (L 268).

That her hair was auburn, her figure slight, and her eyes pale hazel-colored were facts rendered for him through metaphor, in images that implied the characteristics of her personality (or, indeed, qualities she wished that she possessed). She was too forthright and intellectual a woman to be described as "wren"-like; the tenacity she showed Higginson in adhering to her poetic methods despite his disapproval would make that clear. But to the Victorian ideal of the submissive woman, Dickinson always paid lip service, often exaggerating her "small[ness]" to entice or to excite the interest of famous men like Samuel Bowles and Higginson himself. "Bold," she certainly was: in the freedoms she took in her correspondence—writing openly of her love to Bowles, for example, or to the young Susan Gilbert, or to Otis Lord—as in the liberties she took with the strictures of conventional prosody. As for the brilliantly obfuscating image of the sherry in the glass left by the guest: Was that image plaintive, implying need on the part of someone who, at thirty-two, felt that she herself had been abandoned by some she had loved? Or was it simply a way of saying that her eyes were "liquid," for the Victorians a mark of beauty?

However unappealing, the 1847 daguerreotype is revealing. It is vivid proof of the poet's dislike of being seen by a predatory world that, she thought, "looks staringly" (L 107). The photographer's subject confronts him patiently but without pleasure. She has been made to assume a traditional pose: her right arm rests on a table covered by a Persian rug, her left hand approaches her right, and there is a closed book on the table next to her. (Otis Bullard's painting of her as a child presents her prophetically with an open book and a rose; see Fig. 35.) This was so conventional a pose for mid-Victorian women that thousands of similar portraits have been preserved in American libraries and museums.[2] Emily Dickinson's daguerreotype differs, however, from most. In her left hand she holds a small bouquet of flowers.

12. Emily Dickinson, daguerreotype taken in 1847 at age seven-
teen. "The quick wore off . . . in a few days" (L 268).
Amherst College Archives and Special Collections.

With the rise of interest in highly specialized flower gardens of so-phisticated cultivars, oil portraits of women both before and long af-ter the Civil War depicted them in the presence of luxurious blooms.

Colonial American painters, from whose depictions of their sub-jects Dickinson's daguerreotypist might have learned, frequently pre-sented women holding flowers, thus following a tradition in Western painting that began in the early Middle Ages. The subject of John Sin-gleton Copley's *Mrs. Moses Gill (Rebecca Boylston)* (1773), for exam-ple, was painted in a luxurious embroidered gown and fashionable turban against a sylvan backdrop, holding a sheaf of exquisite alabas-ter lilies of the Casa blanca variety that were intended by their costli-ness and scarcity to proclaim her husband's great wealth and sophisti-cation. Copley's ladies holding flowers (or sometimes fruit) did not inhabit gardens but, rather, drawing rooms that gave immediately upon theatrical and artificial-looking woods or rivers. The image of Woman seated or standing in a garden enclosure, however, was to be-come a prominent theme in nineteenth-century American art. In lit-erature, it had found superb expression in Milton's *Paradise Lost,* the favorite epic poem of so many mid-Victorian American poets and art-ists like Ralph Waldo Emerson, Thomas Cole, and Emily Dickinson, who playfully called Milton "the great florist" (L 1038). Milton envi-sioned Eve as the "fairest unsupported flower" among the flowers of Eden, his fond conceit probably earning him Dickinson's epithet. That purer Eve, the Virgin Mary, of course, imagined seated in a gar-den—herself a *hortus conclusus* or inviolate garden—had appeared in thousands of medieval and Renaissance images that form the anteced-ents of this theme.

With the rise of interest in highly specialized flower gardens of ele-gant cultivars, oil portraits of women immediately before and after the Civil War envisioned them in the presence of luxurious blooms. There were three essential ways of conceiving the women's relation to flowers: they might be near and in some form of association though essentially separate; they might be attracted to the flowers; or they might lapse into complete communion with nature, epitomized in the floral bloom. Thus, in Mary Cassatt's *Lydia Crocheting in the Garden at Marly* (1880; Fig. 13), for example, the painter's sister is shown near but still distinctly apart from the garden to her right. Dutifully occupied, she seems indifferent to the lush garden while it, in turn, is separate from her: she is not a romantic or even a married figure. In Eastman Johnson's *Hollyhocks* (1876; Fig. 14), the ladies of the household play at gardening and are watched by their maids who titter in the background, probably at their mistresses' awkwardness. There is a suggestion of womanly oneness with nature in the actions of the

13. Mary Cassatt, *Lydia Crocheting in the Garden at Marly* (1880). The Metropolitan Museum of Art, gift of Mrs. Gardner Cassatt, 1965. (65.184) Photograph © 1993 The Metropolitan Museum of Art.

14. Eastman Johnson, *Hollyhocks* (1876).
   Oil on canvas, 25 x 31 inches. New Britain Museum of American Art,
   Harriet Russell Stanley Fund. 1946.7. Photograph by E. Irving Blomstrann.

15. Frederick Frieseke, *Hollyhocks* (c. 1912).
Oil on canvas, 25½ x 32 inches, National Academy of Design, New York
(479-P).

women, however. In both these paintings the flowers are highly decorative, and in different fashions they imply the appearance and/or demeanor of the women. But in his painting *Hollyhocks* (c. 1912; Fig. 15), Frederick Frieseke depicts a lady who nearly disappears into the garden surround, as if she herself were another flower. His is the apotheosis of that yielding to love for the natural that Dickinson voices in many poems. The speaker of her poems, in fact, conceives of herself in all the relationships I have mentioned: as one associated with flowers, as an observer of flowers, as a grower/tender of flowers, but most significantly, as a woman whose emotional sympathy with her garden is so intense that she literally becomes one of her flowers: "I — inhabit Her —" (F 779).

Like painters and poets, photographers also followed the custom of suggesting that Woman was the superior flower in her garden of flowers—or, as Tennyson wrote in the fashionable but complex poem that Dickinson admired, "Maud is here, here, here / In among the lilies." In 1847, however, such representations of women among flowers—a continuance of the late medieval and Renaissance tradition of portraying the Virgin and female saints with flowers and books—were not customary. Usually a daguerreotypist gave women clients flowers to hold only when they were excessively nervous.

May Brawley Hill was the first to note that in Emily Dickinson's daguerreotype, she clasps a small bouquet of "heartsease"—pansies— which signified both faithfulness and modesty in the American flower handbooks.[3] (The pansy-violet or heartsease was also said to be the flower of those able to love eternally. Thus it was noted that a stricken Georgiana Burne-Jones brought a wreath of heartsease to the grave of her husband, the painter, whose allegories about art and life may have been known to Emily Dickinson.) What I wish to emphasize here, however, is that Emily Dickinson, requiring a flower to hold and having probably been given her choice, selected the violet (*Viola*). Until Mary Elizabeth Kromer Bernhard's discovery of the name of the itinerant daguerreotypist who took Dickinson's picture and her mother's in the same period between December 1846 and January 1847, she was thought to have been photographed at Mary Lyon's Seminary. (In my novel about Dickinson's school years, *I Never Came to You in White,* I was faithful to this traditional conception.)[4]

But the real setting, it now appears, was the Amherst House (hotel), not far from the North Pleasant Street house in whose garden Mrs. Dickinson grew a variety of roses—"love-for-a-Day" roses that bloomed from sunrise to sunset, Calico roses of varied crimson and white, and blush roses, mixed with myrtle, box, and peonies—that were later transplanted to the Homestead garden. The rose was the most beloved flower of Victorian art and poetry, the flower most often held by photographed women, especially brides, and the one that appears most often in Dickinson's poems. The scent of roses would fill the Homestead when the Dickinsons entertained during Amherst College commencements. For her photograph, however, Emily must have chosen violets made of paper or silk from among William C. North's store of props. She would tell T. W. Higginson in 1862 that when she was "caught" with the dawn or the sunset, she knew herself to be "the only Kangaroo among the Beauty" (L 268). To hold a rose, symbol in her lyrics of all that is beautiful, might have seemed inappropriate. Instead, she clutches the heartsease that blooms in the same season. One of the oldest of flowers in the Northeast, the pansy or woodland violet may be annual, biennial, or perennial, exotic or naturalized, depending on the specimen. In Dickinson's day, "pansy" and "violet" were terms used indiscriminately. The flower itself, hardy, fragrant, appealing, and richly colored, grew close to the ground from springtime until frost. By 1847, it was an emblem of sincerity as well as modest circumspection in mid-Victorian culture. Not only did Dickinson seek out violets in the woods as a child; her poems often represent her as small and timid, "the slightest in the House" who takes "the smallest Room," as if she herself were a type of the "meekest flower of the mead" like the violet that she loved to praise (F 473, 147).

Dickinson's botanical textbook at Amherst Academy, Almira H. Lincoln's *Familiar Lectures on Botany* (1815), contained a short disquisition on "The Symbolical Language of Flowers." This suggests that the first books on floral language (which were French, typified by Charlotte de la Tour's *Le Langage des Fleurs*) had an immediate effect on British and American horticultural writers. Although Lincoln's *Familiar Lectures* presented a floral dictionary nearly identical in its interpretations to Waterman's *Flora's Lexicon,* the book's approach to plants and flowers was scientific, not sentimental. Its exploration of the importance of woodland flowers like the violet emphasized their naturalness—the fact that they could grow unassisted, unbidden, and in remote places. Dickinson's personal fondness for the violet may have arisen from the fact that, like her (with her secret garden nook from which, unnoticed, she could watch passersby), violets prefer hidden spots, and like the poet who celebrated the superiority of solitary endeavor, they are able, once naturalized, to cultivate themselves.

When in 1862 Higginson asked Emily Dickinson who her favorite writers were, she named Keats, Robert and Elizabeth Barrett Browning, and then "Mr Ruskin – Sir Thomas Browne – and the Revelations" (L 261). (Her favorite writer was of course Shakespeare, but she probably assumed that Higginson would wish to know her more idiosyncratic preferences.) That she put John Ruskin first among prose writers is significant for anyone interested in Emily Dickinson: her life, her art, her gardens. It was probably Volume III of *Modern Painters* (1856) that was especially important to her.[5] But, given her thoroughness and remembering its popularity among the cultivated and among educators in New England, it is likely that Emily Dickinson also read Volume I (1843). In his Preface to the second edition, Ruskin analyzed the distinction between the scientific study of plants and flowers and the "studies" being made of them by poets such as Ralph Waldo Emerson or William Cullen Bryant and painters like Thomas Cole, Frederic Edwin Church, and the American Pre-

Raphaelites. The scientist or botanist—the "Savan" of "'Comparative Anatomy,'" as Dickinson put it (F 147)—

> counts the stamens, and affixes a name, and is content; the other observes every character of the plant's color and form; considering each of its attributes as an element of expression, he seizes on its lines of grace or energy, rigidity or repose; notes the feebleness or the vigor, the serenity or tremulousness of its hues; observes its local habits, its love or fear of peculiar places, its nourishment or destruction by particular influences; he associates it in his mind with all the features of the situations it inhabits, and the ministering agencies necessary to its support. Thenceforward the flower is to him a living creature, with histories written on its leaves, and passions breathing in its motion.

Emily Dickinson, who like a botanist "knew her chemistries"[6] but, like Ruskin's poet, always approached her flowers as quasi-human presences, would address the flowers of the field with subtle understanding of corolla, calyx, and stamen, using such words to delineate their "faces" yet contemplating the specimens in her hand with deep sympathy for their vegetable life. She could *feel* her flowers' condition no matter where she was, she said, writing to Susan from Washington, D.C. in 1855: "as for my sweet flowers, I shall know every leaf and every bud that bursts, while I am from home" (L 178). For her, the gardens without and within the house provided the apotheosis of the artistic subject; she could write of them with an awe she usually reserved for cosmic themes such as God, immortality, the Muse: "I wish I could show you the Hyacinths that embarrass us by their loveliness," she wrote James D. Clark in 1883, "though to cower before a flower is perhaps unwise – but Beauty is often timidity – perhaps oftener – pain" (L 807). That Emily Dickinson associated writing poetry with relieving the pain she experienced "if caught with the Dawn – or the Sunset see me" or the "palsy" she suffered in perceiving "a sudden light on Orchards" was a confidence she made to Higginson in her earliest letters (L 268, 265). She wrote poetry, she confessed, to assuage the painful ecstasy of her encounters with beauty. Together with more cosmic apparitions like sunrise and sunset, her flower gardens were her quintessential experience of beauty. Thus, growing flowers was never a mere avocation but an activity that contributed directly to her poetic project.

The craze for floral paintings that preceded the Civil War and increased when it ended was at first affected by one of Ruskin's central pronouncements: that common flowers or wildflowers in a realistic out-of-doors setting were the best floral subject for all artists, visual and literary.[7] The violet or heartsease was his favorite. In the paintings and watercolors of American Pre-Raphaelites like John Henry Hill, Robert Brandegee, Thomas Charles Farrer, and especially Fidelia Bridges, violets (and other low-growing flowers like the anemone and arbutus) were frequent subjects. William Henry Hunt's *Hedge-Sparrow's Nest with Primroses and Violets* (c. 1840–1850) was characteristic of this genre, which became most fully developed between 1858 and 1870, in the years of Emily Dickinson's greatest productivity.

Such watercolors as John Henry Hill's lovely and reverent *Dandelions* (1858) reveal the same intense respect and fondness for this ubiquitous "weed" that Dickinson demonstrates in her lyrics and letters praising dandelions. Hill's painting focuses on the brilliance and plump opulence of the *Taraxacum officinale,* with its rosette of toothed leaves and bright flowers on hollow stems. His picture is a roundel, the roundness of its shape suited to the roundness of his subject. Like so many nineteenth-century floral still lifes, it is small—only six inches in diameter—and, in the manner of the brief incisive floral poems of Emily Dickinson, it emphasizes the precision of its insights by their intense concentration. Yet Hill's watercolor is also dense, the inner picture space almost completely filled with a variety of leaves and grasses as well as the dandelion's peculiar jagged leaf, suggesting the utter intimacy of this flower with its surround. (Any gardener who has tried to detach a dandelion from the earth knows that even knives and poison will frequently fail to do so permanently. One aspect of nineteenth-century respect for the wildflower had to do with its insistent attachment to nature.) The very fact that two of the best mid-Victorian American artists—Hill and Thomas Farrer—made studies of so humble a wildflower as the dandelion proves the influence of Ruskin's teachings.

One of Dickinson's meditations on the nature of the dandelion, like Hill's, contemplates its roundness, akin to the sun's, and she is fascinated by its arrival and appearance in a winter landscape:

> The Dandelion's pallid Tube
> Astonishes the Grass —
> And Winter instantly becomes
> An infinite Alas —
> The Tube uplifts a signal Bud
> And then a shouting Flower —
> The Proclamation of the Suns
> That sepulture is o'er — (F 1565)

Her poem reveals how closely this poet enjoyed observing a flower's growth in stages: from "tube" or stem to bud to flower, a characteristic her niece Martha recalled vividly in her images of the poet peering absorbedly at each new development of her flowers. In Dutch Renaissance floral painting, it was conventional to depict not just birth but decay and death; often, a broken stem, dying leaves, scattered petals, or even a snail—enemy of gardens—would be shown within the picture space, even though the most gorgeous and brilliant of blooms was the ostensible subject. Likewise, in the American tradition of floral design, watercolorists like Gabriella F. (Eddy) White in her album *Flowers of America* (1876) took obvious pleasure, as did Emily Dickinson, in depicting stages in the career of the dandelion [Fig. 16]. White shows its enclosed and unfolding bud, its near-bloom, full bloom, past-bloom, and then the point of decay when the dandelion turns to white particles, ready for the wind to scatter. In the poem quoted above, Dickinson does not show decay. Rather, her

16. Gabriella F. (Eddy) White, "Dandelion," from *Flowers of America* (1876).

emphasis is on the "shouting Flower" in its assertive butter-colored roundness, which she associates with the "Suns" or succession of sun-lit spring days that proclaim the end of winter, nature's season of "sepulture"—burial. Like Gabriella White's dandelion, depicted with earth still clinging to it, this floral poem imagines the natural setting.

But there is another, more poignant picture of the dandelion that Dickinson set down in pencil on a fragment of wrapping paper in 1879:

> It's little Ether Hood
> Doth sit opon it's Head —
> The millinery supple
> Of the sagacious God —
>
> Till when it slip away
> A nothing at a time —
> And Dandelion's Drama
> Expires in a stem (F 1490).

The Victorian versifier John Bannister Tabb wrote a ditty about the dandelion that, like many poems of the period about violets, reveals the ubiquity of wildflower subjects and the complexity, by contrast, of Emily Dickinson's characteristic approach. In "The Dandelion," Tabb sees the career of that weed as related to humanity's:

> With locks of gold to-day;
> Tomorrow, silver-grey;
> Then blossom-bald. Behold,
> O man, thy fortune told!

Tabb strikes off the stages of the flower's decay facetiously, as if it were a human head. Dickinson also sees a hood, hat, and head in the first quatrain of her poem, but she then shifts in the second quatrain to a vision of the flower's "expir[ation]," entering into the experience of its death with a sense of its microcosmic importance.

Some of the most beautiful of Emily Dickinson's lines were lavished on her garden and its tenants as they sank from color, scent, and liveliness into decay. "I trust your Garden was willing to die," she wrote her Aunt Katie Sweetser in 1880, "I do not think that mine was – it perished with beautiful reluctance, like an evening star –" (L 668). When the outdoor garden, like the planet Venus, "perished" or slowly faded and was extinguished, Emily would immediately begin "prospecting for Summer" in various catalogues with Lavinia (L 689). She cultivated the conservatory flowers more intensely and began to force bulbs in her bedroom. But the deaths of her plants always mirrored human death to Dickinson; they were mystical events to her. In the poem quoted above, the dandelion is seen in its penultimate form or "fruiting stage," corresponding to the filmy fourth "flower" in Gabriella White's watercolor. It wears an "ether" or vaporous "hood" in the first quatrain that cleverly shifts to "a nothing at a time" in the second; that is, the dandelion wears no hood except the one that scatters in near-invisible particles. These particles, like ether, the poet imagines as the "millinery" of God (in his kingdom of air). The "sagacious God" orders the design and array of nature, and for Dickinson, loss and death in particular are parts of his inexorable plan. Still, though the "Sun" and "Drama" of the dandelion in bloom may "expire," both exist in her recollection. To her beloved friend, Mrs. Holland, she wrote in January 1881, "Vails of Kamtchatka dim the Rose – in my Puritan Garden" (L 685). She meant that her garden was veiled by snow, for "Kamtchatka" is a peninsula in northeastern Siberia. Elizabeth Holland was sage enough to infer from the phrase "*dim* the Rose" (emphasis mine), however, that Dickinson's June roses still shone out in her memory.

William H. Gerdts reminds us in *The New Path* that Ruskin "railed . . . vehemently against" the formal floral subject drawn from Dutch seventeenth-century prototypes, and that it was "the casual wayside growth" that inspired American painters and watercolorists of floral still life from 1840 to around 1880.[8] It is exciting to realize that Emily Dickinson—partial recluse though she may have been—was an important member of a whole movement in American art and culture, and that the wildflowers she loved best—clovers, buttercups, daisies, gentians, arbutus, anemone, orchises, daylilies, Indian pipes, violets— were painted with serious care by the most important artists of her time. Dickinson's poem about the Calla lily, for example (discussed in Chapter 1), would find counterparts in many still lifes of the 1860s when that form of lily was "a particularly popular subject." Fidelia Bridges' luminous *Calla Lily* (1875; Fig. 17) with its serene emphasis on the flower's slender perfection does not include a humorous element, as Dickinson's poem does, but both poem and picture focus on the lily's upright integrity. Each still life follows Ruskin's preference for the study of single flowers. Dickinson's acquaintance with contemporary art was not inconsiderable, a fact that I have tried to demonstrate elsewhere. Her poems and letters reveal a sympathy with Hudson River School subjects and Pre-Raphaelite design methods— careful scrutiny of line and color—in particular. When one reads her poems on wildflowers in the light of these movements, it is often with a thrill of recognition.

The violet *(Viola)* was another flower frequently depicted by the American poets and painters of Dickinson's day. Violets were then associated with the coming of spring and the birth of sentiment, as Dickinson shows in a long letter to Susan Gilbert, written at a time when she felt lonely and anxious about the future. She observed, "I write from the Land of Violets, and from the Land of Spring, and it would ill become me to carry you nought but sorrows" (L 85). Yet one of the young Emily Dickinson's most poignant allusions to spring flowers like the violet is tinged with precocious meditations on death and eternity. Thus she muses of a friend who has died, "She gathers flowers in the *immortal* spring, and they don't fade, tho' she picks them all morning, and holds in her hand till noon; wouldn't you and I love such violets, and Roses that never fade" (L 86). Skeptical of the orthodox Christian doctrine of heaven (though yearning to believe in

17. Fidelia Bridges, *Calla Lily* (1875).
Brooklyn Museum of Art, Museum Collection Fund.

it, continually engrossed by it, and longing to see heaven at last), she saw in the garden, with its cycle of birth, decay, death, and rebirth, an idea that rendered heaven plausible. Such paintings as D. G. Rossetti's *The Blessed Damozel,* with its sensuous poem on the same subject, reinforced in the popular imagination the conceit of heaven as garden in Dickinson's time, even in the United States. Death, the enemy depicted so mordantly in her youthful letters, the brutal caller who stole away her childhood friends, could be made bearable by thoughts of a handful of anemone or a sheaf of trailing arbutus, or by a violet cluster or snowdrop, wildflowers that rose each spring and therefore augured eternal life.

Ruskin's later works like *Proserpina* (1875–1881) were filled with allusions to other than woodland flowers, and such charming drawings as his "Twig of Peach Bloom" (c. 1874) would reflect his subsequent interest in studying "the symmetry or order" of all flowers, cultivated or wild, in any setting. At first, however, he described "flowers [such as the violet] relieved by grass or moss" as "the most beautiful position in which flowers can be seen" and viewed humble flowers like the daisy or dandelion as the most natural and excellent of blooms. Like Wordsworth, Ruskin and his followers regarded wildflowers as godly because they seemed closer to God's hand and to the original flowers that must have grown in Eden before human methods of cultivation and hybridization intervened. Samuel Bowles's fondness for roaming the woods for wildflowers (as did Dickinson in childhood) was construed as evidence of his instinctive, rather than systematic, religious piety.

At seventeen, when she clasped the pansies that appear in her daguerreotype, Emily Dickinson could not have known that the greatest art critic of the age would declare a preference for violets and all woodland flowers. Quite simply, they were *her* preference. "Thank you for remembering me when you found the wild flowers," she wrote fondly to Austin in April 1853 as a young poet of twenty-three. She was still, as in her childhood, given to roaming the woods beyond the Dickinson mansion in search of pansies and arbutus, even as she had combed the woods for them near Mary Lyon's Seminary as a lonely girl of seventeen. With the pansy-violet or "heart's ease," she was to hold one of her earliest poetic conversations in 1860. She imagines the small flower speaking to her, perhaps as she comes across it during a walk:

> I'm the little 'Heart's Ease'!
> I dont care for pouting skies!
> If the Butterfly delay
> Can I, therefore, stay away?

The pansy, like the anemone, was a favorite of Emily Dickinson because it came up early, announcing the longed-for spring, and, as a type of bravery, could withstand cold and even an April snow flurry or two in her Amherst garden. In her poem the pansy announces itself boldly, telling her it has been "resoluter" than the "Coward Bumble Bee" that loiters by a warm hearth waiting for May, or the delaying "Butterfly." "Who'll apologize for me?" demands the pansy of the poet, who immediately and playfully warms to her task:

> Dear – Old fashioned, little flower!
> Eden is old fashioned, too!
> Birds are antiquated fellows!
> Heaven does not change her blue.

Personified as flowers sometimes are in Dickinson's poems, the pansy is pleased to be told that her color is "Heaven['s]" color and that, since she is "Old fashioned"—that is, not among the complicated new hybrids and sophisticated cultivars being introduced to the public in 1860—"Eden" is her analogue. That the pansy is spoken of in the context of Eden, mankind's first garden (and Dickinson's metaphor of sensuous delight in poems that enshrine the word), is more evidence that woodland flowers like the violet had a special excellence for her, founded on the quasi-religious conception of their simplicity. Told that her "blue" is heavenly and that Heaven does not alter in color— that is, character and significance—the pansy replies,

> Nor will I, the little Heart's Ease –
> Ever be induced to do! (F 167)

Dickinson implicitly argues a point in this playful poem about the superiority of the natural to the artificial, the simple and traditional to the new and complex. What can truly give the heart ease? Not those things of artificial or, as she liked to say, "Cosmopolit[an]" nature (F 1592). She would make the same point again and again throughout her work, as in her famous early letter to Thomas Wentworth Higginson which declared that "the noise in the Pool, at Noon – excels my Piano" (L 261).[9] Although she loved music, Mozart's especially, and although her piano lessons had been a joy to her at Mary Lyon's and she was known for composing what Susan's friend Kate Anthon Turner called her own "weird & beautiful melodies,"[10] Dickinson tells Higginson that nature's music—water in movement— is more beautiful. Her readers, however, are forced by her poems to reflect upon this rivalry between nature and art and to decide which is more lasting and effective: poems about violets or the violets themselves? In one brief lyric Dickinson herself decides in favor of the "flowers" of art:

> When Roses cease to bloom, Sir,
> And Violets are done –
> When Bumblebees in solemn flight
> Have passed beyond the Sun –
> The hand that paused to gather
> Opon this Summer's day
> Will idle lie – in Auburn –
> Then take my flowers – pray! (F 8)

Probably written, like many of her poems, to accompany a bouquet, this lyric has at its center the prospect of the poet's own death: as a gardener, she gives what will surely "cease"; as a poet, she herself will "cease" and lie in her grave (as she imagines it) in Mount Auburn Cemetery. The concept of Mount Auburn, a cemetery planned and laid out as a garden-park and one whose avenues were named for the flowers she preferred—"Gentian," "Heliotrope," "Violet," "Anemone," "Tulip," "Harebell," "Orchis," "Geranium," "Narcissus," "Daisy," "Camellia," "Primrose"—always strongly appealed to her. But the "flowers" that are her words have—she imagines in this lyric at least—a different destiny. The contest between nature and art, rehearsed in so many Dickinson poems, would find conclusion in a sentence from a late letter: "Your Hollyhocks endow the House, making Art's inner Summer, never Treason to Nature's" (L 1004).

☙

In May 1845, the fifteen-year-old Emily Dickinson wrote to her close friend Abiah Root, "My plants look finely now. I am going to send you a little geranium leaf in this letter, which you must press for me. Have you made an herbarium yet? I hope you will if you have not, it would be such a treasure to you . . . If you do, perhaps I can make some addition to it from flowers growing around here" (L 6). Her own herbarium, which would eventually include over four hundred plants and flowers from the region around Amherst, was already her treasure. It is now preserved in the Emily Dickinson Room of the Houghton Rare Book Library of Harvard University. Its extreme fragility prevents scholars from examining it today, although I was privileged to spend a few hours studying its aspect and contents some years ago. My first experience with a book that had belonged to Emily Dickinson, however, took place when I was a child, sitting with my mother in the Houghton Reading Room. As I watched her gloved hand turn the pages of Dickinson's Bible—a clover from Edward Dickinson's grave had been pressed opposite a page from the First

Book of Samuel, a note told us—I marveled that Emily could read the book's tiny print and conceived her as a small, uncannily perceptive woman. A link between the grieving daughter who pressed the clover and was once a dependent child like me and the terrifyingly brilliant, prophetic, starry intellect that conceived such phrases as "Grief is a Gourmand" (F 753)—which I could not understand but was still besotted with—formed in my mind. My whole life—as is the case of many who read her poetry—was to be shaped and directed by that early moment, spent with the spirit of Emily Dickinson. When I looked years afterward at the Dickinson herbarium with its handwritten names, coarsely constructed paper, and delicately moribund, faded specimens, her passion for flowers became exceptionally real. The photo facsimiles of the herbarium now available to readers at the Houghton Library still present the girl Emily appealingly: the one who misspelled, who arranged pressed flowers in artistic form, who with Wordsworthian tenderness considered nature her friend.

Herbariums were made to encourage the young botany student to identify the names of plants and flowers in a period when botany and geology were major subjects in the schools. "Nature walks," either accompanied or unaccompanied by a teacher, were keys to understanding the appearance and characteristics of plants—one step in comprehending the workings of the universe and, after Darwin, the progress of evolution. Emily Dickinson alludes to them as part of a round of amusements in 1848: "While at home [from school]," she writes Abiah Root, "there were several pleasure parties of which I was a member, and in our rambles we found many and beautiful children of spring, which I will mention and see if you have found them – the trailing arbutus, adder's tongue, yellow violets, liverleaf, blood-root, and many other smaller flowers" (L 23). Her herbarium, for all the scientific knowledge implied by its Latin names, has a genuinely artistic quality, derived from the appealing placement of the floral specimens and from their loveliness, diminished but not eradicated after a century and a half. Inspiring Dickinson's choice of flowers for pressing was not only availability but what May Brawley Hill calls the "informality" of "Grandmother's garden," the old-fashioned pre–Civil War American garden. According to Anna Bartlett Warner's *Gardening by Myself* (1874), "rich confusion" was its "aim": "You want to come upon mignonette in unexpected places, and to find sprays of heliotrope in close consultation with your roses . . . No stiffness, no ceremony."[11] This kind of garden—asparagus waving near phlox, roses entangled with peonies—was what Martha Dickinson remembered about her aunt's plantings.[12]

Like old-fashioned gardeners, Dickinson also used old-fashioned vernacular names for her pressings as well as Latin ones. Some names are wonderfully aromatic: wild cucumber and coltsfoot, stargrass and climbing fumitory, Sol's Seal and scouring rush, pigweed and bellflower, the passion flower and the plantain-leaved everlasting, the candle larkspur and the whorled loosestrife, the rough bedstraw and the robin-run-away, the butterfly flower and love-in-a-mist, the bastard pennyroyal and Dutchman's breeches, the common lousewort and the hog peanut, the mad-dog skullcap and the turtle head, and—appropriately—the Grass of Parnassus.[13] Some of these flowers were wildflowers: Sol's (Solomon's) Seal is *Polygonatum biflorum,* a native flower of damp woodlands, while bastard pennyroyal is *Trichostema dichotomum,* a wildflower member of the mint family. Many though not all of these curious names may be traced to contemporary equivalents: thus, the bellflower is (and has been since the sixteenth century) the common name for the various flowering plants of the species *Campanula,* an exotic not native to New England, while candle larkspur is our *Delphinium.* On the other hand, Darwin writes of the butterfly-flower of the genus *Schizanthus* in 1881 but apparently did not mean what we now call the buddleia *(Buddleia)* or butterfly-bush of the family *Loganiaceae* but rather *Asclepia tuberosa,* a native wildflower of dry meadows. (The correct botanical names of the plants listed above are given in note 13.) In any case, common names stimulated Dickinson's fancy. The poet who wrote—incorrectly but with colorful precision—"I wish I were a Hay" always preferred the provincial to the scientific term (F 379). In his poem "The Humble-Bee," a punning Emerson would also show his fondness for wild-flowers and the vernacular idiom, writing musical lines about "Grass with green flag half-mast high, / Succory to match the sky," "Scented fern, and agrimony, / Clover, catchfly, adder's tongue." Dickinson's arrangement of her pressed flowers shows decreasing interest in their Linnaean categories. Some pages suggest that she grouped flowers together because they may simply have caught and pleased her eye at the same moment.

To those acquainted with Emily Dickinson's temperament and preferences, certain flowers on the herbarium's pages may inspire pangs of delight and sympathy. Many are wildflowers and her favorites. But on the very first page, the first flower pressed by the girl Emily, was the *Jasminum* or jasmine [Fig. 18], the tropical flower that would come to mean passion to her as a woman. This "belle of Amherst," as she once imagined herself, this poet who liked to think that she saw "New Englandly," was, though Puritan in her disciplined upbringing, profoundly attracted to the foreign and especially to the semitropical or tropical climes that she read about in *Harper's* and the *Atlantic Monthly*—Santo Domingo, Brazil, Potosi, Zanzibar, Italy (L 6, F 256). (Indeed, such a yearning for difference is, by rule of the attraction of opposites, a Puritan's dower.) Domesticating the jasmine in the cold climate of New England, writing sensuous lyrics about forbidden love in spare meters, Dickinson followed a paradoxical pattern that related poet to gardener in one adventurous pursuit. Just as her fondness for buttercups, clover, anemones, and gentians spoke of an attraction to the simple and commonplace, her taste for strange exotic blooms is that of one drawn to the unknown, the uncommon, the aesthetically venturesome.

The appearance of the jasmine as the first flower of the herbarium is symbolic of that aspect of Emily Dickinson's life that is most associated with love and crisis. The poet some think of as a maiden recluse—very "spirituelle," as her minister's wife said of her appearance in death[14]—had her own encounters with eros, as the "Master" litera-

18. Page one of Emily Dickinson's herbarium, with a pressed white jasmine at the upper left corner and a pressed yellow jasmine at the lower left.

ture and her many wistful, ardent, sometimes disappointed letters to Susan Dickinson make clear. In addition, she was fully aware of the embattled lives of many around her. Ultimately, this would include her distinguished brother, whose love affair with Mabel Loomis Todd, wife of an Amherst professor and Emily's first editor, began in 1883 after years of volatile marriage with Sue, Emily's "Only Woman in the World" (L 447). Certainly the poet knew of her brother's unhappiness and that of his wife; certainly it must have pained her. Mabel wore widow's black after Austin's death in 1887 and, fantasizing that they were really married, inscribed "Mabel Loomis Dickinson" on a slip of paper attached to a daguerreotype that revealed her youth and sweet appearance [Fig. 19]. Mabel, too, expressed herself in the floral language; one of her favorite activities was painting floral still lifes and

19. Mabel Loomis Todd, daguerreotype, with a slip of paper on which she practiced her signature as she wished she could write it: Mabel Loomis Dickinson.

flowers on china. Giving lectures to women's clubs after the publication of *Poems* (1890), she especially emphasized the activities of Emily Dickinson as gardener.

Because the past was sacred to Dickinson, because she seems always to have tried to be faithful to her early affections—her "perennials"—she was at pains on occasion to explain what seemed her strange social behavior to those she knew best. As her girlish vivacity altered in the 1860s, she became increasingly shy of strangers and nervous even with friends. The silence and freedom provided by her closed bedroom door could be so alluring as to make ordinary social intercourse almost painful. By 1883, she excused herself for declining to receive Professor Joseph Chickering by explaining, "I had hoped to see you, but have no grace to talk, and my own Words so chill and burn me, that the temperature of other Minds is too new an Awe" (L 798). Words that chill and burn: this sounds like Dickinson's description of poetry, which could, she said, be recognized as true when "it makes my whole body so cold no fire ever can warm me" (L 342a). After a quarter of a century of limited contact with people and intense concentration upon her own self and her art, she had become (as it were) her own text; she and her poems were one. Nevertheless, she often had recourse to her gardening idiom—the language others could easily understand—in order to comfort those friends or relatives she might have declined to see:

> You cannot make Remembrance grow
> When it has lost it's Root —
> The tightening the Soil around
> And setting it upright
> Deceives perhaps the Universe
> But not retrieves the Plant —
> Real Memory, like Cedar Feet
> Is shod with Adamant — (F 1536)

Even "Sister Sue" was occasionally turned away. A tender note to Sue sent before Emily died concludes, "The tie between us is very fine, but a Hair never dissolves" (L 1024). Prompted, perhaps, by Johnson's entry in the *Letters* that "This . . . note, written to Sue, can be dated by handwriting only. [It] sound[s] as if [it] had been written during a period of illness . . . when her brother Austin did not dare leave town," the feminist revisionist critics Martha Nell Smith and Ellen Louise Hart, whose ambition is to elevate Susan Gilbert to the position of Emily's "muse," "collaborator," "imagination," and lover, interpret the note to mean that "even death cannot disengage Emily from Susan nor Susan from Emily."[15] But the notes that Emily sent to Susan in this period are not vigorously ardent and buoyant, like those written in youth when she rhapsodized "my heart is full of you" (L 94). Instead, they seek to reassure Susan that they *remain* friends (no matter what) and, by law and long association, "Sisters": "Remember, Dear, an unfaltering *Yes* is my only reply to your utmost question —"; "You asked would I remain? Irrevocably, Susan — I know no other way — Ether looks dispersive, but try it with a Lever —" (L 908, 874). Emily signs "With constancy" or "Faithfully." "Hair" is the cognate of "Ether" in the earlier letter; it no longer signifies a substantial and confident bond but, rather, the withdrawal of the speaker who nevertheless protests that, because of a shared past, she can never be quite gone, never altogether a stranger. This was the "Emily, Whom not seeing, I still love," as Susan inscribed her utterly inappropriate Christmas gift of *Endymion*, Disraeli's novel of society, in 1880.

This enigmatic but intense friendship, like most of Dickinson's relationships, was often described or charted in floral images.[16] For a short time after Austin and Susan's marriage, Emily was a lively member of their circle. Around 1859, however, after Samuel Bowles became a frequent guest, she wrote this apology to Susan:

Susie,

You will forgive me, for I never visit. I am from the fields, you know, and while quite at home with the Dandelion, make but sorry figure in a Drawing — room — Did you ask me out with a bunch of Daisies, I should thank you, and accept — but with Roses — 'Lilies' — 'Solomon'

himself — suffers much embarrassment! Do not mind me Susie — if I do
not come with feet, in my heart I come —[17]

She ends by thanking Susan for *her* "frequent coming, and the flowers
you bring" and for "the glad laugh, which I heard this morning, tho' I
did not see you." (The close proximity of the Dickinson households is
sometimes impressed upon us by such remarks.) She promises to
"keep [the flowers] till I reach my other Susie"—the private one—
when next she visits.

That Susan's "torrid Spirit" attracted Emily had much to do with
their differences in temperament and tastes (L 855). But as the
women grew older, those differences could apparently be divisive.
Susan in her furs and spangled satin gowns, Susan's evening parties
with venison and oysters for repast and dancing and game-playing for
amusement contrasted decidedly with the appearance and days of
the twenty-nine-year-old Emily Dickinson. "Roses" and "Lilies"—in
this case, probably the Easter or Calla lily rather than the daylily of
the meadow—are perhaps meant to stand for Susan's life: her ele-
gance of dress, her expensive tastes, her stature as a desirable (and
married) woman. She is the costly and select hothouse flower, Emily
the ordinary dandelion, an image in harmony with a train of subse-
quent self-images as "Backwoodsman" or rustic in later letters to
"Master" or Otis Lord (L 248). Moreover, Emily prefers "my other
Susie," the one not associated with a distant laugh or with entertain-
ing others but with face-to-face communion, the vulnerable young
Sue of their girlhood who sat with her "on the broad stone step" of
Edward Dickinson's house, "mingling our lives together" (L 88). Here
the language of flowers has been enlisted to explain Emily's complex
feelings and behavior. This was precisely what Victorians expected
that "language" to do.

❦

The appearance of the jasmine as first flower in the herbarium may in-
trigue the reader of "Come slowly, Eden" and those other Dickinson

poems that imagine the first garden, Eden, in Dickinson's garden and its "jessamines" in hers. On page twenty-eight of the herbarium, the jasmine reappears. But other pressings also foreshadow poems to come. For example, the Showy Orchis *(Orchis spectabilis)* or wild orchid is pressed on page thirty-seven along with delphinium, trillium, heliotrope, the coreopsis, and wild larkspur. These are flowers that Dickinson transplanted or gathered from the woods or the paternal Dickinson meadows all her life. The "Orchis in the pasture" with its ruddy "Gown," she wrote of three times (F 642) in poems. In 1858, for example, she framed a remark about the orchis in a winsome couplet that had the air of a proverb. Summer was ending, which prompted her to observe, "To him who keeps an Orchis' heart – / The swamps are pink with June" (F 31). The pink orchis, like the jasmine, had a special allure for her, associated with erotic feeling and the delight of discovery. In "Some Rainbow – coming from the Fair," the orchis or "lady's slipper" "binds her feather on / For her old lover – Don the Sun!," and the poet makes clear that their assignation takes place where Dickinson often wandered in search of the orchis, "the Bog" (F 162). The orchis was a wildflower that first caught Dickinson's eye in early childhood, but she was forty-six when she happily described her rapture at first plucking one. To T. W. Higginson, who had written about the orchis in *Outdoor Papers,* she wrote, "I had long heard of an Orchis before I found one, when a child, but the first clutch of the stem is as vivid now, as the Bog that bore it – so truthful is transport –" (L 458).

A North American member of the more than five hundred species of the orchid family, the orchis is terrestrial in form rather than an air-plant and is only to be found by digging deep in woodland swamps, one of Emily Dickinson's more rugged pleasures. She probably meant the Lady's slipper or *Cypripedium* when she alluded in her poems to the "orchis"; as the Latin name suggests, the flower itself was associated with Venus and her island, Cyprus. Indeed, *orchis* means testicle in Greek, "probably after the shape of a tuber at the base of the flower of certain species[;] orchids were considered an aphrodisiac in antiquity. Despite this heritage or because of it," writes Theodore E. Stebbins, Jr., "the many nineteenth-century flower books [like] *Flora's Lexicon,* rarely mention the orchid or its symbolic meaning."[18] (Frances Osgood's *Poetry of Flowers* [1841] *did* assign a meaning to the orchid; in her text it stood for "a belle," an especially beautiful woman.) "Lady's Slipper," another watercolor from *Flowers of America* (1876) by Gabriella F. (Eddy) White [Fig. 20], emphasizes the testicular associations of this plant as well as its delicate and interesting shape.

The extraordinary popularity of orchids in Europe and the United States in the nineteenth century[19] and the "grand scale" cultivation of orchids in England after 1818 and in Boston after the 1830s (coinciding with the ability to regulate temperatures in greenhouses and with William Cattley's experiments with the *Catteya labiata* or catteya orchid, named for him) give rise to an interesting question: Why did Emily Dickinson, who so loved the wild orchis, not grow its hothouse equivalent in her conservatory? Orchids were worn as lapel flowers, appeared in bouquets and on dining tables, and were celebrated in still lifes during her lifetime. John Bateman's *Orchidaceae of Mexico and Guatemala* (1837–1843), a volume weighing thirty-eight pounds that included fine lithographic plates, had stimulated production in the United States alone of a great number of art books—many written by women—devoted to tropical flowers, especially the orchid. Yet there is no record whatever of Emily's conservatory housing any of the orchids available for growing in nineteenth-century New England.

Indeed, the orchis or wild orchid was not among those wildflowers such as the anemone or crocus that Emily chose to grow herself in the Dickinson garden. Still, it was one of only three examples of natural presences dear to her in the third letter she sent T. W. Higginson: "I know the Butterfly – and the Lizard – and the Orchis – Are not those *your* Countrymen?" (L 268). In the seasonal narrative made by her nature poetry, spring, summer, and fall wildflowers often represent hu-

20. Gabriella F. (Eddy) White, "Lady's Slipper," from *Flowers of America* (1876).

man emotions and conditions. The orchis represents adventure in that narrative, a symbolism that discloses her independence from more sentimental mid-Victorian writers. Dickinson's friendly "Preceptor," T. W. Higginson, in his courtly essay "The Procession of the Flowers" (admired by Emily Dickinson in her copy of the *Atlantic*) avoided any sexual connotation in his description of the *Cypripedium*. Instead, in an appreciation of New England flora that demonstrates his knowledge, as a Massachusetts resident, of the same flowers that Dickinson knew, he focused on the orchis's connection to the aristocratic orchid. (Higginson was a decorous writer, mindful of his own gentlemanly standing. Two decades later, while editing her first volume of *Poems* [1890], he fretted that Dickinson's sensual poem "Wild nights" might misrepresent her to the public.) In "The Procession of the Flowers" he chronicles his wanderings in the woods, like Dickinson, in search of timely specimens:

> Another constant ornament of the end of May is the large pink Lady's-Slipper, or Moccason-Flower, the "Cyprepedium [*sic*] not due till tomorrow" which Emerson attributes to the note-book of Thoreau, — tomorrow, in these parts, meaning about the twentieth of May. It belongs to the family of Orchids, a high-bred race, fastidious in habits, sensitive as to abodes. Of the ten species named as rarest among American endogenous plants by Dr. Gray, in his valuable essay on the statistics of our Northern Flora, all but one are Orchids. And even an abundant species, like the present, retains the family traits in its person, and never loses its high-born air and its delicate veining. . . . I never can divest myself of the feeling that each specimen is a choice novelty.

If one studies Gabriella White's watercolor of the "Lady's Slipper," this "high-born air" and "delicate veining" are evident in the arching pose of the flower and the light and heavy lines that trace across the sides of the "slipper." But White's watercolor (like Georgia O'Keeffe's paintings of floral stamens and calyxes, the best examples of such sensuous envisioning) also makes it quite clear why even the meadow orchid was thought to be, like all the *Orchidaceae,* amusingly naughty, powerful, or risqué, depending on the viewer's sensibilities. Interestingly, in France the *Cypripedium* is called either "le sabot de Vénus" or "le sabot de la Vierge," a flower lover being made to choose between the sacred and the profane. The London Crystal Palace Exhibition of 1851, "the first grand exposition that brought exotic plants and flowers to the general public," helped make the orchid become "the most adored flower" of the upper classes.[20] British greenhouses were stocked with orchids from Java, Borneo, and all parts of South America, while orchids could demand prices as high as $2,000 "in 1996 dollars." In the United States, the enthusiasm for orchids was at its height in 1860, when the Dickinsons had enjoyed Emily's conservatory for five years. That she did not grow the fashionable orchid is telling. Its lack of scent may have discouraged her, for the other conservatory flowers such as the gardenia, daphne, and oleander were all heavily perfumed. (This absence of orchids in Dickinson's conservatory also casts doubt on the theory of Domhnall Mitchell in his essay "A Little Taste, Time, and Means" that her gardens, interior and external, were specifically dear to her as marks of rank.)

The quest for spring flowers like the orchis that mark the close of winter and signify the temporary defeat of death was to become a genre in Emily Dickinson's poetry. In May 1852, Lavinia Dickinson attached a postscript to one of Emily's letters to Austin, then teaching in Boston: "The garden is made and everything is growing rapidly, the air is full of fragrance and of song."[21] Emily, however, speaks to Austin in biblical cadences about a whole world that is renewing itself because it is May: "This morning is fair and delightful – you will awake in dust, and amidst the ceaseless din of the untiring city, wouldn't you change your dwelling for my palace in the dew?" (L 89). "You will awake in dust" implies not merely the cinders and dirt of the city but the "dust" that is mankind's eventual decay and death, from which Christians hope ultimately to be awakened at the General Resurrection. Spring provides a temporary renewal and brief resurrection that give hope to all who experience them; thus Emily writes from her "palace in the dew," the kingdom of spring, a season that piqued her imagination as vividly as it did Wordsworth's. Like Wordsworth, she chooses spring flowers, often woodland flowers, the first growth of hillsides and meadows, to praise.

Dickinson's early poems include scenes in which the sensitive and wishful speaker, like Wordsworth in the early poems, discovers new growth in out-of-the-way places, newly sprung flowers like the crocus, anemone, clover, or daisy that are all the more precious because they are confidingly, vulnerably, democratically available to all. Austin Dickinson was known to raid the woods outside Amherst for specimen trees that he transported to and planted on his own property. Such rifling is now against the law, and his sister Emily anticipates this in 1859 by writing an arch, mock-guilty anecdote about her own forays into the woods beyond the Homestead:

> I robbed the Woods —
> The trusting Woods —
> The unsuspecting Trees
> Brought out their Burs and mosses
> My fantasy to please —
> I scanned their trinkets curious —
> I grasped — I bore away —
> What will the solemn Hemlock —
> What will the Oak tree say? (F 57a)

A later version of this poem, completed in 1861, disavows the thief but is still fascinated by the pillage of those early spring flowers and seeds that apparently (though she never says so) possess some magical power. In this poem, instead of "I robbed," a question is asked:

> Who robbed the Woods —
> The trusting Woods? (F 57b)

"Who robbed the Woods" is a distinctly Wordsworthian poem; its echoes of the poet of *The Prelude*'s guilt in stealing "A little boat tied to a willow tree," "An act of stealth," should remind us of the breadth and intensity of Emily Dickinson's reading, together with her own quasi-Romantic sensibility. Thomas H. Johnson informs us that two of her letters quote Wordsworth's "Elegiac Stanzas" (somewhat incorrectly), while one alludes to "We are Seven." But it is in her approach to wildflowers and to their personal and transcendental significance that Dickinson exhibits a vision of nature related to yet distinct from Wordsworth's.

Like his, her fondness for small flowers like the primrose, daisy, and violet is aroused by their smallness and ubiquity.[22] Twice in 1802, Wordsworth commended the daisy: "Thou unassuming Commonplace / Of Nature, with that homely face, / And yet with something of a grace / Which love makes for thee!" He imagines himself being greeted as a traveler in the lane or in "nooks remote" by the "sweet Daisy" which is not so proud as to be "grieved if thou be set at nought." The sight of the daisy is able to rid him of "stately passions" and inform his heart with "homely sympathy." He imagines in the small but shining flower many shapes and presences from "queen" to "nun" to (in its decay) "starveling in a scanty vest," yet the daisy, "Nature's favourite," is finally dear to him because it is modest and its "home is everywhere." Wordsworth's lyrics about the daisy find descriptive analogues in those Dickinson love poems already mentioned that tell the story of "Daisy" and "Master." Like Dickinson's "Daisy," the flower's charm for Wordsworth is in her humility.

Some of Wordsworth's encomiums to wildflowers list them with a determinedly naïve enthusiasm, even as Dickinson does in her jaunty "Whose are the little beds":

> 'Tis Daisy, in the shortest —
> A little further on —
> Nearest the door — to wake the 1st,
> Little Leontodon.

'Tis Iris, Sir, and Aster —
Anemone, and Bell —
Bartsia, in the blanket red,
And chubby Daffodil. (F 85)

Dickinson's tone in this poem is cozy, rosy, and purposefully naïve.
No hint, here, of the austere poet who could regard the natural world
with cold despair. But the Romantic idiom often sought the minia-
ture, jocose, and pretty when delineating flowers. (That Dickinson
does not so restrict herself is significant.) Because "The Small Celan-
dine" is his favorite wildflower, Wordsworth seizes upon it last after
listing others:

Pansies, lilies, kingcups, daisies,
Let them live upon their praises;
Long as there's a sun that sets,
Primroses will have their glory;
Long as there are violets,
They will have a place in story:
There's a flower that shall be mine,
'Tis the little Celandine.

Like many nineteenth-century poets, Wordsworth praises his fa-
vorite celandine by declaring it superior to violets, the wildflower all
Victorians seem to have loved. There are two species called "celan-
dine": one is the *Chelidonium majus* of the poppy family, a tiny yellow-
flowered biennial, and the other, *Stylophorum diphullum,* a species
of woodland poppy very familiar to gardeners in the United States.
Wordsworth's "little Celandine" was the yellow one of Europe, whose
florets resemble bird's wings (hence the name from Greek, *Che-
lidonus,* or "swallow"). Like his devotion to the daisy with her "meek
nature"—Dickinson's lines about the "meekest flower of the mead"
(F 147) seem to re-echo his phrase—Wordsworth's affection for the
celandine is aroused by its character as he imagines it: "Modest, yet

withal an Elf, / Bold, and lavish of thyself." If Emily Dickinson's fondness for snowdrops, anemones, crocuses, and violets was piqued by their willingness to bloom amid the lingering gusts of winter, Wordsworth loves the celandine because it, too, is brave but not proud:

> On the moor, and in the wood,
> In the lane;—there's not a place,
> Howso'ever mean it be,
> But 'tis good enough for thee.
> Ere a leaf is on a bush
>
> . . .
>
> Thou wilt come with half a call,
> Spreading out thy glossy breast
> Like a careless Prodigal;
> Telling tales about the sun,
> When we've little warmth, or none.

Small flowers attracted Wordsworth's affection and interest throughout his writing life. One critic, hypothesizing what she calls "differences between male and female art," declares that Dickinson embraced the study of "detail, bounded on one side by the *ornamental* and on the other by the '*everyday*'" and that her floral poems differ from "the poetry of nineteenth-century men," who almost always preferred grand subjects of sublime character and disdained "individual studies of . . . flowers."[23] However, hundreds of thousands of pictures of single flowers done by male artists in the nineteenth century— among them the minute or delicate floral studies made by even such heroic painters as Delacroix—give the lie to such sexist generalizations. In poetry, too, the flower poems of Thoreau, Emerson, or William Cullen Bryant (whose "To the Fringed Gentian" is marked in Dickinson's copy of his poems) demonstrate, like Wordsworth's, a fondness for the very smallness of the flowers they praise that resembles poems by some women. The following well-known lines of Tennyson, published in 1869 and memorized by scores of Victorian schoolchildren on both sides of the Atlantic, are evidence that true art is essentially androgynous and finally eludes delimiting categories. Sentimental, and as fascinated by small forms as any of the floral writings of Mrs. Lydia Sigourney or Susan Fenimore Cooper (in *Rural Hours By a Lady*) or Mrs. Clarissa W. Munger Badger (whose *Wild Flowers Drawn and Colored from Nature* Emily Dickinson might have seen), Tennyson's poem makes clear that the very minuteness of an uncultivated bloom could intimate the grandeur of God's creation to one Victorian mind:

> Flower in the crannied wall,
> I pluck you out of the crannies,
> I hold you here, root and all, in my hand,
> Little flower—but *if* I could understand
> What you are, root and all, and all in all,
> I should know what God and man is.

Tennyson does not emphasize the fact that his wildflower hardily persists among rocks; yet, in spite of the ease with which his powerful human speaker robs it of its resting place, he is still unable to penetrate the tiny flower's secrets. Several of the more popular Victorian poems about wildflowers, written by men, thus elaborate a mysterious connection between the flower's habits and forms, and an unseen Creator whose hand (despite the blow to religious belief furnished by Darwin) they presume to perceive. In Bryant's "To the Fringed Gentian," the speaker is fascinated by the flower's late blooming, precisely as is Dickinson in her own gentian poems:

> Thou waitest late, and com'st alone,
> When woods are bare and birds are flown,
> And frosts and shortening days portend
> The aged year is near its end.

Bryant rhapsodizes that "the sweet and quiet eye" of the gentian reflects the blue sky from which it seems to have fallen, and in an awk-

ward, somewhat confused analogy between the mature gentian and
himself as old man, hopes that at the moment of his death, he, like the
late-blooming flower, "May look to heaven as I depart." To Tennyson
and Bryant, the wonder of wildflowers lay in an abundance so perfect
as to be full of the secrets of life. Why a gorgeous (if cheap, because
natural) wildflower could bloom in a raw, poor place was to them a
ritual and profound question. Emerson, whose influence on Emily
Dickinson was manifest in her lifetime, sought to answer this ques-
tion in his shapely tribute to the *Rhododendron canadense,* the wild
"Rhodora":

> I found the fresh Rhodora in the woods,
> Spreading its leafless blooms in a damp nook,
> To please the desert and the sluggish brook.
> The purple petals, fallen in the pool,
> Made the black water with their beauty gay;
> Here might the red-bird come his plumes to cool,
> And court the flower that cheapens his array.
> Rhodora! if the sages ask thee why
> This charm is wasted on the earth and sky,
> Tell them, dear, that if eyes were made for seeing,
> Then Beauty is its own excuse for being;
> Why thou wert there, O rival of the rose!
> I never thought to ask, I never knew;
> But, in my simple ignorance, suppose
> The self-same Power that brought me there brought you.

Not technically a sonnet but similarly arranged in rhymed lines of
exposition followed by apostrophe and a shift in thought, "The Rho-
dora" meditates on the difference between the ugly setting in which
the flowers of this delicate shrub of the heath family often grow and
the flowers themselves. Significantly, Emerson makes the rhodora a
"rival" to the rose in a form of comparison typical of mid-Victorian
verse and horticultural description whereby the rose was the belle,
and best, among flowers. Far more confident of God's providence

than Emily Dickinson, Emerson (once an ordained minister) infers that the rhodora's growth in dark, cramped swamps, like his own life and acquaintance with them, is God's will. For Dickinson—far more desperate in her world view than he—who could describe life as "Murder by degrees," who observed that "'Tis Life's award – to die –," God was not so benign, as the "Gash" that frost visits upon gardens made clear (F 485, 911). In 1884, two years before she died, she jotted this bleak poem on the back of an envelope addressed to her Aunt Elizabeth Currier:

> Apparently with no surprise
> To any happy Flower
> The Frost beheads it at it's play –
> In accidental power –
> The blonde Assassin passes on –
> The Sun proceeds unmoved
> To measure off another Day
> For an Approving God – (F 1668)

In words, in tone, "The Rhodora" argues, as in Emerson's essay "The Poet," "the great, calm presence of the creator" and the fullness and perfection of that power's ends. Although Dickinson often concurred in her poems and letters with Emerson's view that "Beauty is its own excuse for being," she also recognized the cruelty with which beauty is destroyed in nature. Since the garden was her cherished metaphor for the world, the careers and fortunes of her flowers signified the bitter struggles of humanity. The death of a flower was like a "behead[ing]"; the "happ[iness]" of the flower before it is murdered by forces like frost, intrinsic to divine design, proved in miniature the truth of the chilling aphoristic lines she wrote in 1860:

> A *wounded* Deer – leaps highest –
> I've heard the Hunter tell –
> 'Tis but the extasy of *death* – (F 181)

Dickinson could write easily and cheerfully to neighbors who brought her field lilies or gillyflowers (today's dianthus) that they were heavenly, thus employing the idiom of the floral dictionaries and garden books; but there was a grave difference between her more complex vision of flowers and that of one "W. Martin," for example, who wrote in the preface to Mrs. Clarissa Munger Badger's first book, *Floral Belles*, "Beautiful Flowers . . . were your tints and odors given to grant the spirit, in the shade of this dull world, some glimpse of heaven?" Martin's accents characterize the general mid-Victorian response to wildflowers in particular (always excepting the reactions of Darwinians, for whom they chiefly illustrated ancient vegetable forms). In optimistic moments, Emily Dickinson could indeed imagine a paradise in which her beloved dead peaceably picked eternal blooms. But she was far too well acquainted with pain, outer and inner, with storms, and with "Doom's Electric Moccasin" not to depict the inevitably wretched fate—death—of all flowers and all persons who live (F 1618).

Thus we do not find in Dickinson, whose more independent mind usually perceives an end to the triumphant moment of spring bloom even as she notes it, the cheerfulness of such celebrations of violets as Mary Russell Mitford's in *Our Village* (c. 1835). Like other Victorians, Mitford cherishes the Wordsworthian sight of thousands of violets whose number causes her to understand for the first time how beautiful they are. Her reflections upon the violet typify those of the writers of Dickinson's day in which, as for Emerson in "Flower Chorus," the "murmur" of the violet makes spring. But her vision lacks the radiant inclusion of another—the prospect of death and resurrection—that complicates Emily Dickinson's. Mitford enthuses:

> Now a few yards farther, and I reach the bank. Ah! I smell them already—their exquisite perfume steams and lingers in this moist, heavy air. Through this little gate, and along the green south bank of this green wheat-field, and they burst upon me, the lovely violets, in ten-

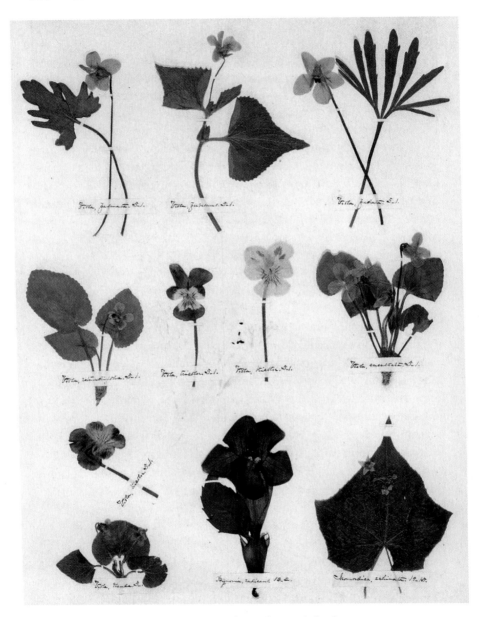

21. Pansy violets *(Violae)* from Emily Dickinson's herbarium, page 46.

fold loveliness. The ground is covered with them, white and purple, enamelling the short dewy grass. . . . There they lie by hundreds, by thousands. . . . What happiness to . . . fill my basket with the blossoms! What a renewal of heart and mind!

Emily Dickinson once promised Samuel Bowles, when he was ill, "Estates of Violet — Trouble ne'er looked on!" But if violets were especially precious to her, it was because their loveliness came up in meadows often "unsuspected" or unseen or too late (F 272, 69). On her "estate," even violets encountered trouble.[24] Indeed, so vulnerable could they seem to her that ultimately she translates them into the purple hue of heaven or the violet color of noon or the deep blue haze over the mountains at evening.

On page forty-six of the herbarium, Emily Dickinson pressed eight kinds of pansy violet together with a spray of trumpet creeper and prickly cucumber [Fig. 21]. The violets were *Viola palmata, Viola pubescens, Viola tricolor* (two colorations), *Viola pudata, Viola rotundifolia, Viola cuccullata,* and *Viola blanda.* This page is one of the most artistically conceived in the herbarium, the differences in leaf shape and flower size imparting a sense of variety and plenitude. Even as "Daisy" was the wildflower Dickinson later chose when describing herself as the loving friend of Samuel Bowles, her "Sun," the violet appears in her first tribute to Susan Dickinson, in whose dark eyes, she wrote in 1858, "the Violets lie / Mouldered" for many Mays—a fine Dickinsonian instance of courtly imagery (L 197). But even as a child she had already claimed the violet as a subject.

❧

In "A Little Taste, Time, and Means: Dickinson and Flowers," Domhnall Mitchell discusses the poet's regard for flowers—even wildflowers like the violet—as an aristocratic espousal of class distinctions.[25] His essay cites and is sympathetic to Betsy Erkkila's "Emily Dickinson and Class," in which Erkkila declares, "Dickinson was the 'lady' and the intellectual whose leisure, freedom, and space 'to think'"—Lavinia Dickinson once whimsically isolated Emily's duty in the family as "think[ing]"—"were made possible by the manual labor and proletarianization of others."[26] At one point in an analysis that in substantial measure attributes Dickinson's gardening skills to her superior education, and her success with flowers to her family's financial ease (they could buy the right equipment—for example, a Franklin stove to help warm the conservatory), Mitchell asks this question: "Can the accident of [Dickinson's] birth as a white, upper-middle-class woman be held against her?" His reader may well ask, held against her in what way? As a person? As a poet? In posing such a question, essays like Mitchell's shift attention away from Dickinson's achievement as a writer in order to judge her sociological sympathies, her "politics," according to the standards of a time other than her own. Because it specifically touches upon the topic of Dickinson as a gardener—the subject of this book—I would like to consider Mitchell's essay in more detail here.

Emily wrote in 1881 that her sister Vinnie appealed to "Bliss's catalogue" when "prospecting" for seeds (L 689), but Mitchell proposes—interestingly—that both sisters may have used L. W. Goodell's *Catalogue of Choice Selected Flower Seeds and Bulbs* since Goodell lived in Amherst, although his business was situated at "Pansy Park" in Dwight, Massachusetts. By 1881, Emily's increasing frailty was causing Lavinia to take over more and more of the garden, but I think it likely that in the 1860s and 1870s both sisters used Joseph Breck's *The Flower Garden; or Breck's Book of Flowers* (1851), reissued as *The New Book of Flowers* (1866), for instruction. Joseph Breck of Boston (1794–1873) was far better known than Goodell; indeed, he was the chief New England authority on horticulture, president of the Massachusetts Horticultural Society, editor of *The Horticultural Register and Gardener's Magazine,* which he began publishing in 1838, and a seedsman of note besides. Although Breck's chief interest was floral cultivation, he was also an authority on trees and shrubs. It seems unlikely that the Dickinsons, tutored by Edward Hitchcock, would have patronized a plantsman less famous or distinguished than Breck. Since the Norcross sisters of Cambridge often sent their cousins seeds, moreover, they were probably bought at Breck's. Breck's catalogue business was widespread; it survived into the early 1900s. His poetic vision of the importance of gardening to the human spirit is far more congenial to that of Emily Dickinson than Goodell's, as Mitchell describes it.

Goodell advertises his flowers as "choice" and "select," just as seed companies often do today, thus suggesting that the buyer will not receive underdeveloped or infected bulbs or mixed seeds from different species. Mitchell, however, understands his advertisement as an "appeal to class distinctions." Prompted, perhaps, by Goodell's promise of exquisite specimens, Mitchell declares that horticulture in Dickinson's world was "a measure of refinement." Emily Dickinson's "literacy," "comparative leisure," and "privacy," he concludes—not to mention her family's comfortable circumstances—enabled her to become a gardener and, in turn, "part of a network in which women belonging primarily to the middle and upper-middle strata of society shared their advantages and affinities." He rightly observes that Dickinson regarded her poems and plants as related works of art but continues to frame a reductive argument about her passion for flowers, delimiting it in social terms by remarking that she never did the "*physical* work of the garden," confining herself to the "'luxury of apprehension'— choosing, growing, picking, arranging, and sending flowers for display and as emblems of taste." Since "flowers are beautiful but (to a large extent) useless—except as markers of taste and gentility," Mitchell writes, "establishing a flower garden was [largely] a means by which a reputation and even a sphere of influence could be secured." In addition, he finds Dickinson's conservatory, even more than her garden, a means of "demonstrating . . . good taste and individual talent," as well as her family's prosperity.

Much could be argued against these observations if Emily Dickinson's approach to gardening and flowers is to be more sympathetically understood. It would be absurd, of course, to claim that personal refinement and wealth do not frequently accord with a love for gardening. Certainly E. M. Forster's worldly narrator in *Howards End* is only too brutally correct in saying that the arts, especially the decorative arts, are substantially closed to the desperately poor. When they are starving, people have no strength, time, money, or will to plant flowers. Still, a deep interest in cultivating flowers and a true affection—even a yearning—for them have traditionally been experienced by rich and poor alike. In her important book *American Gardens of the Nineteenth Century,* Ann Leighton chronicles the development of the English garden as a means of reducing distance between the social classes: "The nineteenth century [saw] the common man . . . emerging and flexing his muscles—especially those used in gardening. Glasshousing of plants was being developed . . . on a great range of social scales." She describes the "revolution in domestic horticulture" that came to England and the United States after 1810, writing that "the onus—as well as the honor—of promoting the propagation of new flowers descended from being the province of a very few rich individuals and their expert gardeners to becoming a backyard hobby of the so-called working classes." Americans, especially New Englanders, experimented with cultivating new floral strains (as Emily Dickinson appears to have done with the double narcissus) or made "conservatories" (whether designed by architects or improvised from sheds with cut-out glass windows). In this, they resembled their English cousins:

> Men home from work earlier than ever before—and with more time and money to spend—bent over their specialties in little glass-covered cold frames, squeezed into brick areas beside washing arrangements, and readied them for shows. . . . There everyone . . . competed on equal levels, and merit alone won the prize.[27]

If the gardens at Wilton were regarded as national treasures, the novels of Charles Dickens envisioned tiny London plots with struggling, soot-choked blooms dear to the unlucky tenants who hover over them. Breck writes for Emily Dickinson's generation in an early passage of the *Flower Garden,* "The cultivation of flowers is an employment adapted to every grade, the high and the low, the rich and the poor."

It is true that nineteenth-century American women were encouraged to garden and even to learn the principles of botany in order to beautify their homes, inspire spirituality in their children, and improve their health. But authors did not conclude that only the rich would welcome their advice. In 1843, Andrew Jackson Downing (whose *Treatise on the Theory of Landscape Gardening* was owned by the Austin Dickinsons) wrote a preface to Mrs. Loudon's appealing *Gardening for Ladies and Ladies' Companion to the Flower Garden.* He urged every American female "high or low" to turn to "Flora," explaining that "there is nothing in the plan of a house or garden that may not be realized by a family living on a very small income."[28] In her turn, Mrs. Loudon provided instructions for "Window Gardening, and the Management of Plants in Pots in Small Greenhouses." Considering such indications of the presence in Dickinson's time and place of strong inducements to garden, I think we cannot assume that her devotion to flowers and their care was an effort to proclaim her social superiority.

In the same essay, Mitchell regards the poet's encounters with her garden as superficial; she arranged flowers but did not *work* with them: "Dickinson left the heavier physical work in the garden to the hired man and to her sister, Lavinia, while she focused her energies on the 'luxury of apprehension'—choosing, growing, picking, arranging, and sending flowers for display and as emblems of taste, or transforming them into 'flowers of speech.'" Here, growing flowers and writing poems about flowers are equated, while neither is regarded as "work."

To consult Dickinson's poems about the writing process is to discover how exhausting she found the construction of a phrase. At the same time, Emily's girlhood letters reveal that she did what amounted to laborer's work in her father's orchard. She wrote ruefully in August 1861 that paring fruit outdoors was freckling her complexion. Much of her mature correspondence describes the difficulties of keeping flowers healthy in heat and cold. To state the obvious, growing flowers requires bending, lifting, carrying, spading, weeding, fertilizing, separating tangled roots, and "dead-heading," or removing dead flowers to encourage new ones. To enjoy such success as Dickinson's with the camellias, gardenias, and jasmine of her conservatory requires a complex, vigilant pattern of misting, fertilizing, mulching, draining, potting, and protecting against insects. MacGregor Jenkins recalled the poet kneeling on a rug as she potted her plants—probably transplanting the contents—in the twilight. Martha Dickinson Bianchi remembered her aunt firing the adjoining dining room stove during winter nights so that the conservatory flowers would not freeze. Seeding and grooming a garden may not require the kind of brute strength that mowing—Mitchell's example of real labor—does, but they constitute *work*. (In fact, the Dickinson acres were mostly scythed.)[29] That Emily Dickinson, a woman who was not physically strong, left the clearing of her father's land to Horace Church and other hired men before she made the spring garden was only sensible. But she reports in August 1885 that Vinnie is "still subsoiling," or turning over the earth, which Breck recommended before planting fall bulbs (L 1000). Though a "gentlewoman," Lavinia seems to have done heavy work in the garden; Emily did not find it beneath her. "I am very busy picking up stems and stamens," she wrote to their sick servant, Maggie Maher, in 1882, "as the hollyhocks leave their clothes around" (L 771). This kind of cleanup, both painstaking and extensive, would be hard work for a delicate woman. But "I will work with all my might, always, as soon as I get well," Emily had typically written her sister from Cambridge in 1864, apologizing that her eye malady was depriving Lavinia of household help (L 295).

Nor was Dickinson's floral passion an avoidance of the useful. In his *New Book of Flowers* (1866), Joseph Breck raised the issue of "The

Utility of Flowers," calling it "sheer nonsense to tell us it is useless to cultivate flowers" and attacking "a class of men who would pare down everything to the mere grade of *utility*." The "decorative aesthetics" that Breck laid down for Dickinson's era had to do with the "beautiful": Flowers "render [our homes] more attractive," he wrote, and flowers had their uses, both practical and spiritual. Dickinson's nasturtiums appeared in her sister's salads; she knew that digitalis came from the foxglove; indeed, that essential oils pressed from flowers created perfume. Remembering the poet's preference for wildflowers, one must also balk at the idea that "Emily's floral preferences" are "saturated with the language and suppositions of class division." Dickinson traced her affection for violets and dandelions to her rustic nature. But Mitchell remarks that if she was able to find wildflowers, "her [aristocratic] education taught her where to find them, which ones to value and why, and how to cultivate them." Long before Emily Dickinson went to Miss Lyon's establishment at Mount Holyoke, however, and before she made the herbarium as an adolescent schoolgirl, she walked the woods with her mother, brother, and sister. "When we were little children," Lavinia recalled, "we used to spend entire days in the woods hunting for treasures." The Dickinson children were country people whose study of wildflowers began long before their training in Edward Hitchcock's botanical principles.

There is, finally, the case of Dickinson's much-quoted letter to Dr. and Mrs. Josiah Holland, written during a fever epidemic that afflicted Amherst in 1858. Here, the poet had recourse to her conceit of the garden in order to describe her state of mind. (Dr. Holland was the editor of *Scribner's* and the *Century* magazine; that he wrote the misogynistic novel *Miss Gilbert's Career* revealed his purely literary ambitions as well. Emily's letters to the Hollands are often metaphoric exercises designed to impress.) Domhnall Mitchell, like Betsy Erkkila and Alfred Habegger, finds this letter's "infuriating blindness" "painful," a proof that Dickinson was fond of "social distinctions" and could be "callous" about humanity. The letter ends dramatically:

Good-night! I can't stay any longer in a world of death. Austin is ill of fever. I buried my garden last week — our man, Dick, lost a little girl through the scarlet fever . . . Ah! dainty — dainty Death! Ah! democratic Death! Grasping the proudest zinnia from my purple garden, — then deep to his bosom calling the serf's child. (L 195)

Habegger remarks of this passage, "Readers are shocked by Dickinson's equating 'the serf's child' with her frost-killed flowers," although he points out that "epidemics [often] inspire a strained . . . dance of death [response] with all sense of scale abandoned."[30] Mitchell, on the other hand, observes that the child's death was caused by "poor standards of health and housing" and laments that Dickinson's letter makes no acknowledgment of the fact since hers was "not a consciousness that is sensitive to such issues."[31] But how could she have known that fevers like typhoid, the child's real illness, are caused by poor sanitation? Even Queen Victoria was not aware that Prince Albert's death in 1861 may have been the indirect result of bad drains at Windsor Castle.

That her letter employs the frequent, classic comparison of a girl to a flower may well strike the modern reader as callous because it implies that flower and girl are equal in importance, equally to be mourned. In addition, her use of the word "serf" for the family's groundsman may seem highly inappropriate in a republican society and incorrect besides: he was in no way her tenant. Dickinson's language here may simply appear to be that of "Squire" Edward Dickinson's daughter, taking herself and her provincial, if privileged, family very seriously.

While acknowledging the insensitivity it projects—Austin's illness and the natural coming of winter to her garden are also equated—I think a slightly different interpretation of this letter's diction could be helpful in understanding the poet as both writer and gardener. To begin with, it is simply the case that Emily Dickinson loved flowers quite as much and as if they *were* human; her implicit comparison was undoubtedly not intended to diminish the "little girl," as she is rather tenderly called. (More ambiguous is the fact that Dickinson selects the "proudest zinnia" from her "purple"—that is, royal—"garden" as a term of comparison since the zinnia, newly introduced from Mexico, was considered a highly valuable exotic in the 1860s. The child is identified as working class.) With the cadences of Ecclesiastes and the Elizabethans always vivid in her ear, it was only natural that Dickinson should express the communion and equality of all living forms in death. Indeed, her letter's zinnia and child commingling in Death's grasp calls up such lines as *Cymbeline*'s "Golden Lads, and Girles all must, / As Chimney-sweepers come to dust." Her oft-used diction of hierarchies in which "serf" plays its part may be traced among other things to the constant reading of Shakespeare—"why is any other book needed[?]"—which made his monarchical society very real and consummately available to her for imagistic and narrative purposes [L 342b].

Dickinson translated this imagery into a kind of fairy-tale language in which kings and queens, realms and royalties substituted for persons and places she knew. Thus, on a trip to the Willard Hotel in Washington when she was twenty-five, she wrote—also to Mrs. Holland—"you will not care to know the value of the diamonds my Lord and Lady wore," suggesting that the Willard, then run as a superior boarding house with a common table, was very grand indeed (L 179). In 1883, she used this quasi-Elizabethan, fairy-tale diction of princes and paupers with whimsical affection, commenting to Susan Dickinson of her daughter's photograph, "I knew she was royal, but that she was hallowed, how could I surmise" (L 886). Since Susan could be proud and the Dickinsons were not just anybody in Amherst, Emily was telling a kind of truth in using the adjective "royal" while at the same time teasing Martha's mother for her maternal complacency.

Not snobbery but the power of the aesthetic impulse to which she was subject is chiefly manifested in Dickinson's much-discussed letter. As in other letters, the energy and embellishment of her narrative are what chiefly concern her. Another mention of flowers that is troubling to some also queries the poet's vision of herself in society. This letter was written to Samuel Bowles, then in Europe, in August 1862 when the Civil War was at its height. In it, Dickinson writes:

A Soldier called — a Morning ago, and asked for a Nosegay, to take to Battle. I suppose he thought we kept an Aquarium. (L 272)

Reading these sentences that appear impatient and vacant of empathy, I often wondered: Did Emily, so generous with gifts to friends, grant the soldier a flower? Perhaps he saw her conservatory from the street and imagined that the Dickinsons kept an "Aquarium" or artificial tank for growing, then selling, flowers and plants. Her tone is arch. The soldier's intrusion was probably unacceptable, possibly frightening; certainly her cherished flowers were not dispensable. The soldier was a stranger; the War seemed to her stranger still. Therefore, perhaps, Dickinson's sympathy—so eloquently expressed in the case of the dead Union soldier Frazar Stearns—was not quickly excited and may even have been withheld. Like her elegy for both her flowers and the groundsman's daughter, her attitude to the soldier seems cold. This is one of a few occasions when Emily Dickinson's humanity failed to make itself known. There are scores in which it did not fail.

Thus, she invoked the rose to write an elegy for Susan Dickinson's niece, dead at two years of age. The uncommonly beautiful and vulnerable flower becomes a metaphor of the fragile and precious child:

> She sped as Petals from a Rose —
> Offended by the Wind —
> A frail Aristocrat of Time
> Indemnity to find —
> Leaving on Nature a Default
> As Cricket, or as Bee,
> But Andes — in the Bosoms where
> She had begun to lie (F 897C)

"Offended by the Wind"—adversity and illness?—the little girl is wafted from this world, speeding from it as frail rose petals do in a storm. The exquisite and susceptible nature of roses is described in the first four lines to explain the child's early death, while their delicacy and material refinement—their "aristocracy"—commemorate her importance to Susan Dickinson's family. The child is so little that she resembles a bee or a cricket, two of Dickinson's favorite insects, and ordinary; yet she leaves a monumental loss, large as the Andes mountains, in the "Bosoms" of those who had begun to know and love her. Dickinson's line "She had begun to lie" is especially poignant, for nineteenth-century families often hesitated to love or even name their children, so terrifyingly high was the rate of infant mortality. If Emily Dickinson's poem appeals to the long-established language of social distinctions, it is that she wishes to emphasize the child's great intrinsic worth. (In alluding to the other little girl as the "serf's child," thus achieving a lyrical-sounding balance of opposites, she slighted a *truly* "democratic" fact.) There are fewer "aristocrats" or highly cultivated members of any society than other folk, fewer roses than the ubiquitous wildflower. Moreover, her appeal to the British traditions of nobility—"King" appears twelve times in her poems, "Queen" sixteen times, "Prince" six times, and the mysterious, sometimes mystical "Earl" nine times—may be explained not by snobbery but by the need for a recognized system of ranking, with connotations of rarity, power, elegance, or beauty. Once again, it was to her not a political but a fantastic, fairy-tale diction that could easily convey excellence or its opposites. To call the heroine of her poem a "citizen" of time would say nothing.

❧

Finding Emily Dickinson "imperious" and subject to the same kind of snobbish narcissism he attributes to her brother and sister, Alfred Habegger remarks in the course of an innovational character study,[32] "Those who would like to democratize the poet should give some thought to how she might have patronized their forebears." Yet the

descendant of early Connecticut River Valley stock who wrote, "I'm
Nobody! Who are you?", who clearly relished praising "A Weed of
Summer" that "did not know her station low" and whose tender civil-
ity to the Dickinson servants was well-known, certainly exhibited no
snobbery when it came to flowers (F 260, 1617). Whatever evidence
there might be for Dickinson's imperiousness, her approach to the ar-
chitecture of gardens was simple; her feeling for flowers, democratic.

Thus, two years before she wrote her elegy depicting the rose, she
wrote a love poem to the simple clover. Once again employing the
language of social distinctions, Dickinson describes the clover's chief
attributes in anthropomorphic terms: generosity, bravery, and humil-
ity. It is a "Purple Democrat":

> There is a flower that Bees prefer –
> And Butterflies – desire –
> To gain the Purple Democrat
> The Humming Bird – aspire –
>
> And Whatsoever Insect pass –
> A Honey bear away
> Proportioned to his several dearth
> And her – capacity –
>
> Her face be rounder than the Moon
> And ruddier than the Gown
> Of Orchis in the Pasture –
> Or Rhododendron – worn –
>
> She doth not wait for June –
> Before the World be Green –
> Her sturdy little Countenance
> Against the Wind – be seen –
>
> Contending with the Grass –
> Near Kinsman to Herself –

For privilege of Sod and Sun –
Sweet Litigants for Life –

And when the Hills be full –
And newer fashions blow –
Doth not retract a single spice
For pang of jealousy –

Her Public – be the Noon –
Her Providence – the Sun –
Her Progress – by the Bee – proclaimed –
In sovreign – Swerveless Tune –

The Bravest – of the Host –
Surrendering – the last –
Not even of Defeat – aware –
When cancelled by the Frost – (F 642)

The suggestion of archaism provided by "doth" and by the substitu-
tion of what would normally constitute the subjunctive "be" for "is" or
"are" in this poem imparts a biblical tone to Dickinson's encomium to
the clover. The clover of the genus *Trifolium* is actually a hay plant, a
cover crop of leguminous forage which Dickinson remarks in saying it
"contend[s] with the Grass" for its very life, its "Sod and Sun." As she
does with other small, unsung plants, she praises its selflessness: it
gives honey in proportion to the needs of any who seek it—insect,
bee, butterfly, or hummingbird. "Sturdy," never jealous of "newer
fashions" of flowers that bloom in June, the clover dares the wind long
before spring and dies last, retaining its reddish-purple hue even as
frost kills it. Most remarkably, it blooms in fields and meadows with
no "Public" but the day itself, no caretaker or "Providence" but sun-
shine, and no gardener to chart its growth but the bee that buzzes
more loudly over it when it is full-grown and full of honey. Emily
Dickinson did not often entitle her poems; here she did not, though
the editors of *Poems* (1890) provided the title "Purple Clover." Her

description of a flower-face "rounder than the Moon" and "ruddier" than an orchis or rhododendron might be suitable for a number of flowers, but other characteristics described in this poem eliminate dahlias, for instance, or zinnias or other tended flowers. Dickinson's little clover is cheap as grass and loved for that reason. The fact that, unlike Emerson in "The Rhodora," she does not name her flower but trusts it to be recognized by its features may emphasize the clover's ubiquity. As in her poem for the robin, "You'll know Her – by Her Foot –" (F 604), Dickinson's omission of the name of her subject may constitute a good-humored game, played with her imaginary reader. Readers in her own time, an agrarian age, were far more alive to the names and natures of plants, flowers, and birds than we are today.

Finally, it is no exaggeration to claim that flowers, especially wildflowers, had spiritual significance for Emily Dickinson. (As we shall see, they had sentimental significance as well for her family, preparing her for burial.) It is evident that she regarded flowers as nearly human. "The career of flowers differs from ours only in inaudibleness," she told her Norcross cousins in 1873. "I feel more reverence as I grow"—like a flower?—"for these mute creatures whose suspense or transport may surpass my own" (L 388). Often she chose a floral event to make a philosophical argument or to teach a moral lesson in verse. Sometimes the poems in which she does so have been read wrongly or inadequately because the genus or species of the flowers she selected is unknown to the critic. Thus, I have heard the last stanza of "Some Rainbow – coming from the Fair!" described by a well-known British critic as a "New Englander's dream vision" of a Turkish army, standing in colorful uniforms on a hillside. The lines that provoked his reading form the conclusion of a poem that her editors entitled "Summer's Armies" when bringing out the first edition of her *Poems* (1890). This lyric describes the awakening of platoons of "Baronial Bees" "From some old Fortress on the sun," the reappearance of robins, and of the orchis in spring. It concludes with a vision indeed:

Without Commander! Countless! Still!
The Regiments of Wood and Hill
In bright detachments stand!
Behold, Whose multitudes are these?
The Children of whose turbaned seas —
Or what Circassian Land? (F 162b)

In these lines, Emily Dickinson is writing not about the Turkish army but about the power of beauty: in this case, that of new tulips. Springing up on the hillside, they assume a near-military formation that describes their aesthetic potency. Moreover, she knew that botanical or wild tulips like the *Tulipa acuminata* or *cornuta,* called the "Turkish tulip," came, like all tulips, from Turkey, where men were "turbaned." The tulip was introduced to Europe in the mid-1500s, appearing first in Vienna and later in the Netherlands. "Circassia" is the name of that historic region between the Black Sea and the Greater Caucasus that was ceded by Turkey to Russia in 1829. Circassian women were supposedly famed for their beauty, a legend that may linger in Dickinson's appreciative tag, "Circassian Land." This poem about armies of wild tulips coloring the Amherst "Wood and Hill" as spring overtakes the world demonstrates her visual sensitivity as well as her conviction that nature had magical powers.

A more important instance in which knowledge of flowers—in particular, the flowers Dickinson preferred—renders the meaning of a Dickinson poem more beautiful and suasive to the critical eye is furnished by the following poem, written in early 1864:

It bloomed and dropt, a Single Noon —
The Flower — distinct and Red —
I, passing, thought another Noon
Another in it's stead

Will equal glow, and thought no more
But came another Day

To find the Species disappeared –
The Same Locality –

The Sun in place – no other fraud
On Nature's perfect Sum –
Had I but lingered Yesterday –
Was my retrieveless blame –

Much Flowers of this and further Zones
Have perished in my Hands
For Seeking it's Resemblance –
But unapproached it stands –

The single Flower of the Earth
That I, in passing by
Unconscious was – Great Nature's Face
Passed infinite by Me – (F 843)

This poem is infrequently commented upon or anthologized, although it is one of the most elegant and powerful of Emily Dickinson's poems. The peculiarly modernist pessimism that some of her verses uniquely inflect appears here, thrown into relief by the poem's revelation of her clear understanding of the Romantic mode. The idea that nature may teach moral virtues; that it often does so by offering an object of extraordinary value, beauty, or meaning to the receptive eye of the poet; that nature does this in a single priceless moment which can never come again, and that the poet-seer will live thereafter altered by the recollection of that time: these are characteristics one meets in archetypal Romantic poems—Wordsworth's essential "I wandered lonely as a cloud," for example, in which ten thousand daffodils "at a glance" bring him sufficient "wealth" that his "inward eye" is permanently endowed with radiant vision and his heart with joy. The speaker of Dickinson's poem, however, does not accede to this experience of happiness—and through her own fault.

The setting of Emily Dickinson's poem is a garden through which she recalls "passing," clearly with other objectives than viewing in mind. The poem, set in the past, constitutes a meditation on a deeply felt experience that, like Wordsworth's in the daffodil poem, is understood only after much thought. The poet confesses to having seen a brilliant flower, one that was both "distinct" and "Red," a flower that stood out and commanded attention. Negligently, she passed it by, however, enabled to do so, perhaps, by the fact that it died as soon as it had bloomed. No flower does this *precisely,* and thus Dickinson's first line is dramatically synthetic. Yet there was indeed one flower grown by the Dickinsons that blooms for only one day and then drops from the stem, often in noontide heat: the daylily or *Hemerocallis.*

In *Emily Dickinson's Imagery,* Rebecca Patterson identifies the flower that "bloomed and dropt, a Single Noon" as a "red rose of love" that Dickinson left unplucked.[33] Martha Dickinson Bianchi writes of the Dickinsons' Cinnamon or "Love-for-a-day roses," called thus "because they flare and fall between sunrise and sunset."[34] But the characteristics of the *Hemerocallis* better fit the poem. "Distinct and red" is Dickinson's flower, she says; as gardeners know, daylilies—tall, lean, often singular, and ending in a burst of bell-shaped color—make a profoundly dramatic appeal in any garden. Like lilies-of-the-valley *(Convallaria majalis)* or lily-of-the-Nile *(Agapanthus africanus),* they do not belong to the genus *Lilium* at all, though they have lily-like blooms. *Hemerocallis* "lilies" were known colloquially in the nineteenth century as the "Blooms-for-an-hour" flower, and Dickinson makes unspoken but clever use of the fact in this poem. That she chooses a daylily to pass by, to ignore, succinctly indicts her speaker; Susan A. Roth summarizes the reactions of most gardeners by writing that daylily "flowers are truly amazing—huge trumpet-shaped affairs," whose stalks can be five feet tall.[35] To pass by *this* most distinctive flower without worshipping is proof of a failure to be thankful for the bounty of nature.

Daylilies, moreover, produce numerous blossoms on a single stalk. If one has dropped, the speaker assumes (with some justification) that

"Another in it's stead / Will equal glow." To her surprise, however, when next she passes the place where the daylily died—presumably a plot or clump full of them—the entire planting has disappeared. We learn from the second quatrain that the speaker has visited the spot the very next day, yet in that short time, the "Species" has vanished. This is strange behavior indeed for the *Hemerocallis,* even if the blossom that died was the last of five or six blooms on the "scape" or stalk. But Dickinson intends our surprise. For her poem is not realistic; it seeks to describe a mysterious event and an equally exquisite punishment that avenges mysteriously primitive powers that deserve more respect than has been accorded them.

The event becomes the impressive and poignant source of the speaker's grief and shame in the last three stanzas. It teaches her her own "retrieveless blame," blame that can never be lifted because the flower she passed by turns out to be "The single Flower of the Earth." The poem's forcefulness is like that of a fairy tale in which the transmogrified Prince reveals himself in all his superb humanity but is not recognized by the careless heroine. At the same time, the speaker is an Eve, seeking the lost Paradise. She roves the "Zones" of her garden—*zone* is the plantsman's name, Webster reports, for "a biogeographic region that supports a similar . . . flora throughout its extent"—in quest of a flower made in the red flower's likeness. But it remains peerless. The poem ends in tones of dignified but anguished remorse: "Great Nature's Face"—the face of this single flower, representing all creation—"Passed infinite by Me —."

To appreciate the degree of Dickinson's fondness for wildflowers, it is enough to cite this poem wherein not the rose or the elegant *Lilium* but the field flower *Hemerocallis,* probably the *Hemerocallis fulva* (see Fig. 11), becomes the metaphor of all nature. The poet's funeral, however, offers another proof of her love for the humble flowers of woods and fields. When Emily Dickinson's mother lay in her coffin in 1882, a bouquet of violets was placed near her dead hand. Four years later, a sorrowing Lavinia Dickinson, her sister's nurse, had the painful task of choosing flowers for Emily's coffin. (It was said that in youth Emily never seemed dressed without them.) Since Emily imagined roses in her poems more than any other flower, it might have been appropriate for Lavinia to pick a few of the Dickinsons' Harrison's Yellow roses, which would probably have been blooming since May first. T. W. Higginson had written in his essay "Letter to a Young Contributor" (which prompted Emily Dickinson to write to him forty years earlier), "Literature is attar of roses, one distilled drop from a million blossoms." One of Dickinson's acute poems on the poetic process takes the making of perfume from roses as a central metaphor and might have been a meditation on Higginson's conceit. For her, poetry—an essential oil, an attar—was earned ("wrung") through hard work and by understanding form ("Screws"). As with flowers, "Suns" (natural genius alone) were insufficient to produce it:

> Essential Oils – are wrung –
> The Attar from the Rose
> Be not expressed by Suns – alone –
> It is the gift of Screws – (F 772)

But for the poet's funeral, Lavinia chose one of the wildflowers they had gathered together as girls.[36] She selected fragrant heliotrope for Emily to "take to Judge Lord," but also the *Cypripedium* or lady's slipper. The nineteenth-century *Cypripedium* [Fig. 22] was less articulated and picturesque in form than today's lady's slippers; its apparent timidity as it nestled among leaves gave it a quaintness that Emily had treasured as a child. Lavinia must have culled the heliotrope from plants in Emily's conservatory, but the lady's slippers would have been fetched from the woods beyond the Homestead. She also tucked a "knot of field blue violets" into the poet's white shroud at the neck. Blue violets were thick upon the Dickinson lawns that day. They had been at Emily's side, she said, when she wrote her mysterious letters to "Master" in the 1860s; that they were "transitive," she wrote Olive

22. Lady's slipper *(Cypripedium acaule)*. From *Curtis's Botanical Magazine,* 1792.

Stearns in the spring of 1875, was their "only pang" (L 435). Later, Clara Newman Turner marveled that "a wreath of the same modest [violets] was the only decoration of her casket." Although pansy violets meant modesty in the floral dictionaries, the etymology of the word "pansy" includes *pensée* or *pensez à moi,* a wistful irony that may have occurred to Dickinson's mourners as they followed her narrow white coffin to the grave.

CHAPTER THREE

The Enclosed Garden

My flowers are near and foreign, and I have but to cross the floor to stand in the Spice Isles.

Emily Dickinson to Elizabeth Holland, March 1866

A REMARKABLE REVIEW in the *Amherst Record* (December 1891) of the second volume of Emily Dickinson's poems edited by Todd and Higginson warned people "who understand the word poetry to mean lines smoothly written" to look elsewhere; for the Amherst poet's lyrics were unconventional, more concerned with "spirit" than form. Calling his townswoman the genteel "answer" to the rough if capacious muse of Walt Whitman, the reviewer declared her "close in touch with the unwritten harmony in forest and glen" and praised both Dickinson's poems and the poet herself in floral images:

> After one has visited some grand conservatory and feasted the eye on the richest and rarest products of floriculture, has been surfeited with the glory of color and the weight of perfume of the floral aristocracy, it is a relief to turn to the wild rose growing by the wayside hedge.[1]

To the *Amherst Record*'s commentator, the aristocratic daughter of Edward Dickinson who herself kept an exquisite conservatory that contained the "rarest products of floriculture" wrote poems like wild roses. Accustomed to the hothouse verse of the "Gilded Age," the commentator clearly relished the work of what Austin once called Emily's "wild" heart.[2] Lingering in the reviewer's metaphors was the familiar equation of the poet herself (despite her connections) with a wild rose; implicit was the classic comparison of all women, especially poets and the unmarried, to flowers. Thus, when Mabel Loomis Todd, lecturing on Dickinson's poetry four years later, compared it to "the orchid growing among ordinary flowers of the field,"[3] her audience was free to conclude that the reclusive poet herself was an orchid among dandelions, a writer whose life and methods were rare, refined, unusual, and not to be judged by ordinary standards.

In our own time, using floral metaphors to characterize Dickinson's texts is less frequent a habit than it was in the nineteenth and early twentieth centuries, while contemporary criticism likewise resists describing the poet herself as flower-like. Recalling Edna St. Vincent Millay reading her poems to an audience of Yale students in the 1940s, Dickinson's biographer Richard Sewall once said, "She stood before us like a daffodil."[4] Sewall was doubtless remembering the picture Millay made then, with her profusion of curly red-gold hair like a flower atop a long black velvet cloak like a stem, and his remark complimented her beauty. (Millay's sonnets about April and free love in the springtime may also have prompted the playful simile.) Edna Millay, like Elinor Wylie, often made her personal loveliness a subject of verse, attiring herself for her role as poet-actress in romantic garb worthy of the ornate flowers of Lalique. Dickinson's self-consciousness was not quite so manipulative, and certainly she wrote no poems to her own beauty. Still, her dainty white dresses and her custom of denying visitors her company while offering them instead a sprig of jasmine or a white clover on a silver tray acted to efface the distinction between her body and the bodies of her flowers: both were fragile, both were from sheltered worlds, both were doomed to die.

Writing to Sarah Tuckerman in July 1878, Dickinson spoke of herself as a rose in danger. It is one of the most striking examples of her identification with the flowers she grew; only the more prosaic part of her letter makes a distinction between them. Mrs. Tuckerman had apparently proposed to see Emily Dickinson and received this reply:

> Would it be prudent to subject an apparitional interview to a grosser test? The Bible portentously says 'that which is Spirit is Spirit.'

> Go not too near a House of Rose —
> The depredation of a Breeze
> Or inundation of a Dew
> Alarm it's Walls away —
> Nor try to touch the Butterfly,
> Nor climb the Bars of Ecstasy —
> In insecurity to lie
> Is Joy's insuring quality — (L 558 / F 1479)

Dickinson indicates that "apparitional" interviews by mail must be enough for her constant correspondent; she has sent Mrs. Tuckerman her spirit in letters, but the "grosser test" of having her body seen must not be tried. Her homily takes its exemplum from the nature of roses, a flower subject to more than fifty diseases, whose petals are easily swept away by a few drops of dew or the least of winds. The "house" of her body is like a rose, but she is also the untouchable butterfly. Mrs. Tuckerman must not try to see her, to "climb the Bars of Ecstasy"—that is, to enter Dickinson's "magic Prison," where, as she exults in another poem, she is "Immured the whole of Life" (F 1675). After all, their joyful friendship will only be heightened, she says, by surmise.

Despite such poems of psychic revelation, the manifest intellectuality of Emily Dickinson's art and an ever-developing awareness of its cosmopolitan sophistication have almost eliminated the Victorian habit of imagining her as a shrinking violet or air-fed orchid. On the other hand, the custom of decorating book jackets of Dickinsoniana with flowers, a custom that began with the Indian pipes of the first volume of her *Poems* (1890), continues today; indeed, it thrives. Contemporary illustrators usually alternate between choosing sheaves of sturdy wildflowers or bouquets of fragile camellias, Calla lilies, or white roses, as if to emphasize either Dickinson's "barefoot heart" and natural themes or her image as the poet of delicate insights and romance.[5] This tradition of illustration tends to sentimentalize Dickinson's poetry, taking no account of its austere, aphoristic, and prophetic elements. Yet at the same time it serves as a kind of shorthand to advertise what was for her a central artistic focus. Her attraction to exotic flowers and her affection for the woodland kind, moreover, reveal two aspects of her personality and character, each carefully guarded from danger of extinction: the quest for vivid, even dangerous experience, represented (ironically) by the sequestered plants of her conservatory, and the pursuit of good sense and duty, emblematized by woodland flowers.

In *The Botany of Desire,* Michael Pollan writes of gardening as a contest between the apollonian quest for balance and form and the dionysian quest for ecstasy. Developing flowers like the tulip, he argues, requires a will toward both. Reading Emily Dickinson's poems and letters about her special flowers—their shapes, colors, and enchanting effect upon her—one recognizes both the apollonian and the dionysian, the passion for form and the need for delight. Two other categories, two kinds of beauty, preoccupied her in this double quest. In an early poem, she contemplates them: a simple type represented by "all the Daisies / Which upon the hillside blow" and a more exotic, complex form illustrated by butterflies from Santo Domingo (Haiti), where sugar cane was grown and the landscape, different from Amherst's, could be imagined as intoxicatingly bright and colorful:

> Flowers – Well – if anybody
> Can the extasy define –
> Half a transport – half a trouble –
> With which flowers humble men:

Anybody find the fountain
From which floods so contra flow –
I will give him all the Daisies
Which opon the hillside blow.

Too much pathos in their faces
For a simple breast like mine –
Butterflies from St Domingo
Cruising round the purple line –
Have a system of aesthetics –
Far superior to mine (F 95)

The idea of flowers prompts Dickinson to reflect with colloquial intimacy upon the mingling of joy and pain—"transport" and "trouble"—that beauty causes in the heart of a beholder. These oppositional ("contra") "floods" flow from what she calls a "fountain" whose origins are unknown, perhaps unknowable, but which she yearns to locate. In "Dejection: An Ode," Coleridge mourned that, for him, "the passion and the life, whose fountains are within" could no longer be animated by the sight of "outward forms." Dickinson's poem suggests that *her* "fountain" springs from a response to secrets of nature that still move her. Nevertheless, until the close of her life she confessed both the rapture and the anguish that the sight of things beautiful caused her, as well as the ambivalence that such an intense response could engender. (In an undated poem, for example, she would write an aesthete's prayer: "Beauty crowds me till I die / Beauty mercy have on me / But if I expire today / Let it be in sight of thee –" [F 1687].) Failing to "define" or limit the ecstasy flowers awaken, she deems it "humbl[ing]" and overwhelming ("too much"), even in the case of daisies. This reflection prompts another, cryptically stated in the last four lines: that the beauty of the foreign and unknown may be more compelling than that of the near and familiar; that, indeed, butterflies "on their passage Cashmere" (F 98), traveling great distances past the "purple line" of the equator in search of nourishment, have a "system of aesthetics" superior to hers. By virtue of not being "simple"—provincial—and not being human, they inhabit the beautiful in its various aspects with painless ease.

No lepidopterist, Dickinson seems nevertheless to have gleaned real knowledge of the butterfly's migratory habits, which delighted her. We now know that the monarch butterfly regularly migrates three thousand miles from Canada through the United States to forested slopes high in the mountains of Mexico. Possibly in the service of a private symbolism, Dickinson chose to imagine her butterflies as Brazilian and conceives them appearing in Amherst at high noon. Like the birds that were her "posts" (F 780) or the hummingbird that brought her mail from Tunis, they were foreign yet at home in her garden. In 1872, the painter Winslow Homer depicted a lady asleep

23. Winslow Homer, *The Butterfly* (1872).
Oil on canvas, 15⁹⁄₁₆ x 22¾ inches, Cooper-Hewitt, National Design Museum, Smithsonian Institution, gift of Charles Savage Homer, Jr., 1917-14-1, photograph by Michael Fischer.

in her garden in what appears to be noonday heat. She holds a large unfurled fan whose shape repeats the smaller one of a monarch butterfly resting on her hand [Fig. 23]. Like Dickinson's poem, Homer's elegant *The Butterfly* declares the conjunction of the foreign and the near, the exotic and the commonplace, his New York/New England settings with those he would paint of Jamaica or the Bahamas. Just so, Dickinson's Amherst garden entertained brilliant visitors from afar:

> Some such Butterfly be seen
> On Brazilian Pampas —
> Just at noon — no later — Sweet —
> Then — the Licence closes — (F 661)

By their ritual wanderings (both poem and painting show), butterflies join the northern with the southern hemisphere, the strange with the familiar, as Dickinson (disingenuously modest) claims she cannot, with her "simple breast" and New England restraint. Her poem, however, proves otherwise. Sarah Burns speculates that the butterfly in Homer's painting, which "flutter[s] near the heart he wished to win"—that of Helena deKay, who later married the poet Richard Gilder—is the emblem of Homer himself.[6] Dickinson would sign "Butterfly" as her pseudonym in 1885 (L 1013), and she wrote about the butterfly more than fifty times, somewhat less than the pollinating bee. The Dickinsons grew asters and marigolds in an effort to attract butterflies. Butterflies also had an important place in the hierarchy of Dickinson's literary garden, their fine radiance seeming heavenly to her, as her play on the word "assumption" in a musical set of triplets makes clear:

> The Butterfly's Assumption Gown
> In Chrysoprase Apartments hung
> This Afternoon put on —
>
> How condescending to descend
> And be of Buttercups the friend
> In a New England Town — (F 1329)

Just as flowers traditionally appear in *vanitas* art from the Renaissance through the nineteenth century to suggest the ephemeral nature of life, so the butterfly often appears on the stalk of a tulip or narcissus as an emblem of the immortality to which perennials aspire. Flowers, like butterflies, emerge in their final form from shapes that had draped and obscured their jewel-like brilliancy. Sometimes Dickinson imagines the butterfly arising from a moth-like shroud, like Christ who broke open his chrysalis or grave clothes to assume the beauty of his godhead or real nature. In her version of the doxology— either a playfully impudent substitution of nature for God or an emphasis on the God of nature—she prayed "In the name of the Bee" (God the Father), "In the name of the Breeze" (the Holy Spirit), and "In the name of the Butterfly" (God the Son, who came from far-off eternity into this world) (F 23). The butterfly in its gem-like gown, attracted to the buttercup, was one of her emblems of the union and attraction of divine and human. To be sure, butterflies often perch on exotic flowers in the classic eighteenth- and nineteenth-century botanical drawings to which Dickinson's education would have introduced her. There, they resemble elegant floral forms [Fig. 24]. In sympathy with this tradition, Dickinson depicts "Navies of Butterflies" sailing among the "Roses . . . from Zinzebar – / And Lily tubes – like wells," emerging from "Straits of Blue" and "firmamental seas" to adorn both her "Puritan Garden" outside and the interior one on glass shelves (F 266, L 685). In poems like "Flowers – Well – if anybody / Can the extasy define –," this migratory pattern of the butterfly becomes emblematic of the poet's blending of the exotic with the homely.

☙

When the poems discussed above were written, Emily Dickinson had taken practical measures to ensure that she could grow her beloved flowers in any season. Perhaps she also intended that the enrichment of the exotic, represented by tropical butterflies and blooms, should

24. Maria Sibylla Merian, Plate 31 from *Dissertation in Insect
Generations and Metamorphosis in Surinam,* second edition, 1719.
Bound volume of 72 hand-colored engravings, National Museum of
Women in the Arts, gift of Wallace and Wilhemina Holladay.

be continually available to her. Four years earlier in 1855, she had accepted (indeed, may have entreated) Edward Dickinson's gift of a small conservatory, built facing south and east and adjoining the dining room of the mansion [Fig. 25]. Entered either through her father's library or from the outer garden, the conservatory was architecturally commonplace and serviceable rather than elaborate, imaginative, or large. But it did pay tribute to her gardening skills and her taste in flowers, and it was a sensitive present that showed her father's familiarity with his daughter's temperament. She literally suffered when

25. The Dickinson Homestead in the nineteenth century, with Emily's conservatory at the viewer's right (off the garden).

winter robbed her of her garden; she might speak of "the happy Sorrow of Autumn," but it filled her with real pain, if wryly expressed on occasion (L 945). The example of a dead flower might seem an inadequate index to the finality of human loss, but to Dickinson, for whom gardening made up so great a part of life, it was not: "My acquaintance with the Irreparable," she wrote, "dates from the Death Bed of a young Flower to which I was deeply attached" (L 945). Her grief on such occasions was very real, although her employment of the solemn phrase "Death Bed" suggests an awareness that it might be thought extravagant, even ludicrous.

Her need to be in the presence of flowers was genuine and doubtless arose in part from the fact that they constituted major subject matter for her poems and letters. The painter Odilon Redon (1840–1916) declared in his memoir *À Soi-Même* that he must have flowers near him daily: he needed to *see* them for their "intensity" and "profundity"; they were the "confluence of two streams: that of representation and that of memory"; they kept in his mind both the beginnings of life and the approach of death. For Redon as for Dickinson, the opulence of flowers on one hand and their simplicity on the other formed two aspects of the beautiful. When her Aunt Katie Sweetser marked the anniversary of Mrs. Dickinson's death by sending Emily lilies in November—perhaps from Mrs. Sweetser's own conservatory or, more expensively, from a greenhouse—the poet's heart, she said, was "so high it overflows" (L 952). Flowers were "qualified as saints" (L 991). When they were gone from view, the landscape lost its mystery, magic, and sanctity. Because of her father's gift, she could write Maria Whitney in early 1885, "The little garden within, though tiny, is triumphant. There are scarlet carnations, with a witching suggestion, and hyacinths covered with promises which I know they will keep" (L 969).

The formidable "Squire" Dickinson was himself moved by the sight of blooming flowers. In April 1828 he had written his fiancée, Emily's mother, just before their marriage, "I have been down to [our] house, and . . . found one of our Peach trees in blossom . . . I . . . [cannot] feel happy enough amid such beauties."⁷ To preserve such flowering trees as well as tropical and subtropical plants, conservatories had long been popular in America. Bananas, mimosa, and pineapple were grown in eighteenth-century "hothouses." George Washington's "pinery" at Mount Vernon displayed pineapples but roses too. While kings maintained orangeries to preserve the illusion of summer amid snow, the glass house of the nineteenth-century horticulturalist kept tropical flowers before the eye all year round. Emily Dickinson's "garden within" contained no trees, only what Breck's *New Book of Flowers* listed as shrubs: the *Daphne odora* and the Arabian jasmine. It was a refuge for rare, glamorous plants and also a warm place where she could overwinter field flowers like buttercups, usually considered far too ordinary for a conservatory.

Indeed, the contents of the "garden within" illumine Emily Dickinson's sensibility. Its most precious occupants were the exotic plants and flowers that would be difficult to grow outdoors at any season in Amherst: the Eurasian *Daphne odora* "with its orange-bloom scent astray from the Riviera"; oleander *(Nerium)* with its white, red, and pink flowers; ferns (possibly the popular "maidenhair fern" or "cheveux de Venus" [*Adiantum capillus-veneris*]); two Cape jasmines (now called gardenias, *Gardenia jasminoides*); camellias *(Camellia)*, a subtropical flower from Asia; the dainty oxalis or wood sorrel from South America; and eventually the "poet's jessamine"⁸ or jasmine given to her by Samuel Bowles. (Some of these exotic plants like the camellia were fairly recent introductions to western gardens and greenhouses, the camellia itself having been brought to Charleston, South Carolina from China in 1785. That Emily's conservatory contained such "exotics" implies her horticultural sophistication and her attraction to charming, sensuous flowers.) These visually alluring imported flowers had heady scents that caused the poet to write happily that she could inhabit "the Spice Isles" merely by crossing the dining room floor to the conservatory, where the plants hung in baskets or were placed in rows on glass shelves (L 315). Interspersed with the uncommon blooms, however, were the wildflowers—often plain, sometimes awkward-looking—that Dickinson could not live without. Thus, she tended her queenly Daphnes and gardenias together with her transplanted lady's slippers, achieving a generous horticultural perspective.

Considerable attention has been paid to Emily Dickinson's visual imagination and auditory sensibility, very little to that fondness for strong perfumes that seems to have prompted her to grow plants that emitted them. Her attraction to assertive blooms is another evidence of a powerful personality that was anything but "timid" or "little" or girlish, despite her frequent recourse to those words in an effort to create a childlike or unthreatening self-image. Dickinson's preference for the perfume of the tropical jasmine—sweet and overpowering, delicate and acute—or for old ("Bourbon") roses with their ripe, intoxicating scent indicates a sensibility that found intensity delectable. In a short poem that is rarely if ever discussed, she calls the perfume of her flowers equivalent to poetry itself and the flower whose scent she inhales, the equal of a poet laureate:

> They have a little Odor – that to me
> Is metre – nay – 'tis Poesy –
> And spiciest at fading – celebrate –
> A Habit – of a Laureate – (F 505)

At first she imagines scent as one of the several features of a poem: meter, the "jingle" that accompanies the poet's "tramp," his artistic excursion (L 265). But that comparison is insufficient, just as "melody," the alternative option recorded in fascicle 39, was insufficient. No, the perfume of flowers is poetry itself. (Recall the later poem "Essential Oils" [F 772] that compares the manufacture of attar of roses to the making of a lyric.) The flowers that inspired the last two lines may have been Oriental lilies, which, more than any other flower she may have grown, yield a rush of perfume just before they wither and become scentless. Dickinson compares this "habit" to the most beguiling poems of an aging ("fading") poet laureate. (Perhaps she had Tennyson in mind—England's laureate since 1850—whose *Maud* and *Idylls of the King* were immensely popular.) Her use of the word "spiciest" suggests that she was writing about the flowers of tropical origin maintained in the conservatory.

Like so many of her preferences in literature and painting, tropical flowers indicated the depths of Dickinson's intellectually venturesome nature. That she was deeply attached to "my *own* DEAR HOME" (L 20) is shown by the fact that the word "home" appears more than five hundred times in her extant letters, usually in a context of love or longing. Yet she was always moved by the idea of those far-off places—Sicily, Vevay, Buenos Aires, Peru, East India—and even those threatening ones—Vesuvius, Etna, Chimborazo, the Cordilleras—that she showed no inclination to visit except in dreams, poems, magazines, pictures, and (probably) greenhouse catalogues. In fact, the imagination that preferred Shakespeare's *Antony and Cleopatra* above all his other plays was remarkably at home with gorgeous display, with opulence and people of fiery temper, even if the woman who possessed that imagination was shy, quiet, and clothed in a colorless dress. She once told Samuel Bowles that it was as "delicious to see [him]" as to eat "a Peach before the time" it is ripe (L 438). Devouring a peach is a bold metaphor for enjoying a man's company, since sexual appetite is so often imaged as eating. Yet Dickinson risks the phrase (a phrase that implies a measure of dissatisfaction: peaches before they are ripe can be like stones, which suggests that his company was insufficiently loving). Reliving the experience of hearing his voice, she tells Bowles that she misses the "besetting Accents, you bring from your Numidian Haunts" (L 438). It was merely from his newspaper offices in Springfield, Massachusetts, that Bowles had driven over to visit her a few days earlier. But her letter teases him confidently, imagining that he comes from Numidia, the North African section of the Carthaginian Empire (modern Algeria). His Byronic good looks, his daring speech, his dashing manner made her speak of him in exotic and foreign imagery, even though Bowles was the most American and practical of men. He liked to travel in Europe and Yosemite, not the tropics (F 1432a).

Emily Dickinson, however, displayed a pronounced fascination for the tropics, especially South America—an attraction that she shared with the geologists, horticulturalists, anthropologists, poets, and artists of her time. The *Personal Narrative, Cosmos,* and other writings of the naturalist-explorer Alexander von Humboldt (which Darwin said gave him "preconceived ideas" about the tropics) caused scientists and such painters as Thomas Cole, Frederic Edwin Church, George Catlin, and Martin Johnson Heade to travel to South America, where they hoped to discover a landscape like that of the biblical Garden of Eden. In what Katherine Emma Manthorne calls a "mix of science and romanticism, fact and fiction,"[9] the image of Latin America—particularly Brazil—was proposed in nineteenth-century literate discourse as a contemporary Eden, while the word "Eden" itself was widely used to describe the superb scenery of its tropical "paradise." Indeed, an issue of the *Southern Illustrated News,* printed at Richmond on October 17, 1863, contained, in addition to a profile of Robert E. Lee and reports of the blockade of Southern ports, a poem entitled "First Love" by one "Leclerc." Leclerc's literally florid stanzas compared the "young heart's first awaking" to the blooming of "a tender violet," while the lover's eyes "Seem to stray in search of Eden." (The *Southern Illustrated News* followed this poem with another about a "blue flower in my garden": "The bee and I, we love it both, / Though it is frail and small." Such random examples demonstrate the broad currency of Emily Dickinson's imagery—bees, the private garden of the self, the small frail flower—while at the same time reminding us of the distinction such images attain under her hand.)

A familiar synonym for joy to those who knew their Bible, the word "Eden" figured importantly in the high art of the nineteenth century. Thus we recall that in a note to Susan Dickinson, written in

1859 with an accompanying drawing of a forked creature, Emily Dickinson signed herself "Cole." That she drew a reptilian form suggests that she was familiar with Thomas Cole's famous painting *Expulsion from the Garden of Eden* (1827–1828) wherein Adam and Eve, tricked by the serpent, are sent forth in sorrow from their paradise of palms and brilliant blooms. In 1878, she would greet a new neighbor with a bouquet, enclosing the note cited earlier: "Expulsion from Eden grows indistinct in the presence of flowers so blissful, and with no disrespect to Genesis, Paradise remains" (L 552). Her first phrase was Cole's; so was the idea that "Paradise remains" which Cole expressed in his "Essay on American Scenery" (1836), saying, "We are still in Eden." This essay, which was of great significance to all Americans and especially to painters and writers, urged them to turn from European subject matter—ostentatious buildings associated with corruption and decline—and take pride instead in native American scenery, whose glorious purity brought Eden back to earth. Cole's glowing landscapes made him venerated, popular, and greatly mourned when he died. Hundreds of thousands of copies of his *Voyage of Life* series (1847–1848)—originally painted as a course of moral instruction for the young Julia Ward Howe—were hung in schools, churches, railway stations, hotels, and private homes. Its first panel, *Childhood,* presents a paradisal world of both tropical and woodland flowers, a new Eden that represents the innocence of a newborn child. What seem to be Dickinson's several allusions to its scenery and subject matter make it highly likely that she knew *The Voyage of Life*. Robert Hinshelwood's etchings and James Smillie's engravings of various paintings in the series were sold and displayed throughout the 1850s, widely advertised and easily available.

Certainly Dickinson thought of Cole as America's foremost landscape artist, and she used the word "Eden" several times in precisely his connotation of paradise regained. She wrote Elizabeth Holland in the summer of 1873, "Eden, always eligible, is peculiarly so this noon. It would please you to see how intimate the Meadows are with the Sun" (L 391). Eden with its "jessamines" became her synonym for passionate love in her poem of bashful delight, "Come slowly – Eden!" (F 205), whose speaker sips bliss from the tropical jasmine apparently transported to her New England garden. In general, Eden meant paradise to Dickinson, though occasionally she joined that meaning with others: Eden as passion yet also as shelter, as home. She summoned the word in praising Samuel Bowles to the newly widowed Mary: "As he was himself Eden, he is with Eden, for we cannot become what we were not" (L 567). Bowles had been a refuge for Dickinson, especially after her father's death, while her loving regard for what she deemed his "Arabian" glamour also justified her use of the word (L 643).

She liked to imagine those far-off floral regions where "in the Isles of spice – / The subtle Cargoes – lie –" (F 426). But Emily Dickinson shared that proclivity with writers and painters of her day. She read Tennyson's poems closely from girlhood to death; his landscapes where "Droops the heavy-blossomed bower" and his "Summer isles of Eden lying in dark-purple spheres of sea" disclosed a fascination with the tropical that could symbolize either paradise or spiritual peril. Milton's *Paradise Lost,* which she studied at Mary Lyon's Seminary, was "the primary source of edenic imagery in the post-Renaissance world" and the shaping referent of such Edens as Tennyson's and Cole's. Dickinson's respect for *Paradise Lost* is evident in her fond, facetious description of Milton (mentioned earlier) as "the great florist," and it is specifically to his edenic garden that she often alludes (L 1038). Nineteenth-century geologists and natural scientists hypothesized that Brazil was the site of the biblical Eden. In Emily Dickinson's poetry, "Brazil" is also symbolic of the pleasure and peace of an Eden she cannot attain. "I asked no other thing –," she writes, offering her life in exchange to a sneering but "Mighty Merchant" who resembles the devil of Faust but is actually Dickinson's cruel "Burglar! Banker – Father!" (F 39), the God who gives and takes away:

Brazil? He twirled a Button –
Without a glance my way –

'But — Madam — is there nothing else —
That We can show — Today'? (F 687)

Martin Johnson Heade's departure for Brazil, where he hoped to
paint "the richest and most brilliant of the hummingbird family" in
forests of entangled passion flowers, orchids, and vines, was reported
on August 12, 1863, by the *Boston Transcript*.[10] Heade's earlier sub-
jects had been confined to North America, but now, planning his
Gems of Brazil (hummingbirds, captured so acutely by Emily Dickin-
son, were called "gems"), he was following the mid-Victorian trend of
traveling to South America for artistic stimulus. The subject matter of
his Brazilian paintings—gleaming blue morpho butterflies, the ruby-
throated hummingbird, or delicate trumpet vines observed with great
care—show a remarkable similarity to Emily Dickinson's subjects
during the same period. Although the *Gems* went unfinished as a se-
ries, they gave Heade a place among painters like Thomas Cole and
his brilliant (and only) pupil Frederic Edwin Church, who estab-
lished the tropics as a central nineteenth-century theme. Heade's ex-
quisite paintings of the 1870s—innovative outdoor still lifes of sensu-
ous flowers in tropical mists—were associated with the very concept
of the unspoiled Eden [Fig. 26]. Whether Dickinson was aware of
Heade's work (often celebrated in Boston and its newspapers), as she
was of Cole's and probably Church's, we cannot tell. Certainly she re-
sponded in her own life and writing to the contemporary absorption
with lavish tropical imagery and the new Eden.

The tropical flowers brought back by nineteenth-century explorers
were continually depicted in edenic literature and art. Conservatories
grew in number with the increasing Victorian rage for tropicana.
Cole included water lilies, palms, and giant ferns in *The Voyage of Life;*
Heade painted single magnolias or Cherokee roses against velvet
backdrops in the 1870s; Church's smoldering sunsets of the 1850s
and 1860s flickered over misty jungles full of ruddy, mysterious
blooms. The rare flowers and ferns that Emily Dickinson tended in

her conservatory—opulent gardenias, silken-fleshed camellias, cling-ing jasmine—disclosed an aspect of her personality that might not be surmised from the cheerful native flowers (asters, phlox) that she ar-ranged for the drawing room. In the enclosure of the conservatory she made December "arable as Spring," writing poetry at a small table near the daphnes, the heliotrope with its deep vanilla scent, the gar-denias with their lavish sweetness (F 1720). North and south, summer and winter, foreign and homely were thus joined for her in a single purview, a "Compound manner" (F 815). Like Dickinson's bed cham-ber, the conservatory was closely associated with the intimate act of composition, but the sultry flowers she kept there—different from the

26. Martin Johnson Heade, *Orchids and Hummingbird,* c. 1875–1883. Oil on canvas, 14⅛ x 22⅛ inches, Museum of Fine Arts, Boston, gift of Maxim Karolik for the M. and M. Karolik Collection of American Paintings. Photo-graph © 2003 Museum of Fine Arts, Boston.

plain geranium at her window upstairs—"spoke" to her of thrilling foreign skies. In 1865 she requested that her cousin Louise Norcross "give my love to my lamp and spoon, and the small Lantana," a tropical greenhouse plant with flowers that change in hue from yellow to red as they age (L 302). Apparently the Norcrosses, too, grew tropical plants in Cambridge.

Joseph Breck had proscribed such flowers for the drawing room; like orchids, they all had sexual connotations that he found too ostensible. By the 1860s, however, respectable women did not hesitate to fill their conservatories with plants of Mexican, African, or South American origin. Emphasis fell upon their probable likeness to flowers that must have grown in the biblical Eden. Nevertheless, hothouse (or conservatory) flowers of tropical species continued to preserve the connotations of sexual danger and intrigue that they manifest so brilliantly, for example, in a novel the Dickinsons owned: Hawthorne's *Blithedale Romance* (1852). In that story about the Transcendentalists' Brook Farm and the efforts of reformers such as Bronson Alcott to restore Eden to earth, the heroine Zenobia, with her "fine, frank, mellow voice," glossy hair, and full figure, is continually adorned with "a single flower . . . an exotic, of rare beauty, and as fresh as if the hot-house gardener had just clipt it from the stem." The voyeuristic narrator who likes to imagine the young woman in "the garb of Eden" understands the flower as an emblem of its wearer: "So brilliant, so rare, so costly . . . and yet enduring only for a day, it was more indicative of the pride and pomp, which had a luxuriant growth in Zenobia's character, than if a great diamond had sparkled among her hair." Being grown in a hothouse and lasting only from sunrise to sunset, Zenobia's flower is probably a hibiscus of the large and showy rose mallow *(Malva)* genus, a flower native to southern climes. That she wears an exotic flower which thrives on heat and sun rather than a primrose or violet, emblems of modesty, indicates Zenobia's deeply sexual nature: Hawthorne punishes her for it by drowning her, but he is one with his narrator Miles Coverdale in being fascinated by her independent mind. His appeal to the symbolism of tropical flowers in *The Blithedale Romance* was a sign of his times. Dickinson told Higginson, "Hawthorne appalls, entices —" but she knew his work well enough to speak of it easily (L 622).

From girlhood Emily Dickinson invested the word "Eden" with different shadings in different instances. In her letters to friends, as to the mysterious "Master," the conceit of Eden had biblical overtones of salvation. But she also founded poems on a symbolic Eden that meant pure peace, perfect joy. One poem stands out among them and uses the word with stunning originality. Disclosing the vibrant essence of the sheltered but daring sensibility that chose to grow jasmine in icy New England, "Wild nights" was written around 1862 when both Dickinson's actual and artistic lives were secretly *"at the 'White Heat'"* (F 401). It is a brilliant, deceptively simple erotic poem that, for all its fleet music, spondaic emphases, and bold repetitions of "wild," boasts a containment that tempers voluptuousness:[11]

> Wild nights – Wild nights!
> Were I with thee
> Wild nights should be
> Our luxury!
>
> Futile – the winds –
> To a Heart in port –
> Done with the Compass –
> Done with the Chart!
>
> Rowing in Eden –
> Ah – the Sea!
> Might I but moor – tonight –
> In thee! (F 269)

The setting of this vibrant poem is imagined, since the second line makes clear that its action takes place only in thought. In Genesis, Eden is a garden; in *Paradise Lost,* Eden includes a river; for Dickinson, Eden is—paradoxically—either the sea itself or a "port" upon it. The opening quatrain, whose first words might be either cries of pleasure or calls for help, conflates the wild waters with abandoned lovemaking. Being on the sea—or rather *at* sea: overwhelmed by *luxurie,* by the sumptuous excesses of passion—is one aspect of the speaker's imagined experience.[12] It is tumultuous as waves of desire. Calm as the aftermath of love, it is also a harbor. For "Wild nights" is among Dickinson's most adroit manipulations of poetic time. The poem savors a rapturous encounter that—despite the sensation of or-gasmic peace and release furnished by the middle quatrain and the fully realized opening lines of the third stanza—has *not* been experi-enced. Only in contemplation has the excited speaker been "Rowing in Eden." Yet because she has found her beloved, she can tell what their "rowing" might be like. The poem itself is a seductive prayer that she might seduce (and be seduced); the speaker begs, "Might I." But it is founded on the emblem of life as a voyage on water that we associ-ate, ironically, with hymns like "O God, our help in ages past" with its cruel conceit of Time, the river. For a nineteenth-century reader, more intimate with the Bible than we, the "Eden" myth would be evoked in all its poignancy by this poem: the angels with their flaming swords, the closing of the garden forever, the impossibility of perfect love. The very word "Eden" lends the poem dignity and even tender-ness. In October 1869, Dickinson approximated its opening phrase in a letter to her cousin Perez Dickinson Cowan: "Dying is a wild Night and a new Road" (L 332). The violent dissolution that is physical death and the shattering alteration of self experienced through passion were joined in her imagination. She found, after all, but two subjects to write about: "Love and Death" (L 873).

While reading the correspondence of Samuel Bowles with the Aus-tin Dickinsons, I came upon a letter, dated May 21, 1863, which was sent them from "East Eden," Maine. ("Eden" or "East Eden" was a vil-lage sheltered by a harbor. After a lighthouse was built there in 1875,

Eden was renamed Bar Harbor but remained a famous refuge for nineteenth-century painters and vacationers.) In his sprawling hand, Bowles reported that he was learning to row in Eden on wild waters. The similarity between his description of rowing along the rugged coast and the language and perilous scene of Emily Dickinson's lyric "Wild nights" struck me. Was it coincidence? Intended? Austin shared "Mr. Bowles'"s letters with Emily; Susan shared Emily's poems with Bowles. Was this extraordinary poem with its classic scene of an adventurer alone in a boat—perfect emblem of enterprising love— founded in part on the details of Bowles's letter, or even meant for him?

In any case, it seems clear that the quest for the biblical Eden that motivated nineteenth-century American scientists and artists to some extent underlies Emily Dickinson's appeal to "Eden" as myth and metaphor. Near the close of her life, whenever any flower was mentioned, she was apt to speak of Eden in Cole's context as paradise regained. Thus she wrote her cousins Louisa and Frances (who had sent her seeds), "The divine deposit came safely in the little bank. We have heard of the 'deeds of the spirit,' but are his acts gamboge and pink? A morning call from Gabriel is always a surprise. Were we more fresh from Eden we were expecting him – but Genesis is a 'far journey'" (L 690). Lou and Fanny seem to have been in the habit of sending "little gifts" of seeds and bulbs to Emily, who thanks them again in mid-April of the same year: "The bulbs are in the sod – the seeds in homes of paper till the sun calls them" (L 691). The Norcrosses probably found it easier to buy from Breck of Boston (the likely choice for any serious Massachusetts gardener) than the Dickinsons did. To Emily, the post carrying its "divine deposit" of seeds was like the angel Gabriel's visit to the Virgin Mary. Gabriel announced the coming of the Messiah; the seeds in their yellow ("gamboge") wrappers were announcing the coming of spring.

The seed envelopes were yellow, simply. But Emily Dickinson

chooses to describe them as *gamboges:* a strong yellow manufactured from the gum resin of Cambodian trees. This was another of her characteristic, increasingly systematic allusions to tropical countries as sources of beauty and satisfaction. "Tropic" became her synonym for dazzling, thrilling, even nourishing and sustaining. Reminding Higginson that he had not answered one of her letters, she wrote in 1879 with her usual directness: "Must I lose the Friend that saved my Life, without inquiring why? Affection gropes through Drifts of Awe – for his Tropic Door –" (L 621). Higginson lived in Worcester, Massachusetts, but his eccentric "poetess"—always alluded to by him with mild astonishment—locates him in some tropical place to suggest his importance to her. In "The Bible is an antique Volume –," she humorously wished that the forbidding narrators of its stories could be more "warbling," like the voice of the legend of Orpheus (F 1577). One of the several adjectives she discarded for "warbling" had been a favorite: "tropic."

❦

Walter Howell Deverell's 1853 painting *A Pet* [Fig. 27] captures what might be considered the paradox of the mid-Victorian woman's conservatory. His well-dressed subject, pet dog at her feet, holds a captive bird that is an emblem of herself: dependent (like Emily Dickinson) on the male(s) of her family, protected yet enclosed. She stands at the very limit of her house, the greenhouse, where she conserves her flowers and is herself conserved, being (like Milton's Eve) a human flower. By placing an allée to the outside garden/world behind her at the inviting center of the picture space, Deverell makes his lady's plight intelligible. The grounds in/of the painting appear as her entire sphere of existence. The external garden suggests a measure of sunny release, but the inner garden of the conservatory, with its terra-cotta pots of colorful geraniums, implies her inner world: one of limited opportunity and hungry affections. *She* is the pet, presumably, of her husband; like the shut-up if petted bird, she may be safe but she cannot fly. In "Captive," a poem by Dickinson's contemporary,

27. Walter Howell Deverell, *A Pet* (1853).
Tate Gallery, London. Photograph © Tate, London 2003.

Rose Terry Cooke, a caged bird complains of her condition to her mistress, also caged:

> The Summer comes, the Summer dies,
> Red leaves whirl idly from the tree,
> But no more cleaving of the skies,
> No southward sunshine waits for me!
>
> You shut me in a gilded cage.
> You deck the bars with tropic flowers,
> Nor know that freedom's living rage
> Defies you through the listless hours.

Summer and the south mean freedom to this bird, whose earlier "soaring flight" in Cooke's third stanza has been replaced by the "listless hours" of northern captivity. The bird's mistress interlaces the bars of its cage with "tropic flowers," but providing such familiar warm colors and rich scents to make it feel at home is useless; the bird pines. In Cooke's poem as in Deverell's painting, "tropic flowers" signify the joy of the self set free. The "one Geranium" (F 473) in Emily Dickinson's "I was the slightest in the House —" (a poem about writing at night in her bed chamber) was probably Cranesbill, the scented geranium common to North America, while Deverell's geraniums are the tropical species *(Pelargonium)*, native to South Africa. By choosing them for his lady's conservatory, he suggests both her imprisonment in convention—geraniums were popular—and her inner desires which, like the bird's freedom, have been denied.

In both England and New England, tropical flowers were usually consigned to the conservatory, although a brave gardener might bring a camellia or a gardenia into the parlor on warm days.[13] In the 1860s, hanging baskets like Dickinson's, full of Asian or South American flowers that were difficult to keep, spoke fashionably (said Breck) of "a pure-minded and intelligent family" of good taste. By the 1890s, however, John Singer Sargent's portrait *The Wyndham Sisters*—a gorgeous arrangement of three flower-like women in diaphanous white gowns with camellias (brought in from a conservatory?) at their feet—showed that what made tropical flowers attractive was their costliness, not only their beauty. Earlier in the century, Hawthorne's fable "Rappaccini's Daughter" had recorded the lingering Puritan anxiety about foreign cultures and customs by representing an anti-Eden, a poisonous garden of tropical blooms. Written in the 1840s when horticulturalists were experimenting with hybrids and when botanists, geologists, and other naturalists were returning from primitive sites with unknown plants and herbs to test for many uses, "Rappaccini's Daughter" conveys Hawthorne's fear of science gone mad, intoxicated by what might constitute its powers over nature. In an ancient garden in Padua, tropical flowers alter the humanity of an experimental gardener and his beautiful daughter. "Tall, emaciated, sallow, and sickly-looking" because of the tropical plants he develops and whose scents he continually inhales, the scientist-gardener Rappaccini has succeeded in growing "flowers [as] gorgeously magnificent" as gems. He must mask himself in their presence, however. Only his daughter Beatrice, with her "voice as rich as a tropical sunset," is able to tend them unprotected because she has grown up among them. With one "magnificent plant that hung its purple gems beside [a] marble fountain," she is especially intimate; like that plant (whose purple "stars" suggest that it might be a Persian lilac), Beatrice makes one think of "deep hues of purple or crimson, and of perfumes heavily delectable." When the youthful scholar Giovanni falls in love with Beatrice, however, he learns that her breath, like the purple flower's scent, is poisonous: a "winged brightness"—a butterfly—attracted by it immediately falls dead at her feet.

Hawthorne's Beatrice, in the "Oriental sunshine of her beauty," is a tropical flower in human form. She is also a second Eve, destructive to her lover. Rappaccini's "poisonous garden" is the result of his drastic misguided experiments, the "adultery of various vegetable species" which produce plants that are "the monstrous offspring of . . . depraved fancy, glowing with only an evil mockery of beauty." Underlying this fable is Hawthorne's fear of meddlesome scientific excess. In *The New Book of Flowers,* written two decades after "Rappaccini's Daughter," Joseph Breck warned readers of Emily Dickinson's day to avoid growing hybrids that defy classification and become "monsters." "Adam and Eve," he reasoned, "were put in possession of a truly botanic garden: God gave wild flowers as he made them, and left it with them and their successors in horticultural pursuits, to find their pleasure in making improvements. But . . . the efforts of man to improve certain flowers are futile." Breck did not condemn the manufacture of all hybrids, however; his example of a "monstrosity" was the newly developed double garden lily in which one of Emily Dickinson's favorite flowers, the *Hemerocallis,* was contorted from a slender bloom into an "assemblage of green leaves" in the empty quest to double the size of the flower.

I have suggested that the contents of Emily Dickinson's conservatory may tell us much about her sensibility. The concept of the "double flower or hybrid" as Breck describes it in his *New Book of Flowers* provides an example of her bravery as an amateur horticulturalist and her taste for richness without vulgarity. "By high cultivation," Breck explains in his chapter on "Double Flowers," "the stamens of the flower are converted into petals, to the great delight, in most cases, of the florist. In what estimation . . . would a single rose be held, in comparison with a full double perfect variety, or a single Aster beside an improved Paeony-flowered one[?]" Although he warns against "futile" experimentation that produces the monstrous lily described above, Breck recommends that a gardener attempt double flowers because they are exceptionally beautiful and fragrant, if difficult to seed and maintain.

Dickinson seems to have written about her flowers most specifically and often to her Norcross cousins. In late May 1862, she communicated her anxiety when faced with her father's commencement teas: "I am still hopeless and scared, and regard Commencement as some vast anthropic bear, ordained to eat me up." Then she added a few words that her cousins, gardeners too, might appreciate: "Commencement would be a dreary spot without my double flower, that sows itself and just comes up when Emily seeks it most" (L 264). Since Dickinson speaks of her double flower "sow[ing]" or naturalizing itself, it seems likely that it was a late-blooming double narcissus of the family *Amaryllidaceae,* one of the finest plants in all of horticulture for naturalizing. The double narcissus has been evolving in the United States for more than two hundred years. Breck's *The Flower Garden* describes the "Two-flowered Narcissus" or "Primrose-Peerless," of a pale-cream color, as well as the "Poet's Narcissus," a double flower that is "snow-white with a pale-yellow cup in the center," sweet-scented and flourishing in late May.

Since Emily Dickinson was writing to her cousins in late May, her beloved double flower may well have been related to Breck's "Poet's Narcissus" *(Narcissus poeticus).* The nineteenth-century double narcissus was at first both slender and tentative in form [Fig. 28] by comparison with the contemporary bloom. Breck's catalogues no longer survive; we do not know how he might have advertised the double narcissus to gardeners of Emily's day. However, the catalogue of White Flower Farm in Litchfield, Connecticut, which seems to me a modern equivalent of the sophisticated nursery catalogue likely to have been disseminated by the literary Breck, describes daffodils of the *Narcissus poeticus* family with emphasis on their fragrance, delicacy, grace, and refined, almost spectral whiteness. Like her "childhood's Indian pipe" that Dickinson loved for its modesty and elegance of form, the Poet's Narcissus peeks out among a garden's fat and jaunty jonquils late, replacing them yet giving a poignant hint of already evanescent sweetness (L 479). White Flower Farm advertises the split-corona double narcissus called "Cassata" that resembles a heavily petalled daylily, not a daffodil, and yet is no monster but a perfect hybrid of the sort Breck would approve. "Subtle they are not, but . . . 'curious,' 'frilly,' and 'exuberant'"; "intricate blooms of . . .

Pub. by W. Curtis St Geo. Crescent July 1 1792.

Sansom del et sculp

28. Double narcissus *(Narcissus poeticus)*. From *Curtis's Botanical Magazine*, 1797.

stunning variety [that] could be the creation of a gifted pastry chef
. . . tufts of petals as delicate as crepe": thus these modern growers
rhapsodize about the double narcissus.[14] Clearly the flower has en-
joyed an even more opulent pattern of beautification since Emily
Dickinson praised it to her cousins. Her taste for these flowers, which
she both grew in the garden and removed in pots to the conservatory,
reflected her temperament. For they were still uncommon, both ex-
otic in their "doubleness" and perfume yet like wildflowers in their
ability to naturalize. Guy Leighton notes in his study of the Dickinson
garden that only Emily's daffodils remain after a century and a half.

The Victorian conservatory was usually given over to rare or so-
phisticated plants; the difference between a conservatory and a green-
house usually lay in the uncommon nature and finish of the plants dis-
played in the former. Yet, once again, we can learn much about the
personality of Emily Dickinson by reflecting on the final contents of
her conservatory. On the fourteenth of January 1885, she wrote again
to her cousins Lou and Fanny, "Had we less to say to those we love,
perhaps we should say it oftener." This salutation, often found on
greeting cards today, was qualified by the important addition: "the at-
tempt comes, then the inundation, then it is all over, as is said of the
dead." No letter could begin on a more serious note; this one contin-
ues by recounting Vinnie's dream about the cousins, by recalling a
photograph that included Samuel Bowles, by alluding to the cousins'
account of their removal from Boston to Cambridge ("like moving
to Westminster Abbey," Emily teases), and finally, by sending "love
from Vinnie and Maggie [their servant], and the half-blown carnation,
and the western sky"—that is, the sunset. "The whistle calls me,"
Dickinson explains, by which she probably means the village whistle
that announced 6:00 P.M., at which time, a little over a year later,
she would (as she cryptically notified the same cousins) be "Called
back" during another sunset to that Eternity she had always imagined
(L963, 1046). Placed in the same important context as Lavinia and
the sundown is "the half-blown carnation"—a flower that must have

been overwintering, then, in her conservatory. The carnation *(Dianthus caryophyllus)* was an important greenhouse crop in New England, but it was not considered rare. Dickinson, who found the clover as compelling a subject as the lily, did not hesitate to keep carnations in her glass garden, however; for her "garden within" was not, finally, consecrated to special flowers but to any that she loved.

Thus, she enjoined Elizabeth Holland in February of the same year, "Tell Katrina about the Buttercups that Emily tills, and the Butterflies Emily chases, not catches, alas, because her Hat is torn – but not half so ragged as her Heart, which is barefoot always –." The letter acknowledges the sway of that "Winter which you feared," and its picture of the poet running barefoot in pursuit of summer butterflies is a fantasy (L 966). But the buttercups themselves were real, maintained in her conservatory as lovingly as the *Daphne odora,* the camellias and gardenias—"flaunting" flowers as Breck called them—exhibited by the usual conservatory gardener.

As the years went on, bringing with them the deaths of people she loved—her eight-year-old nephew Gilbert, Samuel Bowles, Otis Lord, Charles Wadsworth, her parents—Emily Dickinson's letters alluded more often than ever to flowers she remembered to send, flowers she yearned to see when winter ended, flowers she tried to keep alive in place of the loved ones she could not. Thus, she writes Elizabeth Holland in 1884, "I have made a permanent Rainbow by filling a Window with Hyacinths, which Science will be glad to know, and have a Cargo of Carnations, worthy of Ceylon, but Science and Ceylon are Strangers to me, and I would give them both for one look of the gone Eyes, glowing in Paradise –." Images of brilliant ("Arabian") eyes she usually assigned to the deceased Bowles; in this letter, however, she adds, "There are too many to count, now, and I measure by Fathoms, Numbers past away" (L 882). The windowsill lined with hyacinths was probably in her bedroom, where her niece Martha recalled their scent. But Dickinson's "Cargo of Carnations" was kept in the conservatory, which in her imagination becomes a ship sailing the wintry seas with an exotic freight from "Ceylon." In such elegiac messages near the close of her life, she makes the value of her loved ones plain by wishing she might sacrifice her most fragrant, opulent flowers to bring them back.

In 1859, when her friendship with the Bowles family and Samuel in particular was especially absorbing, Emily Dickinson wrote Mrs. Mary Bowles to thank her for the gift of Theodore Parker's *The Two Christmas Celebrations*. "I never read before what Mr Parker wrote," she said, "I heard that he was 'poison.' Then I like poison very well" (L 213). This airy dismissal of reservations made on moral, even sexual, grounds was typical of Dickinson. Unlike Hawthorne's Coverdale, she did not deeply fear and deplore the sensuous yet crave it cunningly; rather, she respected its power and charm while recognizing its danger to a settled life. It is probably true that the full experience of sexual passion was never hers, yet she declares in numerous aphoristic passages that "Water, is taught by thirst" and "Transport — by throe —" (F 93). Kept hungry at the banquet of love by various circumstances including her own reluctance, her writings suggest that Dickinson tasted of it keenly through desire.

At the same time, she seemed to understand that the "frosts" in which the "garden" of her house of art was sown were necessary to her genius (F 596). In a short poem that might be thoroughly baffling if we did not understand her associations with the word "tropic," she seems to explain the circumstances of her life: the abrupt cessation of a great love's development ("summer") and that commitment to the ascetic artistic life ("winter") which is her "sentence":

> 'Twas here my summer paused
> What ripeness after then
> To other scene or other soul
> My sentence had begun.

> To winter to remove
> With winter to abide
> Go manacle your icicle
> Against your Tropic Bride (F 1771).

The poet's "sentence" or destiny is contained in the first two lines of the second quatrain. There, fate makes plain that she must "manacle" her "icicle" against a "Tropic Bride": that is, she must chain herself to the austerity of a single or wintry life, "remove" herself like a flower from the ripe summer in order to repel the sensuous influence of a "Bride" (like a secret self) that is "Tropic"—desirable, but deadly to her true destiny. This elliptical poem with its mysterious first line is a perfect example of what Jay Leyda deemed the poetry of the "omitted center": without explanation or definition, it alludes to an incident or time—"'Twas here"—that ended an important experience or association for the speaker. Moreover, it enlarges upon its central theme with equal mystery. No matter what "ripeness[es]" took place afterward—whatever developments in her experience of love or pleasure?—the speaker states that her sentence stood.

It seems likely that this poem, whose manuscript was lost but transcribed by Millicent Todd, may be a companion piece to "Ourselves were wed" (F 596), wherein the speaker's "Garden" is "sown" in "frosts" while the garden of another woman friend—a new bride—is warmly lit with bloom. The "Tropic Bride" may be passion in the image of Susan Gilbert, the lost bride of Dickinson's early love poems; the "icicle" that must be manacled is, perhaps, that power of self-government that enabled Emily Dickinson to use her energies in a creative life. Frost and icicles appear in Dickinson's verse as the enemies of flowers. Yet here an icicle is a useful weapon; it is shaped like a pen. To manacle it *against* the Tropic Bride implies wielding her art to kill the spell of love, adversarial to industry (though not to imagination). As I observe in *The Passion of Emily Dickinson,* a cycle of Dickinson's poems for a beloved but inaccessible and sometimes malicious woman describes a narrative of both anguish and transport. Her speaker, like Shakespeare's in the Dark Lady sonnets, laments an unseemly desire that draws her to an unsatisfactory and undependable object and away from what should be the unique labor of her life. Because she cannot be trusted, the beloved woman—imagined as "Cleopatra" or an "Avalanche of Sun" or a "torrid Spirit" or the

"Tropic Bride"—is an enemy to Dickinson's peace of spirit and mind (L 755, 855; F 1771). As the word "Tropic" shows, her person and presence are thrilling but, to Emily's New England "Antony," destructive.

Thomas Wentworth Higginson had saved Emily Dickinson's life, she said in 1879, meaning that his interest in her writing had given her the will to live when she was experiencing suicidal "terror" (L 261). The very door through which her letters to him were deposited seemed afterwards "Tropic" (L 621). Collating the two uses of "Tropic" in her letter to the faithful Higginson and her poem about the "Bride," one can see its complex significance for Dickinson. Like tropical plants and flowers, the word signified both glamour and uplift, danger and revelation, and most of all, the unknown—either in the province of art (which Higginson represented) or humanity (about which Sue, she said cryptically, had taught her more than Shakespeare).

❧

Emily Dickinson's schoolmate, the poet Helen Hunt Jackson, author of the exotic novel *Ramona,* remembered the evening of July ninth, 1861, which she spent in Amherst with friends, awaiting the yearly blossoming of a "Night-blooming Cereus."[15] This spectacle-flower of the tropical cactus family was once painted for *Floral Belles* by Mrs. Clarissa Munger Badger, whose *Wild Flowers Drawn and Colored from Nature* Emily Dickinson owned. Jackson reacted to the appearance of the flower by saying it was "the solemnity & poetry of blossoming," thus linking poetry with flowers as Dickinson often did. Although Emily Dickinson never grew a cereus in her conservatory—perhaps because, like orchids, it lacked scent—she delighted in the delicacy and strangeness of her other conservatory plants. Their loveliness was always somehow unexpected—like the butterfly's, apparitional. MacGregor Jenkins, son of the Dickinsons' friend and minister, recalled being summoned to the conservatory by "Miss Emily" on a "bleak winter day."[16] "Unusual[ly] excited," she pointed to "a chrysalis,

long watched among the conservatory plants, [that] had burst its
bonds. Floating about in the sunshine was a gorgeous butterfly. I did
not understand all she said about it," Jenkins recalled of himself as a
child-guest, "but it was beautiful to see her delight." She had wanted
to show him "something beautiful," a beauty that had been shrouded.
Perhaps she intuited a resemblance between the cloistered beauty of
the butterfly, once like a moth, and her own enclosed life. If but-
terflies were among her chief symbols of edenic beauty, so were trop-
ical flowers. Mabel Todd recalled Emily sending her "queer, rare
flowers that I never saw before": flowers of fantasy, flowers like ladies
in strange costumes, flowers akin to the butterflies that emerged like
spangled jewels from dark coverings. The conservatory flowers in
their enclosure finally reflected her taste for the marvelous.

Martha Dickinson Bianchi recalled that "Emily's . . . conservatory
was like fairyland at all seasons."[17] The simile is appropriate, for in
such fairy tales as Charles Perrault's *The Beauty and the Beast,* the ex-
traordinary love of the Prince disguised as the Beast for the young
woman named Beauty is imaged by a rose that magically grows in
his palace even though it is winter. Dickinson's poetry records her
yearning despite the "Gnash of Northern winds" for the flowers of
the "satin Races" (F 400). She herself in winter was like an "Arctic
Creature, dimly stirred / By Tropic Hint —," as she sat near the con-
servatory, writing poems that imagine spring (F 361). Sending olean-
der blossoms tied with black velvet to friends in deep winter, sending
them poems that acknowledged but transcended whatever bitter-
nesses winter or age or death might bring to her "House of Snow,"
Dickinson taught them to look with reverence at the gifts of the "lit-
tle garden within" (L 432). There, homespun crocuses and primroses
bloomed in the middle of February, fuchsias trailed their strawberry-
colored cups in December, and the exotic jasmine "made an atmo-
sphere," as her niece put it, "for the dwelling of her imagination."[18]
While her poems kept flowers alive in every season, Dickinson's un-
common conservatory attempted the same miracle.

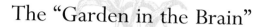

CHAPTER FOUR

The "Garden in the Brain"

Bloom — is Result —

Emily Dickinson, Poems (F 1038)

Exceptional among Amherst residents by virtue of her genius, distinctive in her quest for privacy, Emily Dickinson was perhaps most fully a member of the community by her disciplined commitment to gardening. Lithographs of Main Street, Amherst, in the 1840s with the Dickinson Homestead in the background make the village seem bleak except for a few gracefully arching trees [Fig. 29]. The townspeople's gardens brought the landscape color and gave it a decorative dimension. Writing of Amherst later, in the 1870s, the grown-up MacGregor Jenkins, who liked to recall "Miss Emily" gardening, wrote, "Every one in the town had flowers and planted trees. This was due, in part, to the influence of the Agricultural College, from the greenhouses of which many flowers were supplied for parties."[1] To him, however, Emily's plantings were unique.

The neighbors and friends to whom she sent wildflowers picked from land just outside the village or bouquets made up from her garden or conservatory recalled either the complex artistry of her arrangements or their casual flair. She might send a box of pussywillows to announce the spring or, instead, an elaborate "bouquet in the formal manner of the day" in which "a great variety of flowers, close-pressed together, [looked] like one . . . exotic bloom."[2] In April 1864 her cousin Perez Dickinson Cowan received "a very fine" bouquet of heliotrope, hyacinths, verbena, geraniums, fuchsia, and other flowers, together with the commandment-poem "Partake as doth the Bee — / Abstemiously —" (F 806). Such a bouquet, probably featuring the colors purple, yellow, pink, and white with the sumptuous scents of hyacinth and verbena blending with the sweet odor of scented geraniums, typically caused its recipient long-remembered pleasure. Men as well as women, both the sick and the well, received the poet's extraordinary boxes of carefully chosen blooms. Many who knew that

29. Lithograph view of Main Street, Amherst, in 1840 with the Dickinson Homestead in the background on the left.

she wrote poems fancied a likeness between their intricacy and originality and the beauty and freshness of her floral arrangements. Moreover, the concentration and brevity of Dickinson's poems appeared similar to her habit of giving a single, solitary bloom: one jasmine flower, one sprig of arbutus seemed the cognates of one of her short stanzas.

Perhaps because Amherst was both a college community and a village of churches, perhaps because science vied with religion for converts in the age of Darwin, scientific interest in horticulture accompanied reverent worship of beauty in many Amherst homes. Gardening in the nineteenth century could be pursued with religious fervor and tinged with near-sacramental feeling. The Dickinsons lived during "the nineteenth-century explosion of gardening periodicals" and the publication of such books as Mrs. Loudon's *Gardening for Ladies* (1853), John T. C. Clark's *The Amateurs' Guide and Flower-Garden Directory* (1856), Robert Buist's *The American Flower-Garden Directory* (1839), and many others, designed "to educate and improve as well as to inform."[3] Some books and magazines listed better methods to grow trees and flowers while meditating on their intrinsic spirituality. In his *New Book of Flowers* (1866), for example, Joseph Breck discussed the meadow lily not like a plantsman but as a Christian idealist who knew his Emerson:

> In these lilies of the field, there is a brightness, not of materials prepared and arranged by human hands, but the living brightness that flows directly from the hand of God. There is life in these flowers: every tint glows with the warmth of the unseen love which gives it being. It is not like the beaming stars, nor the glory of western cloudiness, for it shines with the mysterious power of the living principle, it has a breathing and growth toward the source of all true loveliness in this world, and that which is to come.

Today's gardening texts do not usually attribute to flowers such intimacy with a creator and his works. The closest they may come to associating a garden with the principle of eternal love is a promise that I have sometimes encountered in advertisements: If a certain tree or shrub is planted, it will endure long after those who planted it have died, thereby assuring them of immortality. Breck's lines, however, with their implicitly scriptural overtones and their emphasis on "this world, and that which is to come," focus piously on those contrasting but related antitheses that form the Christian religion's essential subject matter—and Emily Dickinson's as well. Though she never formally joined the church, the Scriptures were, like Shakespeare, her continual reference, while the grand categories into which T. W. Higginson divided her *Poems* (1890)—"Life," "Love," "Nature," "Time and Eternity"—may all be subsumed under a single heading: Life and Life Everlasting.

If Breck was moved to write about God, "the power of the living principle," by seeing field lilies, Emily Dickinson declared that "the only Commandment [she] ever obeyed" was "'Consider the Lilies'" (L 904). Her witty allusion was to that passage in Matthew 6:28–29 wherein a vehement Christ eloquently scorns worldliness and urges men and women to trust in God for material sustenance: "Why take ye thought for raiment? Consider the lilies of the field, how they grow; they toil not, neither do they spin; And yet I say unto you, That even Solomon in all his glory was not arrayed like one of these." The passage continues reassuringly, "Wherefore, if God so clothe the grass of the field, which today is, and tomorrow is cast into the oven, shall he not much more clothe you, O ye of little faith?" The *Lilium candidum* (Madonna lily) had been a favorite flower in Puritan gardens since it was first grown in Plymouth colony in 1620. Called the "fair white lily," it may have been just a "grass of the field" but its beauteous white form made it singular. In Christ's injunction, it represents nature contrasted with artifice, the pure silken flesh of God's making opposed to all gorgeous man-made "raiment."

Emily Dickinson's fondness for lilies was intense, and her adherence to this passage was probably won not by its promise of divine support but by its choice of botanical image. (That the lilies neither toiled nor spun also endeared them to her; while sharing the household work, she nonetheless preferred the more aesthetic to the grosser task. "'House' is being cleaned," she confides to Elizabeth Holland in 1866. "I prefer pestilence. That is more classic and less fell" [L 318].) Writing to Mrs. Frederick Tuckerman in late 1884 or to her Aunt Sweetser in the spring of that year, she made it clear that the "liquid Commandment" of Matthew "enchant[ed]" her because it implicitly praised the "fresh" lilies themselves (L 897). Dickinson's reservations about the Calvinist God or "Eclipse" her family "address[ed]" each morning are so well known as scarcely to need repeating here (L 261). She felt tenderness for Christ, the crucified savior, because he suffered. She often felt resentment and contempt, on the other hand, for the God of the Old Testament—a "Mastiff" (F 1332)—who punished Moses by keeping him from the Promised Land, who tortured Abraham, who made her friends and flowers subject to death. In "I had some things that I called mine –," she makes her anger clear. Her "property, my garden" is claimed by God's "Bailiff," death (F 101), even as her young friends were claimed and as she will be.

Yet both the providence and the existence of God were perpetually worrisome themes. During the course of their long friendship, Dickinson posed to Thomas Wentworth Higginson in his persona as both literary man and Unitarian minister three questions of nearly equal importance, in almost identical terms. In April 1862, her first letter to him demanded, "Mr Higginson, Are you too deeply occupied to say if my Verse is alive?" (L 260). In May 1886, the last letter to him before her death asked, "Deity – does He live now? My friend – does he breathe?" (L 1045). As her use or abandonment of the capital letter "H" reveals, Emily Dickinson wanted to know if God "live[d]" as her verse lived and also whether Higginson himself, who had been ill, still "breathe[d]." In the case of deity, poetry, and friendship, "the Alive" was what counted to her (L 233).

In this chapter I should like to consider the garden—that most lively of realities—as a fundamental source of narrative, philosophy, and metaphor in Emily Dickinson's art. It was her garden that encouraged her to believe in eternal life and to hazard belief in the existence of God. By observing the cyclic progress of her plants and flowers, she came to have some faith in the development and resurrection of the soul. As a young woman who disliked attending church and would not bow to revivalist fervor to declare herself "saved" at Mary Lyon's Seminary, she nevertheless inferred from her own garden "the fadeless Orchards," the "remoter green" that existed "*beyond the Rose,*" and she could write with apparent confidence in that unseen world because the annual rebirth of her flowers encouraged her (F 54, 13, 53). To drink in the scent of a flower, she wrote, was to forget this world and experience the next:

> 'Lethe' in my flower,
> Of which they who drink,
> In the fadeless Orchards
> Hear the bobolink! (F 54)

Her garden was her church. One of her best loved, puckish poems makes the distinction between organized religion with its ministers, vestments, and buildings and the Church of the Dickinson Garden, whose "Dome" is made of high-arching fruit trees and whose preacher is the author of all nature:

> Some keep the Sabbath going to Church –
> I keep it, staying at Home –
> With a Bobolink for a Chorister –
> And an Orchard, for a Dome –
>
> Some keep the Sabbath in Surplice –
> I, just wear my Wings –
> And instead of tolling the Bell, for Church,
> Our little Sexton – sings.
>
> God preaches, a noted Clergyman –
> And the sermon is never long,

So instead of getting to Heaven, at last —
I'm going, all along. (F 236)

A confident defense of Dickinson's legendary habit of avoiding the formalities of belief, this deliberately winning poem also insists on the exultation ("Wings") her garden gave her. At the same time, it was this garden, the plants and flowers it contained, and the circumstances they encountered that served Emily Dickinson as an essential source of poetic vocabulary and narrative tropes. In describing and charting the human condition, she reflected on the life of her flowers and appropriated it to meditate on love, sex, ambition, duty, death and immortality, failure and success, distress and happiness, yearning and fulfillment. She has been anthologized as a "nature poet" from the first, but the degree to which she pronounces upon the world of human relationships and activities by exploring the little cosmos of her garden, its tenants and visitors, is more remarkable than the phrase conveys. Indeed, her garden served her as a summary synonym for life itself, for various kinds of endeavor, for the developmental process of art, for eternity. Her external garden was matched, therefore, by what she called "the Garden in the Brain" (F 370). Triumphal in summer, dreamed of in winter, her garden was a map of existence yet it was also the metaphor of paradise. And only the idea of paradise could atone for its annual "perish[ing]" (L 668):

> When I believe the garden
> Mortal shall not see —
> Pick by faith it's blossom
> And avoid it's Bee,
> I can spare this summer — unreluctantly (F 51).

An eloquently developed poem written in 1865, a year of great creative activity for Emily Dickinson, concerns the difficult process by which a flower thrusts itself out of the earth into the light. So witty is it, however, especially in its aphoristic last lines, that one suspects the poem of philosophizing on more than the prowess of flowers:

> Bloom – is Result – to meet a Flower
> And casually glance
> Would cause one scarcely to suspect
> The minor Circumstance
>
> Assisting in the Bright Affair
> So intricately done
> Then offered as a Butterfly
> To the Meridian –
>
> To pack the Bud – oppose the Worm –
> Obtain it's right of Dew –
> Adjust the Heat – elude the Wind –
> Escape the prowling Bee –
>
> Great Nature not to disappoint
> Awaiting Her that Day –
> To be a Flower, is profound
> Responsibility – (F 1038)

Although her lyric "Success is counted sweetest / By those who ne'er succeed" (F 112), with its poignant image of a soldier dying amid the sounds of his enemy's triumph, may be one of the best war poems ever written; although one of her strongest poems alludes to "Battle's – horrid Bowl" and she exclaimed "It feels a shame to be Alive – / When Men so brave – are dead –" (F 524); although her elegies for the dead soldier Frazar Stearns are piteous, Emily Dickinson is frequently criticized for telling Colonel Higginson (as he then was), "War feels to me an oblique place" (L 280). It was another instance of her probity as an artist that she would not presume to write at length about what she but slenderly knew. *Certainly* battles and torn corpses were "oblique" to her; unlike Whitman, nurse and camp follower, she had seen none. All her images of warfare were received—except for those dynamic struggles of nature "red in tooth and claw," as Tennyson styles it, that she observed up close in her garden.

"Bloom – is Result –" was probably written in a year when the North's prodigious efforts during the Civil War ended in victory; therefore, it might seem to some readers tamely restricted in subject matter. Yet the crafty wit that surprises with the idea that a flower—flimsy, decorative—might have "responsibility" may, however wryly, be describing heroism in general and in other undertakings of importance: writing poetry, for instance. To "meet a Flower," to encounter a finely finished product, is often not to surmise the multitudinous "minor Circumstance[s]" that contributed to its appearance. What seems ephemeral as a butterfly whose colors at midday dazzle us with brilliancy has actually had a history of hard endeavor. (Here, Dickinson makes an association of butterflies with flowers that reflects her visual sensitivity, perhaps assisted by the presence of a "butterfly garden" on the Dickinson grounds.) True of flowers, this is also true of good poems, whose orderly smoothness may conceal and belie the poet's pains. Since Dickinson associated herself with her flowers, she perhaps affirms here that, though no businessman or politician—though neither her brother nor her father—she, too, labors to use her talents, to be responsible, to acquit "Great Nature"'s plan. The reader concerned with issues of women's life and development may also read the lines "To be a Flower, is profound / Responsibility" as a subtle assertion of the hardships encountered in being a Victorian girl—that apparently carefree, lissome enchantress of the drawing-room whose deeper life could involve many and constant hardships.

Emily Dickinson's horticultural awareness invigorates this poem. The "Bright Affair / So intricately done" is the flower itself. Sharman Apt Russell's *Anatomy of a Rose* reports that "a sunflower, like a daisy or dandelion"—each a frequent Dickinson subject—"is really an inflorescence, a group of individual flowers, acting together as subjects of a community." Their intricacy, accomplished by "'ray flowers'

[that] unfurl one by one a single petal that with other ray flowers form the larger circle," makes a "ring of light that attracts the bee."[4] Michael Pollan tells us that "Honeybees favor the radial symmetry of daisies and clover and sunflowers,"[5] a complex architecture that Emily Dickinson seems to have inspected closely, as she shows in describing the clover's "residences nimble" and "edifices azure" (F 1358). As "Bright Affair[s] . . . intricately done," flowers are fragile, yet Russell provides ample evidence that—dense, leathery, or (like the orchid) able to drown a prowler—they "do what they can to protect themselves."[6] According to Dickinson, flowers must "Escape the prowling Bee"—a surprising remark, perhaps, since she knew that bees were needed as pollinators, but one that reminds us that she often depicts congress between bee and flower as if it were human sexual intrigue. Her witty lyric, "A Bee his Burnished Carriage / Drove boldly to a Rose —," regards this necessary exchange as a genteel if sensual romance in which "The Rose received his Visit / With frank tranquility, / Witholding not a Crescent / To his cupidity" (F 1351).

Yet Dickinson must also have known from characteristically meticulous observation that honeybees "sometimes enter from behind" a flower, stealing nectar "by inserting their tongues between the sepals and petals,"[7] often piercing the corollas, biting through and destroying floral tissues. In sympathy with Dickinson's poem, Russell comments amusingly of the garden realm: "This is not a world of trust. Windows must be barred, doors locked"[8]—that is, flowers must escape certain marauding bees if they intend to be whole and beautiful. Dickinson appears to concur:

> Like Trains of Cars on Tracks of Plush
> I hear the level Bee —
> A Jar across the Flowers goes
> Their Velvet Masonry
>
> Withstands until the sweet Assault
> Their Chivalry consumes —

> While He, victorious tilts away
> To vanquish other Blooms (F 1213).

Thus sexuality as a theme is frequently represented in the Dickinson canon by the "sweet" intercourse between bee and flower. Asking "Did the Harebell loose her girdle / To the lover Bee / Would the Bee the Harebell *hallow* / Much as formerly?" (F 134), she muses wryly on the sexual double standard. The *Campanula rotundifolia*, called the "harebell" or "bellflower," is a soft-fleshed white or blue ornamental perennial much loved in Victorian gardens. In the poem quoted above, the word "consumes" suggests the difference between the bee's visit to the desiring and desirable rose and the "Jar" that destroys the flower's very architecture and being. Dickinson seems to have noted the damage the honeybee's rape of a flower can do, writing with delicate irony,

> The Flower must not blame the Bee –
> That seeketh his felicity
> Too often at her door –
>
> But teach the footman from Vevay –
> Mistress is 'not at home' – to say –
> To people – any more! (F 235)

Vevey (rightly spelled) on Lake Geneva was evidently associated in Dickinson's mind with things "still," "Cool," mannerly, as is Switzerland in general in "Our lives are Swiss –" (F 129). A flower must sometimes primly turn away her avid pollinator if she hopes to last. By "Pack[ing] the bud" in "Bloom – is Result –," Emily Dickinson probably meant the layers of adhesive tissues that compose the flower itself. Some flowers *are* able to "adjust [their] heat," as she says, by stretching into the shade. Others actually do "elude the Wind" by crouching. In the final quatrain of "Bloom – is Result –," Dickinson gives to the flower a role in the universal plan. Her last line is arresting, unexpected, surprising: qualities she assigned to successful poems. For in "This was a Poet –," Dickinson explained the poetic art as a perfumer's: the distillation of "amazing sense" (punning on *scents*) and "Attar . . . immense" from "the familiar species / That perished by the Door –" (F 446). That is, she defined poetry as the refined compression of the ordinary, of the flower in the dooryard. Nineteenth-century Europeans imagined that trees and shrubs planted close to a house brought fevers. Possibly with this in mind, New Englanders planted flowers, often climbing roses, close to their houses. (The Dickinsons' Pleasant Street house had roses in the dooryard, while in *The Scarlet Letter* a rose meets Hester Prynne's gaze as she emerges from prison.) In "Bloom – is Result –," Dickinson makes the characteristic association of flower and poem, gardener and poet that she establishes in her most specific poems about writing poetry such as "Essential Oils – are wrung –," wherein the "Attar" of the artifact is made from pressing "the Rose" of nature (F 772).

Just as the world of flowers represents the world of men and women, so certain flowers represent specific qualities or endeavors, functions, or careers in Emily Dickinson's work. The fringed gentian, for example, is associated with duty and destiny. Commenting on Dickinson's several lyrics about the fringed gentian—a flower popular with Victorians—Mary Loeffelholz observes, "There was clearly something vocational going on with the gentian" in the poet's mind. In Dickinson's first fascicle "The Gentian weaves her fringes" appears, written around 1858, while another gentian poem entitled "Distrustful of the Gentian" follows it (F 21, 26). Loeffelholz hypothesizes that the "conspicuous placement" of poem 21 in the first fascicle may have something "to do with the book and bookmaking"; that the poem itself was a "vocational embodiment";[9] that "the sequence of [Dickinson's] gentian poems" shows how "her relationship to writing and writing practices . . . changed over time," from the desire to publish to her ultimate refusal of the "Auction" of her mind (F 788). This is a persuasive argument, and Loeffelholz's decision that gentian poem 520 in Franklin's text "images a public vindication of her delayed vocation,"[10] that is, of her poetry itself, is credible, given Dickinson's continual association of herself with her flowers and their careers with her own. This poem was written around 1863, when Dickinson was corresponding with Higginson and might still have hoped for public acknowledgment of her genius:

> God made a little Gentian —
> It tried — to be a Rose —
> And failed — and all the Summer laughed —
> But just before the Snows
>
> There rose a Purple Creature —
> That ravished all the Hill —
> And Summer hid her Forehead —
> And Mockery — was still —
>
> The Frosts were her condition —
> The Tyrian would not come
> Until the North — invoke it —
> Creator — Shall I — bloom? (F 520)

Emily Dickinson's garden, her solitary life, was "sown" (she could write symbolically) "in Frosts" while the north was on every side of it (F 596). Like the gentian's, "Frosts were [Dickinson's] condition." In 1871, long after she had written hundreds of successful poems, she begged Higginson to "excuse the bleak simplicity that knew no tutor but the North" (L 368). This continuous identification of her genius and personality with the north and what she conceived of as northern characteristics or virtues—with the Roman Antony, with Amherst, with those who "see — New Englandly —" (F 256)—rather than with the alluring but quixotic south is reminiscent of Tennyson's lines in *The Princess,* favorite reading of the young Emily: "bright and fierce and fickle is the South / And dark and true and tender is the North." It also causes me to wonder whether this association was inspired by the Bible. One of the messianic prophecies in Isaiah, a book to which

Dickinson alluded familiarly at age nineteen, declares, "I have raised up one from the north, and he shall come: from the rising of the sun he shall call upon my name: and he shall come upon princes . . . as the potter treadeth clay" (41:25). The south might represent sensual pleasures to Emily Dickinson, but the bitter north produced the creative spark that made her great among poets. Various kinds of social and emotional deprivation empowered her art, and she admits this in a striking appeal to seasonal garden imagery that served her as basic trope. To be the rose that blooms in the June of weddings, with all they signified of personal happiness and triumph articulated in "Ourselves were wed one summer – dear –" (F 596), would have been wrong for her. Though she toyed with the idea of herself as rose—"A Breeze – a'caper in the trees – / And I'm a Rose!" (F 25)—Emily Dickinson was too realistic to embrace it as a true self-image.[11]

It is for this reason, perhaps, that neither the poems nor the letters of this highly aesthetic gardener-poet contain an extended treatment of the rose. Other less gorgeous, less opulent flowers, such as the gentian or tulip or harebell, provoke her curiosity and an admiration that results in ingenious narrative and analysis. The rose she regards as a classic emblem of love and of the fragility of all things beautiful, but it does not move her to more than praise (explicit or implicit) of a traditional character. "Ah Little Rose – how easy / For such as thee to die" (F 11), she cries in one of her laments for small creatures such as bees and flowers; "When Roses cease to bloom," she says, imagining her own and others' deaths (F 8); he "was grateful for the Roses / In life's diverse boquet," she remarks of a "humble Tourist" who went to heaven as if he were riding in a balloon (F 72). In the third "Master" letter, rapture causes her prose to slip into a couplet beginning "No Rose, yet felt myself a'bloom," using the classic symbol of a woman made beautiful by love (L 233).

On one occasion, Dickinson sent a rose to her cousin Eudocia Flynt with a poem:

All the letters I can write
Are not as fair as this —
Syllables of Velvet —
Sentences of Plush,
Depths of Ruby, undrained,
Hid, Lip, for Thee — (F 380).

Here is Dickinson's characteristic fusion of nature and art: the rose is both message and poem. But it is also a cup that holds depths of red like rubies, her metaphor linking jewels with flowers as in other poems that prefer the floral "blaz[e]" in the "meadow" to a topaz or emerald (F 726). Famous rosarians like David Austin remind us that the noblest Old Roses like Dickinson's have shapes described since the eighteenth century as "Deep Cup" or "Open Cup." The rose sent to Eudocia seems to be a Deep Cup. Like a good poem, it hides its softest velvets or deepest, most intimate petal-sentences for the one who appreciates it. By putting her lips to the rose, Eudocia will "read" the poem that accompanies it a second time. The poem's tone is both sensuous and fond, fusing women, art, and flowers, while there may be a graceful play on the word "cup" that suggests Dickinson's awareness of horticultural terms.

Roses—especially Dickinson's Gallica ("calico") roses, known since the ancients for their prickly canes—have thorns; love can be painful, as Dickinson acknowledges in her letter (cited earlier) to Mary and Samuel Bowles: "I am sorry you came [to visit] because you went away. Hereafter, I will pick no Rose, lest it fade or prick me" (L 189). Thus the rose served her as a classic floral image of desirable beauty. Although useful in this traditional literary fashion, however, the rose does not, like the dandelion, provoke Dickinson to lengthy exegesis of its parts. She celebrates it as the most delicate, sensuous, and precarious inhabitant of the garden, and it is the "House of Rose" that, like "Ecstasy," we must not attempt to confine if we mean it to survive. Yet the daisy, anemone, violet, gentian, and other woodland flowers *interest* her more. Her finest line about the rose is swift yet rich: "A Rose is an Estate / In Sicily" (F 806). Here, the sumptuous array of its petals, like the complexity of buildings and gardens that make up an estate, is placed in a country known for heat, sunshine, and high emotion, lavishly spent. In Dickinson's vision of the rose, its scent is to be experienced "Abstemiously" because it is the sum of all scents, the very essence of beauty (F 806).

Of course, there is one important way in which the life of roses, so subject to disease, might have reminded Emily Dickinson of her own: probably tubercular, she was never strong. Her life was necessarily limited, which she recognized; in one poem she used her garden metaphor both to acknowledge and to defy her limitations:

> On the Bleakness of my Lot
> Bloom I strove to raise —
> Late — my Garden of a Rock
> Yielded Grape — and Maise —
>
> Soil of Flint, if steady tilled
> Will refund the Hand —
> Seed of Palm, by Lybian Sun
> Fructified in Sand — (F 862)

"Bleak" is a strong word. This poem was written in 1864 during the "Master" period when, frustrated in love, Dickinson was turning increasingly to art with manifest "stead[iness]"—although she never metamorphosed into an austere aesthete or became an emotionally remote atheist whose major theme was the act of writing. Instead, Dickinson preserved her steady engagement with both art and ordinary life until she died. Her garden, her self, was like a "Rock" and yet it was bringing forth grapes and corn, nourishing "Bloom." The seed and soil metaphors would serve her more and more as classic means of describing growth and fulfillment, even the fulfillment that was to be found in death:

> The Opening and the Close
> Of Being, are alike
> Or differ, if they do,
> As Bloom opon a Stalk — (F 1089)

Indeed, "to fail / As Flower at fall of Frost" was a theme that ordered her meditations on death; frost was the enemy, and yet in the gentian poems it represents the season of delayed flowering (F 1710). It was as the gentian *(Gentiana crinita)* that she ultimately regarded her artistic self. Its "Tyrian" or purplish-blue color does not appear until late fall when the cold "North" calls it forth; it is different from other flowers, even as Dickinson's distinctive intellect and prosody made her unlike other poets of her time. Will she someday be the "Purple Creature — / That ravished all the Hill —"? she asks in "God made a little Gentian —." The last line of that poem puts the question to the distrusted yet acknowledged author of her destiny.

❧

To Emily Dickinson, the heliocentric daisy represented faithful devotion; the gentian, determination, ability, industry in the face of difficulty and scorn; the violet, modesty and fidelity; the lily, hallowed beauty; the trailing arbutus, affection and pluck; the aster (as she wrote Samuel Bowles), the "everlasting fashion" of eternity (F 374); the rose, romance and/or conjugal joy. Humble flowers like the violet, arbutus, daffodil, or crocus, which struggle courageously against soil hardened by winter and associate themselves with blessed spring and the advent of the royal season of summer, inspired Dickinson to write poems of praise and empathy. As in the case of the gentian, these flowers reminded her of her own need, as a poet and a woman, for courage.

At the same time, bulb perennials had aesthetic connotations for her. The tulip, daffodil, hyacinth, and crocus, radiant springtime flowers that emerge from bulbs that have stored their mature loveliness in compact form, were especially dear to Dickinson, who described herself as having "long been a Lunatic on Bulbs"—perhaps because, as gardeners realize, bulbs, like poems, are rich worlds unto themselves (L 823). They require only a favorable setting or context to be enjoyed. Just as the "rapture" of a "Bud," which economically contained the entire globe of a blooming rose, fascinated her, so did bulbs (F 1365). She wrote to Maria Whitney in the spring of 1883, "is not a bulb the most captivating floral form?" (L 824). Bulbs were the condensed images of beauty, while compression, "Screws," was a major ingredient of her own method of representing it in terse, short forms (F 772).

In making a poem for those spring flowers that lift the spell of winter, she sometimes implied their inscrutable, seemingly magical powers by declining to name them; such poems were like riddles occasionally intended for gardeners who might enjoy guessing their meaning. The *Epigaea repens* or mayflower, a member of the heath family, prompted three versions of a lyric sent to Sue; to the third version, Dickinson signed her name as "Arbutus —":

> Pink — small — and punctual —
> Aromatic — low —
> Covert in April —
> Candid in May —
>
> Dear to the Moss —
> Known to the Knoll —
> Next to the Robin
> In every human Soul —
>
> Bold little Beauty —
> Bedecked with thee

Nature forswears –
Antiquity – (F 1357)

The arbutus recommends itself to Dickinson by its virtues and decorum. It is punctual, bold, or courageous, a "sweet Barbarian" compared to the "civic" Daphne (though both flowers were "as beautiful as Delight can make them" [L 1037]). She also loved the arbutus because, like her favorite conservatory flowers, it was fragrant. The commonplace Victorian language of physical smallness used by Dickinson for herself and for some appealing women of fiction—Dickens's heroines such as Dora Spenlow or Little Dorrit, Thackeray's Amelia Sedley, or Charlotte Brontë's Jane Eyre, dubbed "a little small thing," "low born"—she applies here to this brave "mayflower" that comes up saucily in cold spring. The poet, herself accustomed to stratagems of concealment, admires the behavior of the arbutus that hides itself under low-growing grasses until its appointed season to appear openly, to be "candid." Although Dickinson's last compliment to the arbutus claims that it defeats "Antiquity," making the world feel young again each spring, it is perhaps the subtlety of this flower that knows *when* to show itself that encourages her to sign with its name. One is reminded that she once put an "X" next to these lines from Emerson's "Woodnotes" in her copy of his *Poems:* "For this present, hard / Is the fortune of the bard, / Born out of time." The post-Romantic or mid-Victorian age gave Dickinson a great deal that was valuable: poetic themes and narratives, moral philosophy, a Ruskinian aesthetic, imagistic allusion (for example, when she wrote "Oh Matchless Earth – We underrate the chance to dwell in Thee" [L 347] to Susan Dickinson, did Susan recognize Wordsworth's "matchless earth" in *Peter Bell?*). But her frequently metaphysical style offended many contemporary critics. Thus, in a way she *was* born out of her time. Dickinson's confinement of her poems to the famous cedar chest may have been a "covert" act, but the evidence of her continual "publication" among friends suggests that she hoped one day for "candor," for recognition—that is, for what the arbutus wins at last from a cold world.

The woodland flowers that, in early poems, Dickinson describes herself roaming the woods to find and steal are sometimes left name- less. In one coy poem the unidentified flower—a violet?—is like a woman, "bashful," "ashamed," and "helpless" when she is seized. In- cluded as poem 19 in the first edition of *Poems* (1890), it leaves no doubt about Dickinson's instinctive association of women with flowers, though the speaker herself seems to be "Emily when a boy":

> So bashful when I spied her!
> So pretty – so ashamed!
> So hidden in her leaflets
> Lest anybody find –
>
> So breathless till I passed her –
> So helpless when I turned
> And bore her struggling, blushing,
> Her simple haunts beyond!
>
> For whom I robbed the Dingle –
> For whom betrayed the Dell –
> Many, will doubtless ask me –
> But I shall never tell! (F 70)

Violets may be hidden by their leaves; pink violets may seem to blush. Occasionally they are difficult to pluck and may appear to "struggle." But the adjectives "bashful" and "breathless" enlist the pa- thetic fallacy that Dickinson could often embrace when it came to flowers, equating them with the stereotypically "timid" (a favorite word) Victorian heroine. The speaker's rather nasty avidity and se- crecy in this poem imply that picking a flower (even to give as a pres- ent) is a crime akin to forcibly deflowering a woman. The speaker is a robber, a betrayer, even a rapist. Mary Lyon deplored the stripping of the woods around her seminary so that students could bring botanical specimens to their classes; Dickinson was probably taught to feel guilty about her woodland adventures, yet she pursued them just the same. The poem's tone is airy, lively, kept from seriousness by the rhyming *d*'s in "Dingle" and "Dell" and by the childish last line which implies that all this was just a game. Nevertheless, the helplessness of the flower against the speaker's superior strength inevitably suggests the female's disadvantage when opposing a powerful male. Here again, an action that concerns a flower stands for something else, something more.

This speaker's ambition to possess the beautiful is keen enough to warrant theft, but the speaker of another poem is also guilty, this time of a failure of imagination. She has taken the wrong road to see flowers modestly hidden in the meadows; at the same time, she walked out too early to see them. Therefore, fate conspires with carelessness to rob her of a blessing and a boon:

> Within my reach!
> I could have touched!
> I might have chanced that way!
>
> Soft sauntered thro' the village –
> Sauntered as soft away!
> So unsuspected Violets
> Within the meadows go –
> Too late for striving fingers
> That passed, an hour ago! (F 69)

The excitation and degree of pain in this lyric might be thought out of proportion to the experience it describes, but the experience itself is of course symbolic. "Unsuspected Violets" might be achievements unattained, loves that might have been, goods that the "striving" but doomed persona has failed to envision. Thus, the minor floral poems of Emily Dickinson often speak only metaphorically of flowers since flowers serve her continually as a widely descriptive language.

In his discussion of the power and beauty of flowers, Michael Pollan observes that "flowers by their very nature traffic in a kind of metaphor," taking on "the changing colors of human dreams."[12] The ancient literary idea of the garden imbues actual gardens with poetry. As for sexuality, a garden—especially in summer—is abloom with it. Sharman Apt Russell muses humorously:

> The Jack-in-the-Pulpit is considering a sex change. The violets have a secret. The dandelion is smug. The daffodils are obsessive. The orchid is *finally* satisfied, having produced over a million seeds. The bellflower is *not* satisfied and is slowly bending its stigma in order to reach its own pollen. The pansies wait expectantly, their vulviform faces lifted to the sky. The evening primrose is interested in one thing and one thing only.
>
> A stroll through the garden is almost embarrassing.[13]

Alfred Habegger speaks of Dickinson's "too frequent bees and birds."[14] But Emily Dickinson, a poet of the country as well as the mind, contemplated the sexual arena of her garden daily. There, the careers of flowers and the dramatic career of the bee as their lover/ propagator commanded her attention, for "till the Bee / Blossoms stand negative" (F 999). To Dickinson—both gardener and poet—bees and flowers could not be written of too often, especially since flowers in particular symbolized a broad panorama of persons and actions different from themselves. The mute sexual activity of the garden, noted by horticultural writers like Pollan and Russell, made it an appropriate theater for some of Dickinson's most effective love poems. It is an irony, however, that in two important instances, a blooming garden is the scene of poems concerned with sexual deprivation.

Thus, for example, Dickinson ascribes to a mysterious lover[15] whom she calls the "Bright Absentee" an inability to garden, caused by his absence. Her accomplished poem uses floral imagery and a nervous, teasing, vivid metrical pattern to project the speaker's lonely craving for her "Lord":

I tend my flowers for thee —
Bright Absentee!
My Fuschzia's Coral Seams
Rip — while the Sower — dreams —

Geraniums — tint — and spot —
Low Daisies — dot —
My Cactus — splits her Beard
To show her throat —

Carnations — tip their spice —
And Bees — pick up —
A Hyacinth — I hid —
Puts out a ruffled Head —
And odors fall
From flasks — so small —
You marvel how they held —

Globe Roses — break their satin flake —
Opon my Garden floor —
Yet — thou — not there —
I had as lief they bore
No crimson — more —

Thy flower — be gay —
Her Lord — away!
It ill becometh me —
I'll dwell in Calyx — Gray —
How modestly — alway —
Thy Daisy —
Draped for thee! (F 367)

This poem, like "I envy Seas, whereon He rides —," was probably composed in late fall 1861 or early 1862, at the height of the "Master" period. During that fall Samuel Bowles was often in New York City, while in April he journeyed to England, Switzerland, and Germany. Since 1858 or (possibly) earlier, Emily Dickinson had been accustomed to Bowles's visits to the Homestead. He shared her interest in gardening, telling Austin once that he would have liked to be a gardener; indeed, they often exchanged gifts of flowers. In her poem, Dickinson says she tends flowers to suit one who is luminously absent, one who might be expected to appreciate them. The poem is ironic: as we learn from the appearance of the garden, the gardener has done no "tending" at all. The speaker's self-portrait is sportive, lightly derisive; the degree of her garden's dishevelment would be humorously manifest to a fellow flower-lover. So, the fuchsia or evening primrose is ripped, whether by rain or harsh handling, while the "Sower/sewer"—a pun equating making a garden with making a dress—"dreams" of her absent lord. The (white?) geraniums are tinting or turning color as they wilt and decay or "spot." The daisies "dot" (an older use of the word "spot") or scatter on the ground; they have not been deadheaded, which would ensure a neater appearance and increased bloom. The cactus splits and—here the sexual innuendo of flowers like women dressing and undressing begins to heighten— "show[s] her throat."

As the iambic/trochaic rhythm of the poem becomes livelier, the most fragrant and sensual flowers—hyacinths, roses—shed their scents flirtatiously. The satiny roses even fall apart, symbols of love denied. Interestingly, hyacinths flower in the poem together with roses, yet roses bloom in June and hyacinths, in early spring. Fuchsias begin to drop off in July, but in the poem, each of these flowers from different seasons blossoms and declines together. Thus the "Garden floor" of the poem is really the poet's mind and the poem itself, a mirror of her meditation. In the final stanza, the speaker herself becomes a flower, one "draped" in sorrow. She is a "Daisy," as "Master" likes to call her, but one that is content to inhabit a calyx, never to grow and be seen because her lover is gone.

Here again, Dickinson has chosen a pattern of vivid floral imagery that recalls "The Daisy follows soft the Sun —" (F 161) and her letters to Bowles with his "Sun"-like face (L 908). Alfred Habegger and Polly Longsworth have revived interest in the minister Charles Wadsworth as "Master," but poems like this one do not seem intended for her dark "Man of Sorrow," her "Dusk Gem" (L 776). The most persuasive evidence that Wadsworth may deserve the title "Master" has always seemed, quite simply, the fact of that name she assigned—the same by which the apostles addressed Christ. Dickinson alluded to herself as "Queen of Calvary," enduring "Calvaries of Love" (F 347, 325). Since the Southern sympathizer Wadsworth was called to Calvary Church, San Francisco, during the Civil War, these epithets also typify Dickinson's characteristically teasing, cunning kind of symbolic usage. The trope of a marriage in heaven and the devoutly religious sublimation described in some of her love poems—as Barton St. Armand shows, the traditional materials of Victorian romance—have also been cited to support Martha Dickinson Bianchi's seductively formulated legend of the minister-lover. But none of these elements except the place names—even the appellation "Master," applicable to a commanding and tutelary presence—excludes Bowles. To him, Dickinson assigned the imagery of Resurrection; a Christ figure, he had "[led] us by it" (L 415). He, too, like Wadsworth, "carried [grandeur] with himself to whatever scene —," and he was famous as a good and generous man associated with noble causes and as a patient sufferer like the "Master" himself (L 776).

In the poem quoted above, Dickinson's "Bright Absentee" is reproached for a temporary absence. Wadsworth, who always lived far from Dickinson either in Philadelphia or San Francisco and who visited her but twice in his life and misspelled her name (addressing her distantly as "Miss Dickenson"), could not have been so scolded. But she is known to have chided Bowles on many occasions for his business trips and recuperative voyages. In any case, if a real man was being addressed in "I tend my flowers for thee," he was one with whom the speaker is on very easy and familiar terms, one who might

have enjoyed the poem's teasing, sensual rhythms and its floral panto-
mime. This could indeed describe "Uncle Sam Bowles," whom Susan
Dickinson called "a true knight, with the fine flower of courtesy on
his invisible shield," but who, for all his sympathetic feminism, had a
hearty, even crude side.

In "I tend my flowers for thee –," Dickinson's flowers dramatize the
speaker's inner feelings. They empathize completely with her, as
might be expected since we have been told again and again through-
out the Dickinson corpus that she and her flowers are one: "A single
Bloom we constitute / Departed, or at Home –" (F 986). Very rarely
do her flowers violate the speaker's wishes, although they appear with
their "unthinking Drums" during one tragic spring when she dreads
them most (F 347). Just as Dickinson is able to conceal herself in a
"Calyx," just as a flower can transmogrify itself into her, the whole
world may be regarded as a flower. So entirely did that image serve
Emily Dickinson as a means of exploring reality that she twice de-
scribed one of the most dramatic and important natural events—sun-
set—in floral language.

In "The Lilac is an ancient Shrub," for example, Dickinson con-
trasts a flower of great age and beauty with one "ancienter": "The
Firmamental Lilac / Opon the Hill Tonight –." She knew that the li-
lac was Persian and took obvious joy in comparing each of its parts—
corolla, calyx, seeds—to the changing lights of sundown, the "Flower
of Occident" (F 1261). It was probably about 1872 when she wrote
this poem, a period of heightened philosophizing in the letters: "An
ill heart," she wrote Louise Norcross, "like a body, has its more com-
fortable days, and then its days of pain, its long relapse, when rally-
ing requires more effort than to dissolve life, and death looks choice-
less" (L 380). Sundown preoccupied her imagination more and more.
Barton St. Armand has written eloquently of her sunset poems, relat-
ing them to what he calls her concept of "the mystic day" and observ-
ing that "Dickinson studied the death of the sun with as much inten-
sity as she brought to the scanning of the dying faces of her friends,

relatives, and loved ones."[16] If the latter could be seen with or even as flowers, so could the sky in its different moods and aspects.

Using precise horticultural imagery in order to establish the similarity between the "efflorescence" or bursting forth of a flower and the gradual revelation of the sunset, Dickinson had written around 1863:

> Bloom opon the Mountain stated –
> Blameless of a name –
> Efflorescence of a Sunset –
> Reproduced – the same –
>
> Seed had I, my Purple Sowing
> Should endow the Day –
> Not – a Tropic of a Twilight –
> Show itself away –
>
> Who for tilling – to the Mountain
> Come – and disappear –
> Whose be her Renown – or fading –
> Witness is not here –
>
> While I state – the Solemn Petals –
> Far as North – and East –
> Far as South – and West expanding –
> Culminate – in Rest –
>
> And the Mountain to the Evening
> Fit His Countenance –
> Indicating by no Muscle
> The Experience – (F 787)

This poem—sent to her sister-gardeners, the Norcross cousins—is in part a prefigurement of "The Lilac is an ancient Shrub" wherein the extension of the sunset also matches that of a hypothetical flower. The lilac poem, however, is concerned with the question of religious faith, possibly reflecting Emily Dickinson's increasing age and her persistent skepticism. "Bloom opon the Mountain" is a most painterly poem, finding analogues in the nineteenth-century landscape tradition with which the Dickinsons were very familiar. For example, the Hudson River painters, whose characteristic works and themes were known to Dickinson, frequently painted sunsets, as had their master, J. M. W. Turner. In such paintings as Frederic Edwin Church's *Sunset* (1856), Sanford Gifford's *A Lake Twilight* (1861), or Worthington Whittredge's *Twilight on Shawangunk Mountain* (1865), the sunset in various stages was radiantly—or ruddily, angrily—depicted above a mountain or mountain range. Mountain and sunset, images of exaltation and sublimity traditional to the Hudson River School, were thus joined as they were in the stormy sunsets of Thomas Cole. Probably working consciously within the aesthetic traditions of her day, Dickinson also depicts a mountain "Fit[ting] His Countenance" to the evening that follows sunset. But for her, the sunset itself is not a special kind of light but a strange flower without a name.

That Dickinson sometimes wrote poems to or about nameless flowers, as if to force her reader to guess their identity, has already been noted. In the poem quoted above, she says the "Bloom" she writes of is "*Blameless* of a name" (emphasis mine), which implies that names are limiting and belong to the world to which sinful Adam gave identity. To have a name is to have some measure of fame—and Dickinson distrusted fame, "the one that does not stay," the "fickle food / Upon a shifting plate"; to be a "Nobody" who lacks a recognizable name is therefore preferable (F 1507, 1702, 260). Dickinson's flower transcends botanical nomenclature. It is the unlisted flower "Sunset," whose petals grow and expand like any other bloom.

Her speaker is enraptured by the beauty she perceives. She claims that, were she the sower of such flowers, not one tropical twilight would "Show itself away" from Amherst; every sunset would be apparent to her and enjoyed. Dickinson's allusion to the tropics, of course, suggests her awareness, gleaned from newspapers, art magazines, and books, of the Victorian fascination with the tropics, recorded again and again in the tropical paintings of Cole, Church, Gifford, Winslow Homer, Martin Johnson Heade, and others. If Dickinson's speaker possessed "Seed," she says—were she God or Nature—her "Purple Sowing" would enrich the whole day (here purple means "regal" as well as the color of sunset itself). For the speaker, like Dickinson, is a planter, though she is inadequate to the task of seeding and tilling the majestic bloom, sunset.

In fact, the sunset or twilight's "efflorescence"—Dickinson uses the correct botanical term for blossoming—appeals for care to the mountain. To the mountain it comes and there it disappears, yet no one knows—"Witness is not here"—who owns the twilight or is responsible for its splendor ("Renown") or its "fading." Dickinson's poem is being said (written, "state[d]") while the radiance of the sunset spreads out across the sky to the points of the compass: "North – and East," "South – and West." Composed of "Solemn Petals," the sunset is a bloom that is "stated" over the mountain by whatever natural force created it, an echo of St. John's gospel in which "the Word" creates the world. Sunset is also "stated" in the poem itself since Dickinson links two acts of creation here, the one that produced a natural sunset and the one she produces as creator of her poem. This lyric is thus related to another, "The One that could repeat the Summer Day –" (F 549), in which Dickinson weighs the comparative value of a painting or poem about sunset and a real sunset. She decides in favor of the poetic reproduction because it can be kept, while nature's sunset can never be repeated.

Thus far, I have discussed poems in which that "Bright Affair," a flower, stands for itself yet also for intellectual or artistic accomplishment, sexual experience, social responsibility, the gorgeousness of nature, sublime and unexpected beauty, or the course of life (F 1038). Dickinson may relate the parts of a flower to the points of a compass or to the technical ingredients of a poem: she compares meter to fragrance, for example, and the shimmering tissue of a rose to a well-integrated poetic argument. In Old English usage, a poet was a "scop" or "shaper," while the verb "scapen" was used to describe the making of a garden or, secondarily, a literary work. Emily Dickinson preserves this association.

In some late instances of such a parallel or equivalence, however, she relates the earthly to the heavenly "garden," extending her metaphors beyond the natural to the spiritual realm. In her luminous meditation upon sunset, "The Lilac is an ancient Shrub," contemplation of the "Firmamental Lilac" above the purple shrubs in her garden causes her to hypothesize the heaven of the gospels (F 1261). "Revelation," or the experience growing out of natural and imaginative vision, and the book of Revelation in the Bible, St. John's apocalyptic testimony, become synonymous, causing her to think deeply about "Faith." Thus the lilac, which represents the beginning of lasting love in the nineteenth-century floral books, is displaced by the sunset, metaphor of Christ's passion and death in nineteenth-century religious iconography. Watching the sunset spread across the heavens as a "final plant" at the end of day, Dickinson's speaker considers last things and Christ's promise of supernal sights in paradise.[17] The ease with which contemplation of a flower in her garden could lead to meditation on the infinite is remarkable. It reminds us that Emily Dickinson knew and admired the poems of such metaphysical poets as George Herbert or, indeed, Henry Vaughan, to whom she casually alluded and whose "They are all gone into the world of light" resembles some of her own elegies in theme and imagery.

❧

In the 1870s, Winslow Homer painted several canvases depicting women in reverie before open windows, in sight of a garden or the diminishing light of the sky. One of these works, *At the Window* [Fig. 30], is hauntingly evocative of the Emily Dickinson who writes of seeing the world from her room. A young woman with Emily's auburn hair, facing the viewer, dreams before a window that gives upon a

30. Winslow Homer, *At the Window* (1872).
    Oil on canvas, 57.4 x 40.0 cm. Princeton University Art Museum, gift of Francis Bosak, class of 1931, and Mrs. Bosak. Photograph by Bruce M. White. © 2000 Trustees of Princeton University.

light green lawn. Two geraniums like those kept in Dickinson's bedroom rest on the windowsill; the woman holds a flower, probably scented. The painting's tones are muted: gold, green, cream. The black velvet dress glints with what appears to be the light of coming twilight. It eloquently suggests the young woman's containment—not imprisonment—within doors and yet her familiarity with fields and trees outside and with her flowers, represented by those that keep her company in the bed chamber. Her gaze evokes that of the speaker of Dickinson's poems about twilight and the close of day, traveling within, yet also into, a beyond that transcends the picture space.

Homer's painting is one of many done by him in the 1860s and 1870s in which a woman is seen alone in or in relation to a garden, either reading *(The New Novel),* working *(The Milk Maid),* playing *(Butterfly Girl),* or dreaming. Portraits of women seen solitary in gardens date from the fifteenth century in Western painting; Homer's picture bears a quiet, plain relation to them. Scenes of the Virgin Mary in her enclosed garden, filled with flowers that signify her holy attributes, influenced portraits of noble medieval and Renaissance virgins depicted in gardens that imaged their modesty, dignity, and loveliness. In the eighteenth century, the noblewoman in a richly designed garden or at a window overlooking it represented the apotheosis of the desirable female in the works of such American painters as Charles Willson Peale. But it is especially in nineteenth-century art that Woman in a Garden—not necessarily noble or virginal, but picturesque and at one with her surround—was a primary theme. Again and again she is depicted alone, a flower among her flowers, even as Milton imagines Eve (L 1038).

Such pictures could validate a life like Emily Dickinson's, enabling it to be regarded as chosen and reasonable rather than unfortunate. There are many fleeting impressions of Dickinson, glimpsed alone (indeed, willfully, determinedly alone) in her garden by friends and even relations. Her nearly monastic appetite for solitude and her pronounced love for growing flowers were the characteristics chiefly attributed to her while she was alive. Though regarded as often related, and emblematized by the figure of the solitary woman flower-lover or gardener in nineteenth-century literature and art, these preferences—finally regarded as excessive—made Emily Dickinson a curiosity in Amherst. Even now, it is possible for Alfred Habegger, à propos of what Susan Dickinson protectively called "Emily's peculiarities," to write "her great genius is not to be distinguished from her madness,"[18] thus feeding the old legend of the poet's craziness. Yet Emily Dickinson's sanity is eminently apparent in the wisdom of her poems and in their spirituality, one that was earned from deep meditation on, and in, nature.

One of Dickinson's most enigmatic poems describes what she calls "the Flower of the Soul." To attempt to parse the meaning of this poem is to realize how closely she could, when she chose, relate flowers with words and words with the Word:

> This is a Blossom of the Brain —
> A small — italic Seed
> Lodged by Design or Happening
> The Spirit fructified —
>
> Shy as the Wind of his Chambers
> Swift as a Freshet's Tongue
> So of the Flower of the Soul
> It's process is unknown —
>
> When it is found, a few rejoice
> The Wise convey it Home
> Carefully cherishing the spot
> If other Flower become —
>
> When it is lost, that Day shall be
> The Funeral of God,
> Opon his Breast, a closing Soul
> The Flower of Our Lord — (F 1112)

Dickinson appears to be speaking here about an especially beautiful product of the brain that she expresses as a "Blossom." It is a small but highly emphatic or "italic" seed that is sown by chance or on purpose, then fertilized or made to flower by the Holy Spirit. This blossom of the brain becomes the flower of the soul by a "process" that is "unknown" but that is swift as a rivulet and impossible to confine as a wind. Some who find the flower "rejoice," while those who are wise take it up, bear it home, and tend the plot where it takes root in case more such flowers appear. Should the flower be "lost," however, God's funeral will take place that very day. The poet imagines God in the coffin; on his breast (as by Victorian custom at funerals) is a flower that is "closing" or dying, like the "Soul" which was "The Flower of Our Lord" since Christ came to draw all souls to himself.

This is a complex poem that succeeds, despite its somewhat belabored argument. The poet appears to take pleasure in the riddling character that relates the poem to others about unnamed flowers. Her subject is religious faith. The Holy Spirit causes it to "fructif[y]" in some persons; it lodges with them by chance or by some unknown plan, and "a few" are glad. They cherish it, hoping faith will increase. If faith should be lost, however, God dies as an idea and with him perishes the flower of faith itself. For the flower of faith, Christ the Lord came to earth, taught, and died.

The tenor of this poem is especially intricate since we learn from the fourth quatrain that God's existence is not absolute; it depends upon a "small — italic Seed" that becomes a flower "by Design or Happening." Thus, the mood here is quite different from that of the lyric "I know that He exists" (F 365). God dies if one lacks belief in him. The last two lines are moving, fantastic, grim: God is a corpse adorned with a dying flower.

Representing so many people, powers, properties, faculties, and situations, Dickinson's flowers also come to symbolize eternal truths. Writing of the gentian, she spoke of it as "a Purple Creature — / That ravished all the Hill —" (F 520). It stood for unexpected beauty, the flower that blooms late by God's design. In her own mind, it may have represented Dickinson herself, the late-bloomer associated with north winds and winter, who vanquishes the summer of the commonplace poet.

Emily Dickinson wrote again about a purple flower, however, in a lyric of decided metaphysical temper. Her poem presents a fantasy that is introduced by a line that promises the reader a carefully reasoned argument:

> Of Death I try to think like this,
> The Well in which they lay us
> Is but the Likeness of the Brook
> That menaced not to slay us,
> But to invite by that Dismay
> Which is the Zest of sweetness
> To the same Flower Hesperian,
> Decoying but to greet us –
>
> I do remember when a Child
> With bolder Playmates straying
> To where a Brook that seemed a Sea
> Withheld us by it's roaring
> From just a Purple Flower beyond
> Until constrained to clutch it
> If Doom itself were the result,
> The boldest leaped, and clutched it – (F 1588)

Written by the poet who always sees "New Englandly" (F 256), the second octave of this carefully designed poem presents an apparently simple scene: children playing beside a brook whose roaring sound keeps some of them from leaping over it to pick a purple flower growing on the farther bank. The scene is in one way an allegory, the illustration of both an idea and an event: death. The contemplative formality of the poem emphasizes the importance of its subject,

while the simple pastoral scene—children straying beside a brook—
suggests that death is, after all, universal and commonplace, not to be
feared. Nevertheless, the poem has an air of mythic importance cre-
ated by its use of rhetorical comparison—the Grave as a Well, the
Well as the "Likeness of [a] Brook"—and by the example of a body of
water that must be crossed. By crossing it, the children that stand for
all humankind may reach a "Hesperian" flower—that is, a flower of the
Hesperides, the nymphs in whose glowing sunset garden at the far
west of the universe the golden apples of peace were said to grow.

The speaker explains in the first octave that the brook of her child-
hood "menaced not to slay" or annihilate her and her friends but "to
invite" them to the other bank where the purple flower beckons. The
children experience "Dismay" at the sight and sound of the rushing
brook, just as adults do at the prospect of what was called in the nine-
teenth century "the crossover"—death. But dismay or fear is merely
the "Zest," the spicy ingredient of sweetness, that "invite[s]" us to
leap over the brook to the "Flower Hesperian." Death, then, is really
a "Well," a source of life-giving water, or a "Brook" like the rivers
Styx or Lethe that in classical mythology separate this world from
the next.

In the past, fear of the brook's loud noise once kept the speaker
and her companions from trying to leap over it. It "seemed a Sea,"
Dickinson explains, invoking her personal symbol (and a frequent
nineteenth-century symbol) of eternal life as she did in a letter about
her mother's death: "I cannot tell how Eternity seems. It sweeps
around me like a sea . . ." (L 785). The "roaring"—the dread reputa-
tion as well as the anguish of dying, if we continue the verbal equiva-
lences—that this vast body of water maintains keeps the children
from trying to jump over it. Finally, however, they are "constrained,"
forced, by the "Purple Flower beyond"—because, ironically, they
crave this flower. Although "Doom"—not mere death but punishment,
even damnation—might be the result, the "boldest" of her playmates
leap to clutch it. The speaker does not tell us whether she is among

them; as in other poems, notably "This was a Poet —," she refrains from including herself.

Is it possible to guess the species of flower on the other side of Dickinson's brook? Probably this Hesperian flower partakes of the usual symbolism of purple in Dickinson's art, and thus we may assume that in some way it is regal, superb. There were many flowers Dickinson grew and wrote about that are or can be purplish: heliotrope, clematis, crocuses, iris, phlox, nasturtiums, hyacinths, tulips. She may, of course, intend that we not identify or imagine the exact appearance of this special flower. To be modest and nameless could be, as we have seen, a kind of triumph in her view. To call the flower in "Of Death I try to think like this" *purple* without naming it may be descriptive enough for Emily Dickinson.

Or perhaps she intends the reader to recall her well-loved gentian [Fig. 31], sketched by Mrs. Clarissa Munger Badger in *Wild Flowers of America* (1859), the picture book given her by her father. The gentian, which stands for late blossoming and triumph through industry and self-fulfillment, is a deep purple-blue. Whatever its identity, the purple flower beside the great brook in this poem is yearned for, dreamed of. Hercules must visit the sunset Garden of the Hesperides in order to steal the golden apples and be purified. Humankind must be bold enough to leap into the beyond, to agree to die in order to clutch the purple flower. Though Emily Dickinson declines to name the flower, if her readers know *her,* they will know its name. The flower belongs to those who, like poets, believe in lasting things; it is called Immortality.

This is one of many poems in which a flower provides the crucial structural image. In one visionary lyric, "It was a quiet seeming Day —" (F 1442), Dickinson even compares an especially brilliant sunset to the destruction of the world on Doom's Day: "As those that Dissolution saw / The Poppy in the Cloud —." Hers is a frighteningly grotesque dream vision in which what might have been a charming picture of the sun going down becomes a nightmarish fantasy. Houses

31. Clarissa Munger Badger, "Fringed Gentian," from *Wild Flowers of America* (1859).

vanish with a roar; the sun, a giant poppy bringing death rather than sleep, is entrapped in a huge cloud, and all humanity is overwhelmed as it spins and crashes, beautiful in dissolution.

Such poems, like "Of Death I try to think like this," reveal the degree to which the idea of flowers and gardens met Dickinson's requirements and needs as a poet. The garden was a sustained and exquisite intellectual construct capable of deeply moving the heart. If flowers gave her a lifelong occupation, they also provided images and symbols whose traditional importance she could reconstruct and embellish. Flowers were "Nature's sentinels" (F 9 1 2). As a poet, she imbued them with original aesthetic significance.

CHAPTER FIVE

Gardening with Emily Dickinson

Louise Carter

If a pod die, shall it not live again?

Emily Dickinson, Prose Fragment 18

W HAT FOLLOWS IS AN ACCOUNT, at times speculative, of the plants and flowers grown by Emily Dickinson in both her garden and her conservatory, together with advice about how to grow them in today's United States. A student of botany and a knowledgeable horticulturalist, Emily apparently experimented with a wealth of native and newly available exotic plants with remarkable success. Except for fragrance—one of the most notable features of her conservatory and garden—it is possible to reproduce her floral world in some of its attributes. (Unfortunately, fragrance is one of the first attributes of flowers to disappear when plants are hybridized as they are today.) When attempting such reproduction, we must remember that the modern search for larger, more brilliantly colored, longer-lasting blooms may keep us from fully appreciating the simpler, shorter-lived wild plants such as the fall-blooming witch hazel *(Hamamelis virginiana),* "witch and witching too," that Emily found enthralling, and the other rare native plants that she admired for their pale colors and mysterious appearance (L 479).

Discussing Emily Dickinson's garden is, of course, problematic. With a few exceptions, she did not use botanical names, and there is sometimes uncertainty about which plants she grew and wrote about. Some plants have been reclassified; others have been given different names over the years. In addition, although we have specific, detailed descriptions of Emily's conservatory, the original layout of both of her gardens—on North Pleasant (West) Street and on Main Street—is uncertain. As Guy Leighton reports in a historical study of the Dickinson grounds surrounding the Homestead, Emily's garden was taken over and partially altered after her death by her sister Lavinia. Further alterations took place after Lavinia died, when Emily's niece rented the Homestead to Dr. and Mrs. Norman Haskell. The Haskells tore down Emily's conservatory in 1915 and had little interest in the garden. By 1916, when the house was bought by the Reverend and Mrs. Hervey C. Parke, few vestiges remained of the original garden with the exception of the great white oak tree that still spreads its branches over the rear lawn [Fig. 32]. The Parkes razed the Dickinson barn, graded the land east of the house into terraces with steps and formal gardens, and installed a tennis court at the end of the property. Those of Emily's flower gardens that lay close to the house were moved into the areas once occupied by the orchard and vegetable garden. When in 1938 a devastating hurricane swept through Amherst, it removed any lingering traces of the old Dickinson garden including all major trees but the stalwart oak.

Nevertheless, through the efforts of the Parke family the Homestead was listed on the National Registry of Historic Places in 1963, and at that time the grounds as well as the house were offered protection from future alteration or demolition. In 1965, the Homestead was bought by Amherst College. When the Evergreens, Susan and Austin Dickinson's home, was officially united with the Homestead as one property in 2003, the "Emily Dickinson Museum" came into being as a shrine to the poet, with curators and staff, and as a study center for Dickinson scholars. The Homestead itself hosts occasional classes and receptions for students of Dickinson's poetry and an an-

32. The Dickinson grounds today: the original white oak with the Homestead in the distance.

nual celebration of the poet's birthday on December tenth. It is also open to the public on appointed days. Even as what Emily called "[her] Father's House" (L 261) has been steadily renovated, efforts are also being made to restore her flower garden to its probable appearance during the poet's lifetime [Fig. 33]. (Under the auspices of the Martha Dickinson Bianchi Trust, the Evergreens is also being restored. Considerable interest is being focused on its grounds, too, and on replanting the trees and rhododendrons known to have been planted and energetically cultivated by Austin.) Study of the poet's letters and poems as well as the papers and published memoirs of those who knew the Dickinson garden in Emily's day is proving invaluable in all these restorations.

Although the flower garden was prized by the entire Dickinson family, its care was originally Emily's responsibility: the planting, watering, deadheading, and cutting back. Lavinia's chief project was the extensive vegetable garden filled with rows of beans, corn, cabbages, celery, beets, potatoes, asparagus, and squash. Only when Emily became physically weaker in the 1870s did Lavinia begin to help with the flowers. In fact, by 1884, Emily was calling it "Vinnie's sainted Garden" (L 885). Richard Sewall observes that Lavinia had felt a vocation for tending to the house and grounds as early as 1853, when she was only twenty. She found the heavier garden tasks suited to her "terrific" energy; thus, in 1885 Emily gives us the portrait of Vinnie "subsoiling" or turning over the ground with her spade prior to planting (L 692, 1000). Yet in 1862, Emily wrote Samuel Bowles that Vinnie was "trading with a Tin peddler – buying Water pots *for me* to sprinkle Geraniums with" (emphasis mine). From the 1850s through

33. Emily's garden today, with informal rows of phlox and dianthus.

the late 1870s, both sisters obviously regarded the flowers as Emily's province, taken over from Mrs. Dickinson (L 272). Certainly the conservatory was known to both the Edward and Austin Dickinson families as "Emily's conservatory," an indoor extension of the outdoor garden.

Emily never explained how her flower garden was arranged; she kept no lists or records of her success with various plants. But she did allude to the flowers, their health and growth, in letters. According to the accounts of others like Martha Dickinson Bianchi, Mabel Loomis Todd, and her daughter Millicent Todd Bingham, Emily's garden resembled the naturally designed "cottage" gardens that were evidence of the growing movement away from Victorian and European formalism. Such gardens were described by the horticulturalist Anna Bartlett Warner as exhibiting "rich, soft, mingled bloom, and tender tints, and wafts of nameless sweetness." Emily apparently grew flowers not in formal isolated beds of their own but mixed with roses and other flowering shrubs in the relaxed informal borders that appeal to gardeners today. She designed no flamboyant Victorian shrubberies, winding gravel walks, or extravagant garden "follies"—the usual features of the rich man's garden.

When Lavinia became custodian after Emily's death, she increased the appearance of informality until riotous abandon was the garden rule. Martha Dickinson Bianchi made that clear: "All [Aunt Lavinia's] flowers did as they liked: tyrannized over her, hopped out of their own beds into each other's beds, were never reproved or removed as long as they bloomed; for a live flower to Aunt Lavinia was more than any dead horticultural principle."[1]

Emily, however, relished fragrant masses of seasonal bloom but with an underlying plan. As her niece recalled,

> There were long beds filling the main garden, where one walked between a succession of daffodils, crocuses and hyacinths in spring— through the mid-summer richness—up to the hardy chrysanthemums

that smelled of Thanksgiving, savory and chill, when only the mari-
golds—they called them 'merry-golds'—were left to rival them in
pungency. Many of the flowers were veritable old time perennials,
punctilious in reappearance.

This garden that Emily inherited from her mother had "little flag-
stones" running from the house that "led down to the garden path that
ran through plots of blossom on either sides, under honeysuckle
arbors to a summer house thatched with roses." (Such arbors and
retreats were very fashionable in the Civil War period. The artist
Jeremiah Hardy, in his 1855 oil painting entitled *The Artist's Rose Gar-
den* [Fig. 34], provides a vision of the abundant climbing roses that
typically covered their trellises. The Dickinsons seem to have had
trellises on which roses were intertwined with honeysuckle, since
Martha also spoke of "the roses clap[ping] their hands high over two
old-fashioned arbors [while] the honeysuckle lured the hummingbirds
all day.") The summer house disappeared with the many changes the
Homestead suffered after Lavinia's death, but it must have offered
Emily a private place at the heart of the garden, invisible to others go-
ing by in the street, where she could observe and compose. Martha
Dickinson Bianchi also remembered that in Emily's garden "self-sown
flowers of humbler origins elbowed and crowded their more aristo-
cratic neighbors" and that both were plentiful:

> There were carpets of lily-of-the-valley and pansies, platoons of sweet
> peas, hyacinths enough in May to give all the bees of summer dyspep-
> sia. There were ribbons of peony hedges and rifts of daffodils in sea-
> son, marigolds to distraction—a butterfly utopia.[2]

In her edition of the poet's letters, Mabel Loomis Todd gave her
own impressions of the Homestead garden:

> The old garden [without Emily] still overflows with annual fragrance
> and color. Its armies of many-hued hyacinths run riot in the spring
> sunshine, while crocuses and daffodils peer above the fresh grass

34. Jeremiah Hardy, *The Artist's Rose Garden* (1855).

under the apple-trees . . . And then the roses, and hedges of sweet-peas, the masses of nasturtiums, and the stately procession of holly-hocks, in happy association with huge bushes of lemon verbena! Still later comes the autumn glory, with salvia and brilliant zinnias and marigolds and clustering chrysanthemums, until ranks of seeds their witness bear, and November folds her brown mantle over sleeping flowers.[3]

In her correspondence Emily alludes to her care of many kinds of flowers, yet she never mentions in what manner or style she arranged them or in what combinations of bloom. Those to whom she sent flowers, however, usually found her bouquets both fanciful and unique. Her niece's use of the word "rifts" suggests that Emily was indeed familiar with the garden fashions of the late nineteenth century that preferred a succession of blooms in lanes, or long drifts of bloom made up of many bulbs, rather than orderly geometrical arrangements. We may infer that Emily grew many of the flowers that her poems closely describe, and we may turn to the testimony of others—for example, her niece or Mabel Loomis Todd or Professor George Whicher, who recalls her success at "cultivating the English violet out of doors"—for corroboration. (A list of the flowers known to have been grown by Emily Dickinson appears in the Appendix.) Lavinia's floral preferences were fashionably Pre-Raphaelite: Oriental and tiger lilies, snapdragons, poppies, gladioli. Emily's choices for her outdoor garden were more typical of the late eighteenth or early nineteenth century "Federal" and cottage gardens: lilacs, roses, daisies, daylilies, sweet peas. But as we have seen, she grew flamboyantly exotic plants and flowers in the conservatory.

There were plants and flowers to which she seems to have given devoted attention that are not celebrated in a Dickinson poem, although they may appear in her letters; for example, the sweet pea, the peony, the marigold, and green leafy plants like the maidenhair fern. It is interesting to hypothesize what might have been Emily's reasons for submitting one flower to imaginative analysis and others to mere cordial mention. So, "Tell Vinnie I counted three peony noses, red as Sammie Mathews's, just out of the ground," she writes Louise Norcross in late April 1859 (L 206). (The "nose" is the proper name for the projecting end of the peony.) In New England peonies might not break through the soil until May or be ready to open their buds, or noses, in bloom until June. Emily is obviously eager to familiarize her sister with the precocity of their peonies, but she might rather have exulted in the luxuriously plump, rose-like softness, brilliant color, and entrancing fragrance of the *Paeonia,* which was native to Asia, venerated in China and Japan, and just the sort of gorgeous flower one might expect her to appreciate in verse. Perhaps its very opulence was a deterrent: her favorite flowers like the gentian or the jasmine were not voluptuous but slenderly formed, their fragrance either astringent or sweet yet fresh, neither musky nor heavy like the rich Oriental peony. Often, as in the case of the Madonna lily or the Indian pipe, Emily preferred white or pale-hued flowers. Moreover, plants or shrubs that were popular in the 1850s or 1860s but did not blossom—like box *(B. sempervirens)* or hosta *(hostaceae)*—did not seem to invite much notice from her, while (with some exceptions like the pine and hemlock) the trees that inspired her attention and praise were usually blossoming trees.

In the absence of any proof, Guy Leighton hypothesizes that the Dickinsons' flower beds were "laid out in a symmetrical pattern composed of a central round bed surrounded by three long, rectangular ones." He concludes that the garden lay east of the house and was reached through the flagstone walk that Martha Dickinson Bianchi remembered, which ran in a straight line from the northeast corner of the house through rows of fruit trees. He supposes that the garden consisted of "a central circular bed planted in roses, surrounded on three sides by rectangular beds of annuals and perennials" and that "its formal geometric shape was quite visible from the house and the piazza because the ground slope[d] away down to the garden."[4] Although he does not include a diagram of the Dickinson garden in Emily's time, Leighton does present a diagram of the Homestead grounds as they were from 1813 to 1840, which suggests that the vegetable gardens impinged closely upon the area for flowers. Unfortunately, there are no photographs, no written descriptions, and no drawn plans to illustrate the true layout of the garden in Emily's time or to justify Leighton's hypotheses about its formality.

I am inclined to think that Emily's garden was far less formal than Leighton proposes. Martha Dickinson Bianchi described its arrangement in the 1870s as informal, with two arbors as its main architectural features, the general impression it gave being that of "a meandering mass of bloom." Leighton's judgment was partially based on the fact that Austin Dickinson owned Andrew Jackson Downing's influential *Treatise on the Theory of Landscape Gardening* (1841), a copy of which may be found among the books in the Brown University Dickinson collection. Leighton supposes that Downing's ideas probably influenced not only Austin but also Emily's parents in establishing the architecture of their gardens. Downing enjoined that a garden be laid out in "the form of circles, octagons, or squares." Yet such intensely regular plantings were common to the eighteenth century, not the 1850s and 1860s, while nothing in their remarks about the Homestead garden suggests that Emily and Lavinia desired or maintained such classical regularity.

In fact, Susan and Austin's garden and grounds were different in fashion and taste from those of the Homestead. Austin (who had planted a grove of pine trees behind the North Pleasant Street house) admired sophisticated formality, and Mabel Todd recalled that he much preferred shrubs and trees to flowers. He collected exotic plants such as rose bay and flame azaleas from the surrounding woods for the garden of his Italianate villa. Emily, on the other hand, noted the elements of informality in her garden and delighted in the rippling lawns of the Homestead, scythed only infrequently. Rather than French formalism, the informal lawns of the Edward Dickinson house must have given an appearance of spontaneity like that of a spring meadow. Crocuses and daffodils would dance under apple trees in the orchard on the grassy slope just off the eastern side of the house. Violets, clover, buttercups, and wild geraniums would have followed the hyacinths and daffodils, springing up amid the grass. The lawn would have hummed with insects by May, as Emily records in her letters.

Emily's Garden Flowers and Some Advice on How to Grow Them

ANNUALS, PERENNIALS, AND BIENNIALS

The essential requirements of plants for good growth, like basic gardening techniques, remain unchanged since Emily Dickinson worked with her plants. However, improvements have been made in our understanding of plant hardiness, soil requirements, and insect and disease control that make gardening a less uncertain task. Emily gardened in what is known today as USDA Zone 5. For those who garden in a cooler or warmer zone, it will be necessary to adapt the advice that follows. Emily chose mostly fragrant flowers, whether annual or perennial. Her perennials were closer in form to the original species rather than to the modern cultivars of these plants familiar to us today. (For distinctions among annuals, perennials, and biennials, see the section on "General Instructions" below.)

While we know little—though that "little" is fascinating—about her methods as a gardener, we do know that Emily was regarded as greatly skilled by those who were acquainted with her and who gardened themselves. The wide array of plants she grew—from wildflowers to exotics to shrubs and vines to meadow flowers and bulbs—suggests her competence. She was apparently venturesome, starting seeds as well as bulbs on the windowsills of her bedroom (where, without central heating, the air remained cool and moist) and on the east-facing dining room sills of the Homestead. Although some bulbs can be forced in water, evidence suggests that Emily forced her bulbs in soil. She probably fertilized her plants with the readily available "manure tea," made by steeping a few cups of rotten manure in a bucket of water overnight and using the resultant "tea" to water house and garden plants. Manure tea was—and is still—used because it is mild and does not burn plants. Although we know she gave her plants loving care, we do not know how Emily dealt with insect or disease problems. Certainly she had them. She wrote Emily Ford in 1853, "I found a family of [Rosebugs] taking an early breakfast on my most precious bud, with a smart little worm for Landlady" (L 124). Keeping plants well groomed is very important in controlling plant disease. There is an amusing self-portrait of her stripping off and gathering up her hollyhocks' spent stamens which suggests that Emily knew the importance of grooming to not only the appearance but the health of her garden. Adjusting soil content to prevent disease or death is more easily accomplished today than in Emily's day, but Emily seems to have understood its importance too, writing her Aunt Katie Sweetser in January 1882 about her delayed Sweet Sultans: "One might possibly come up, having sown itself – if it should, you shall share – it is an Eastern Creature and does not like this Soil. I think it's first Exuberance was purely accidental" (L 746).

"Emily had an uncanny knack," George Whicher declares, "of making even the frailest growing things flourish." Whicher, a professor of English at Amherst College, profited from the memories of many who knew the Dickinson family when he wrote *This Was a Poet* (1938), the first substantial biography of Emily Dickinson. In speaking of her garden, he was able to cite the recollections of some of her contemporaries who were still living. One enthused: "Miss Emily's garden had a touch that no one else's had. I think that others planted gardens with lemon verbena, jockey club, sweet clover, and Star of Bethlehem, because Miss Emily had these in her garden."

Today's gardeners may be familiar with some, if not all, of these old-fashioned flowers. Lemon verbena *(Aloysia citriodora, Lippia)*, for example, was an especially popular greenhouse plant in the 1860s. It will remain evergreen indoors and should be grown at a temperature of about 55 degrees; when the pots are put out in summer, the plant can grow to a lush 3 feet. Emily may have used its leaves in cooking.

Star-of-Bethlehem *(Ornithogalum umbellatum)* is a pretty, low-growing bulb with narrow leaves and clumps of star-like flowers on bare scapes. The flowers are white and six-petaled, each petal being lined down the center with green. On sunny days, Star-of-Bethlehem opens in late morning and closes up before evening and is thus another flower like the *Hemerocallis* or Love-for-a-Day rose that might have contributed to Emily's awareness of the mortality of beauty.

Other old-fashioned flowers grown by Emily Dickinson include many to be found in today's seed and plant catalogues, especially because there is now renewed interest in "heritage" perennials and annuals. Many of these have interesting histories and are hardier and less prone to insects and disease than modern cultivars. Aside from roses (which are discussed in a separate section below, since Emily had so many kinds), the following flowers were cultivated in her garden:

Asters. Perennial. Modern cultivars of the New England Aster *(Aster novae-angliae)* and New York Aster *(Aster novae-belgii)* include a variety of sizes, flower forms, and colors, with blooming times from mid-summer to late fall. Plant in full sun.

Baby's breath *(Gypsophyla paniculata)*. Perennial. Useful as a filler over spent bulbs. Mixes well with other flowers, preferring alkaline conditions. Full sun.

Balsam *(Impatiens balsamina)*. A tender annual, balsam can be seeded into the garden two weeks after the last frost date. It will bloom in two months or less and continue until the first frost, becoming bush-like in rich soil. Called "Touch-Me-Not," balsam will shoot out seeds when the ripe seed pods are touched. Like its relative, *Impatiens walleriana*, balsam will bloom in half-shade as well as full sun.

Bleeding heart *(Dicentra spectabilis)*. Perennial with deep pink or white flowers. Wild bleeding heart *(D. exima)* is a native form. Needs sun.

Daisy or English daisy *(Bellis perennis)*. Low-growing perennial. The single form thrives in cool, damp conditions and may self-sow into the lawn. Requires sun.

Daylilies *(Hemerocallis* sp.). Tuberous perennials, so called because each flower lasts for one day. Yellow (lemon) daylily *(Hemerocallis lilioasphodelus* or *H. flava)* is a 3-foot tall fragrant daylily that has become naturalized in New England. Slimmer in leaf, smaller in blossom than the tawny daylily, it is a less aggressive spreader. The tawny or August daylily *(Hemerocallis fulva)* was Emily's favorite orange "cow lily." It is a common sight growing wild in fields and ditches along the East coast. Full sun.

Dianthus *(Dianthus* sp.) In cool climates, the perennial dianthus prefers full sun and a well-drained neutral to alkaline soil. Add lime or wood ashes if the soil tends toward acid. Most dianthus do not perform well under hot summer conditions, and they will succumb from poor drainage and wet crowns during the winter. Where content, they will grow in a garden for years. Mat forming, mounding, and upright forms exist. See Sweet William *(Dianthus barbutus)* below.

Forget-me-not *(Myositis sylvatica)*. The annual forget-me-not that self-sows.

Hardy geranium *(Geranium maculatum* and *G. roberianum)*. Cranesbill, a native perennial (as distinguished from the contemporary *pelargonium,* the showy garden annual of African origin). Scented.

Heliotrope *(Heliotropium arborescens)*. Usually treated as an annual bedding plant, it can be sown indoors and transplanted to the garden in early summer. (The Dickinsons may have done this, since Lavinia placed heliotrope in Emily's hand at her burial, May 19, 1886.) In cooler climates, heliotrope will not attain its full size and may succumb to high summer humidity. Water and fertilize regularly. In warmer areas such as Zone 10 it will become an erect, branching perennial that can be trained as a standard or against a trellis.

Hollyhock *(Alcea rosea)*. A tall background plant, hollyhock is usually a biennial, although some plants will linger on. Since it self-sows, hollyhock gives the effect of a perennial. The single form is more graceful than the double. Originating in China, hollyhock became a popular flower in America because of its mid-summer bloom.

Marigold: French or African annual *(Tagetes erecta)*. An erect, branching 2-foot tall plant with single yellow or deep orange flower heads. The double French marigold *(Tagetes patula)* is the more common kind, small (to 9 inches) and compact, with small yellow or crinkled flower heads marked red or brown, both having a rough, pungent smell. For best bloom, plant in poor soil in full sun. In Emily's day, calendulas *(Calendula officinalis)* were also called marigolds.

Mignonette *(Reseda odorata)*. A tender annual, mignonette is most fragrant in full sun and in poor, alkaline soil. Small-flowered varieties are more fragrant than the large.

Nasturtium *(Tropeolum majus)*. Nasturtiums of the vining type are annuals, first grown in kitchen gardens. The buds and flowers can be eaten in salads, and the buds can be picked like capers. Nasturtiums should be planted in average to poor soil in full sun. Rich soil causes them to produce more leaves and fewer flowers. Unlike modern compact-growing forms, Emily's old-fashioned nasturtiums would have rambled over fences, other vines, and shrubs or, as Martha Dickinson Bianchi reported, run "wild over defenseless peony bushes."

Peonies *(Paeonia offinalis)*. A long-lived hardy perennial of extraordinary beauty and fragrance with heavy-headed pink, white, or red flowers. They should be planted in late summer in well-drained, moisture-retentive soil rich in organics and spaced 4 to 5 feet apart in a well-prepared permanent position in the garden. Take special care not to plant the "noses" too deep. Full sun at least 6 hours during the day.

Primroses *(Primula* sp.) These perennials include the fragrant yellow *Primula auricula* and *P. polyantha* or *Polyanthus.* They prefer rich, moist, but well-drained soil and partial shade.

Salvia *(Salvia* sp.) A perennial. Various varieties of summer-blooming but non-hardy salvias were available to Emily, including *S. fulgens* (crimson), *S. splendens* (scarlet sage), *S. angustifolia* (blue), and *S. patens* (blue). In New England, salvias must be started indoors to be set out when nighttime temperatures stabilize above 45 degrees.

Snapdragons *(Antirrhinium majus)*. Available in Emily's day in red, crimson, white, and variegated forms, these annuals should be planted in sun to partial shade and are best in cooler summer areas.

Sweet alyssum *(Lobularia maritime* or *Alyssum maritimum).* Frequently used as a ground cover or edger, annual sweet alyssum will self-seed in the garden.

Sweet peas *(Lathyrus odoratus).* The tendril-bearing type is a vine rather than a bush form. Long a favorite annual for cutting, sweet peas were first recorded in the seventeenth century. Earlier varieties were more fragrant than our modern ones, but fragrant old-fashioned varieties are still available. Sweet peas are intolerant of hot weather and should be grown in early spring or in areas with long, cool summers. They prefer alkaline soil and moisture. For best results, prepare ground in the fall, digging in compost and manure and sprinkling the area with lime if necessary. They do not self-seed.

Sweet Sultan *(Centaurea moschata, C. suaveolens).* An old-garden, thistle-like perennial with origins in the Levant. It bears fragrant yellow thistle-like blooms on long stems. Sweet Sultans prefer a dry situation in full sun and alkaline soil. In cool climates, they will bloom until frost. In late summer 1880, Emily wrote to her niece Martha, "'Sultans' in Tippets is rather a perversion of Hemispheres, but then we are such a vivacious Climate – The Shah in Mittens will doubtless ensue –" (L 655).

Sweet William *(Dianthus barbutus).* A biennial that comes in all shades of red as well as white with pinked petals, sometimes solid, sometimes zoned or edged in contrasting colors. Its flowers are spicily fragrant. In the summer of 1861, Emily wrote to Mary Bowles, "Are the Pinks true – and the Sweet Williams faithful?" (L 235). In 1880, she sent "the Progeny of the Pinks you so kindly brought Mother in Winter" to Mrs. James S. Cooper, thus demonstrating that she was clever about perpetuating flowers (L 647).

Violets *(Viola* sp.). Perennial, biennial, or annual, depending on species. Some are exotics, some are naturalized. Many varieties grew wild in the Amherst area in Emily's time. They prefer sandy loam and a little shade, although some varieties grow in moist situations. *Viola odorata* varieties are the most fragrant. The garden variety *Viola tricolor,* known as pansy or heartsease, is an import from England, naturalized in North America. It prefers richer soil.

Zinnias *(Zinnia multiflora,* red, and *Zinnia pauciflora,* yellow). Annuals, they originated in Mexico and have been transformed since Emily's day from their humble, simple, single-flowered beginnings to the broad choice of size, color, and flower forms that exist today. Classic zinnias are tolerant of heat, drought, and poor soil.

WOODLAND PLANTS

Although woodland plants are especially hard to nurture, one of Dickinson's contemporaries declared that "it was impossible for a plant to die, even a woodland plant, when [Emily Dickinson] had once taken it under her care." Some of Emily's favorite wildflowers were not native to the United States but became naturalized; for example, the ox-eye daisy, the red and white clover, and the dandelion or leontodon. They arrived in colonial times as seeds in the fodder for animals or in straw used for packing household goods. Most naturalized field flowers grow best in ordinary garden soil in full sun. Soil that is too rich causes them to "flop." They should be watered during dry spells. Many of the following plants and flowers found their way into Emily Dickinson's garden (but keep in mind that meadow flowers can become invasive in garden situations):

American cowslip or marsh marigold *(Caltha palustris)*
Bartsia *(Scrophularia marilandica)* Painted Cup, rarely planted in a flower border
Blue flag iris *(Iris Versicolor)*
Cardinal flower *(Lobelia cardinalis)*
Columbine *(Aquilegia Canadensis)*
Common red clover *(Trifolium pratense)*

Cowslips *(Primula yeris, Primula vulgaris)*
European wood anemone *(Anemone nemerosa)*
Gentian *(Gentiana* sp.), generally used today as a rock garden
  plant
Harebell *(Campanula* sp.)
Leontodon or dandelion *(Taraxacum officinale)*
Ox-eye daisy *(Chrysanthemum leucanthemum)*
Pink lady's slipper *(Cypripedium acaule)*
Trillium *(Trillium)*
White sweet clover *(Melilotus alba)*
Violets *(Viola)*
Yellow lady's slipper *(Cypripedium calceolus)*

BULBS

Spring Bulbs

Spring-flowering bulbs are planted in the fall. In general, bulbs do best if planted in sunny, well-drained, neutral soil. Avoid heavy clay or hard pan as good winter drainage is essential, and beware of summer irrigation systems that may cause bulbs to rot. Crocus and daffodils can be planted in the lawn, where they will naturalize. Bulb fertilizer can be worked into the soil at planting time. For a small number of bulbs, plant in individual holes. For a large number of bulbs, dig up the entire area, set the bulbs, and carefully return the soil. Space and plant bulbs at depths recommended by the supplier for each variety. Water well after planting. When bulbs become sparse after 3 or 4 years because of overcrowding, carefully dig up bulbs in the fall when they are dormant. Use a spading fork to lift large clumps, and divide and replant.

Emily Dickinson wrote her Norcross cousins in mid-April 1881, "The little gifts came sweetly. The bulbs are in the sod – the seeds in homes of paper till the sun calls them. It is snowing now" (L 691). This letter, like others, shows that Emily was accustomed to receiving plant materials from Boston. Probably the bulbs in question were summer bulbs like lilies (*Lilium* sp.), but regarding all bulbs she confessed herself "long . . . a Lunatic" (L 823). Her spring garden included the following bulbs:

Spring crocus *(Crocus vernus)*. These are among the earliest of spring flowers. Tiny in the wild, *Crocus vernus* are the forerunners of the hybrid large-flowering Dutch crocus. They come in various shades of blue and white and are easily grown in the grass. Flowering early, they will have disappeared before the grass needs mowing. Plant early in the fall in rich soil in full sun.

Daffodils (*Narcissus* sp.) These are most effective when planted in sweeps or masses of one variety rather than mingled. Leave daffodil foliage to ripen and turn yellow, for at least six weeks, before removing to nourish the bulb for next year's bloom.

Fritillaria, or Crown Imperial *(Fritillaria imperialis)* [see Fig. 6]. Fritillaria prefers a deep, rich, slightly alkaline soil in full sun or partial shade. It is a heavy feeder and will exhaust the soil. Dig fritillaria up every few years when it becomes leggy and blossoms poorly or not at all. Transplant into newly enriched soil.

Hyacinth *(Hyacinthus orientalis)*. Oriental hyacinths were probably the species grown at the Homestead. Stout and formal in appearance, they are deliciously fragrant. Plant in September or October, and plant deeper than generally recommended in soil that is not too heavy so that they have a chance to multiply.

Lily-of-the-valley *(Convallaria majalis)*. Lily-of-the-valley rootstock, called pips or crowns, are purchased bare-root and should be planted immediately or wrapped in sphagnum moss to keep them from drying out. Plant in partial shade or filtered sun and in rich, moist, well-drained soil containing plenty of organic matter. The creeping rootstock will spread rapidly under optimum conditions that include a month of temperatures under 40 degrees. Expect only moderate bloom for the first year or two until they become established. "Top dress" or mulch with compost, aged manure, or leaf mold each fall and keep moist during the summer months to avoid browned-out foliage. They thrive in cool climates, USDA Zones 2 to 5, and will also grow in Zones 6 and 7.

Summer Bulbs

Lilies (*Lilium* sp.) Lilies can be grown successfully throughout most of the United States. In USDA Zones 3 through 8, lily bulbs can be left in the ground. They will live 4 to 6 years, blooming yearly. In warmer areas, Zones 9 through 11, bulbs must be lifted out in October and refrigerated for 6 to 8 weeks. This chilling period is necessary, allowing them time to rest and prepare to bloom again. When choosing lily bulbs for planting, choose the largest ones as they will produce more flowers. If lilies are purchased through the mail, plant them as soon as possible after receiving them. Unlike other bulbs, they resent being put "on hold." If necessary, they can be kept for a few days in the storage compartment of a refrigerator in their original shopping bag.

Lilies require at least 4 hours of direct sunlight each day and soil that is rich, high in organic matter, and well-drained. They prefer a neutral to slightly acid soil (pH of 5.5 to 6.5). Dig a hole at least 12 inches deep, loosen the soil well, and mix in a large amount of organic matter. Put several inches of gravel in the bottom of each planting hole if in doubt about the drainage. Cover the gravel lightly with soil into which a spoonful of bulb food or bone meal has been mixed. Plant according to directions from the supplier. After planting, water thoroughly, then as necessary to keep the soil evenly moist. In winter, mulch lightly to protect the bulb from freezing temperatures. Stake tall lilies (over 3 feet) by inserting a thin bamboo stake next to the bulb at planting time, being careful not to puncture it, and tie the stem in two or three places to support the lily as it grows. Feed lilies when the stems first emerge in spring, and again just before flowering. Continue to water after they bloom and until the foliage begins to turn yellow and wither in the fall. Cut the stalks to the ground after they have withered completely.

To Charles H. Clark, Emily Dickinson wrote in mid-April 1886, a few days before she died, about a visit paid her by the Reverend Charles Wadsworth: "The last time he came in Life, I was with my Lilies and Heliotropes" (L 1040). Wadsworth's visit took place in the summer of 1880. Since her sentence implies time spent, she may have been staking her lilies—a painstaking task—or watering both the lilies and heliotrope against the Amherst heat.

ROSES (SHRUBS)

In her herbarium, Emily Dickinson identified three roses: the sweet briar or eglantine rose (*Rosa rubiginosa* or *R. eglanteria*), *R. lutea,* and *R. parviflora* (probably the swamp rose, *R. paulustris). Roses grew wild in the Amherst area, and several are identified in Hitchcock's *Catalogue of Plants Growing without Cultivation in the Vicinity of Amherst College: R. corymbosa, R. lucida, R. parviflora,* and *R. rubiginosa.* Emily's sample pressings may have been taken from Amherst gardens. Mary Adele Allen's *Around a Village Green* includes a description of Emily Dickinson's garden as Allen's mother remembered it. According to Allen, Emily grew the heavily scented Bon Silene rose, a Tea or China rose with deep crimson petals identified as *R. odorata.* (Emily speaks of her "crimson scouts" in "Where Roses would not dare to go" [F 1610].)

Robert Buist's *American Flower-Garden Directory* (1832) lists a multifloral variety of rose called "*Grevillia* [sp.], or *seven sisters* rose, a very curious rose," describing it as "a wonder of the vegetable world." The Grevilla or Greville rose had white, pink, red and purple, single, semi-double, and double blossoms in clusters, all in bloom at once. It was very hardy in New England. Some of these roses were brought from Monson, Connecticut, to Amherst by Emily's mother upon her marriage. A Greville rose that Buist listed had clusters with 20 flowers and a mix of 12 to 15 colors covering an area of 200 feet. Such a flower would truly have justified Emily's description of a rose as "an Estate," though Buist listed it as growing in Philadelphia, not—as Emily did—"in Sicily" (F 806).

Buist also lists two Sweetbriar roses, a single pink and a double-flowered one. A species rose of European origin, the sweetbriar or eglantine rose *(Rosa rubiginosa)* was probably brought by the first colonists from England and naturalized throughout New England by the nineteenth century. Fragrant single pink blossoms are produced in abundance in late spring, followed by oval scarlet hips that attract birds and last into winter. (The "hip" is the ripened accessory fruit of the rose, consisting of a fleshy receptacle enclosing numerous achenes or one-seeded fruits.) The eglantine rose is famed for its fragrance, used in potpourri. Sprays of its foliage were frequently made into nosegays. A dense shrub, 9 by 5 feet, sweetbriar rose can be used as a hedge rose, in an herb garden, free standing, or trained against a wall as it was at the Homestead, where it grew at the corner of the conservatory until it was destroyed by a snowstorm in the winter of 1860. Sweetbriar roses are hardy in Zones 4 to 8.

There were other roses in Emily's garden: yellow and white, Blush roses, and a variety of single rose called Cinnamon. Blush roses are Old Roses of great antiquity with healthy foliage, often blue-green in tone, and non-fragrant blossoms that tend to have pale or white flowers and decorative rose hips. Two forms are the Great Double White *(Rosa alba maxima),* with double, flat, creamy-blush blooms and oval hips, and *R. alba semiplena,* a single form with golden yellow stamens against milk-white petals and red hips. A rose "rustler" from central Texas, searching for old canes, discovered by the door of Appomattox Courthouse a shrub of "Old Blush" growing today in the same spot as in Mathew Brady's daguerreotype of Robert E. Lee's surrender. Famous cultivars of the Blush rose are "Felicité Parmentier," "Maiden's Blush," "Great Maiden's Blush," and "Kön   igan von Danemark."

Emily's Cinnamon roses *(Rosa cinnamomea)* bloomed early in the season. They were diminutive, red, and much admired for holding shape and scent throughout the day. A shrub of medium height that grows wild in France, the Cinnamon rose is highly variable. It blooms in June, and its blossom color may be dictated by soil and site conditions.

Emily also grew a variegated crimson and white rose called the "Calico" rose. One hypothesis is that this name derives from the rose's likeness to the cabbage rose found in chintz patterns. Another is that "calico" is a corruption of Gallica rose *(Rosa gallica)*. The Gallica rose, also called the French, Provins, Provence, or Cabbage rose, was an Old Rose, not used in the evolutionary development of modern roses. The variety of Gallica rose known to Emily Dickinson might have been a cultivar of the striped *Rosa mundi (R. gallica var. versicolor)*.

Finally, there were long rows of "Hedge-hog" roses in Emily's garden, whose ferocious thorns made excellent barriers against wandering animals.

"Harrison's Yellow" (a semi-double yellow rose), "Stanwell Perpetual" (a fragrant double blush), and two fragrant striped roses called "Belle de Crécy" and "Gloire de France" were introduced in the early nineteenth century. It is well known that "Harrison's Yellow" was grown by the Dickinsons. The other varieties might have been. By mid-century damask, moss, and noisette roses were also popular; the tea rose arrived soon after. Francis Parkman, a Boston Brahmin and author of the *Book of Roses* (1866), considered "Baltimore Belle" "the offspring of a foreign marriage . . . [or accidental union] with the Tea rose or the Noisette," and the Dickinsons may have attempted to grow all of these fashionable new cultivars. These roses, like the

Old "Deep Cup" Roses, were extremely alluring in color and fragrance. It is easy to understand why, as Judith Farr observes, Emily Dickinson compared inhaling their scent to "drain[ing]" "Depths of Ruby" (F 380).

Although nineteenth-century rosarians were beginning to segregate roses into special beds of their own, Emily continued to grow roses in mixed beds with other shrubs and flowers, and she also trained them on trellises. She may have mulched roses with a mixture of rotted manure and straw as Buist recommended.

Caring for Roses

Roses may be planted at any time of year as long as there is no threat of severe frost. When possible, planting bare-root is the best choice. Depending on one's location and the shipping schedule of the supplier, the correct time to plant will be in autumn, winter, or early spring. Roses will grow well in clay or sandy loam soil provided there is good drainage and pH conditions (5.5 to 6.5) are met. Many roses are sold on their own root; others are grafted onto hardier rootstock. In colder areas, grafted bare-root roses should be set so that the bud union or graft is 1 to 3 inches below the soil line to protect the graft from frost. This will also discourage suckering of understock and encourage the top stock to develop its own roots. In the south (Zones 8–10), roses may be planted with the bud union above the soil line. After planting bare-root roses, mound additional soil up around the stem to steady it. In cold areas this mound of soil will protect the stem from freezing weather and in the south, from desiccating sun and wind. Leave the soil mound over the winter or, if planting in the spring, spread the soil about in the bed after 3 or 4 weeks. Patience is required. Roses grow at different rates of speed, some pushing up rapidly the first year, others needing more time to establish themselves. Directions for container-grown roses are given in the following section.

OTHER SHRUBS AND VINES IN THE DICKINSON GARDEN

Lilac *(Syringa vulgaris,* common lilac). Lilacs were among the first plants imported by the colonies and are inseparable from most people's vision of a New England garden. Their flowers and fragrance are their only redeeming features, but they are so beloved that gardeners put up with these plants during the rest of the year. They are plagued by insects and disease, especially powdery mildew, yet some manage to live on indefinitely. They are most effective if planted in groups or used at the back of a shrub border. Plant them in neutral soil supplemented with peat moss or leaf mold. The problem of mildew can be lessened if shrubs are sited in full sun and provided with plentiful air circulation. Lilacs need a lengthy dormant period in winter if they are to maintain their vigor and blossom reliably each year. Since lilacs bloom on the previous year's wood, careful pruning is needed to preserve the following year's bloom buds. (Zones 3 to 7.) Emily Dickinson's affection for lilacs may be inferred from two letters that joyfully associate them with pollinating bees and the "divine Perdition" (L 712) of spring and from her superb celebration of their form and color in "The Lilac is an ancient Shrub" (F 1261).

Mock orange *(Philadelphus coronarius).* Frequently confused in name with the lilac, both have shared the name "syringa" and a common origin in Turkey. Heavily scented, mock orange, like the lilac, has little to recommend it as a shrub once its white flowers have faded. A vigorous grower, it transplants easily and prefers moist, well-drained, rich soil. It is best used as a background shrub. Mock orange requires little care. Prune after flowering to remove old wood and to shape. There are numerous cultivars with improved growth habits, but not all are fragrant.

Pinxterbloom azalea *(Rhododendron periclymenoides)* and swamp azalea *(R. viscosum).* Austin's fondness for azaleas was well known in Amherst, but Emily never mentions her own azaleas in her surviving letters. She compliments Mrs. Thomas P. Field for a spray sent to her in spring 1885: "Your azaleas are still vivid, though the frailer flowers are flitted away" (L 980). Her grateful note was accompanied by a Daphne bud.

Familiar Hall's Japanese honeysuckle *(Lonicera japonica cv. "Halliana").* An imported Oriental species, it is appreciated for its rich fragrance but has become a weed in the eastern United States. It should be grown in a tub to curb its invasive nature. Some modern *Lonicera sempervirens* cultivars are fragrant and should be substituted for Hall's honeysuckle when scent is desired. A climber, honeysuckle needs a fence or trellis and is effective mingled with climbing roses or clematis. (Zones 4 to 7, depending on variety.)

GENERAL INSTRUCTIONS FOR GROWING EMILY'S GARDEN PLANTS

Today we are more fortunate than were the Dickinsons in the number and kinds of plants available to us. In the nineteenth century there were nurseries that specialized in bare-root trees and grape vines, bulbs and vegetable seeds—that is, plants that stay viable for long periods. But for the most part, gardeners relied on family or friends for live plants, cuttings, or perennial and annual seeds. Some plants Emily received as gifts; some, she gathered from the surrounding woods and fields. Others she grew from collected seeds or cuttings, and still more, from division of plants in the garden. The more unusual plants probably came from greenhouses or special growers, who gradually emerged to fill the growing demand for new and hitherto-unknown species.

In both her garden and conservatory, Emily grew annuals, perennials, and biennials. An annual is a plant that completes its life cycle within one growing season. It can be started indoors if early bloom is desired and transplanted to the garden after all danger of heavy frost is past. The seed packets will provide information on sowing, germination times, and times to transplant. Annuals benefit from deadheading or light shearing back after blooming if they become leggy. For repeated bloom, keep annuals well watered and feed biweekly with a good liquid fertilizer.

A biennial requires two years to complete its life cycle. It begins as a seed and produces a leafy plant during the first year. In the second, it flowers, produces seed, and then dies. (An occasional biennial will rebloom for one additional year, while some modern varieties of Sweet William and hollyhock bloom the first year.) Its care is essentially similar to an annual's.

A perennial lives for more than two years and may be herbaceous (surviving the winter chiefly by rootstocks, like the iris) or woody (surviving by roots, stems, and sometimes leaves, like most shrubs and trees). Growing perennials from seed or cuttings requires great planning and patience as it can take several years for them to reach the blossoming stage. Most perennials are acquired as plants that are ready to go into the ground.

Instructions for Planting

Plants other than shrubs: First, prepare the site in advance, cultivating deeply and removing any weeds, grass, or other debris. Next, test the soil for its pH level and adjust if necessary. If the pH level is too alkaline—that is, higher than 7.0, which is neutral—acid peat moss, oak leaf mold, or other acidic organic materials should be incorporated into the soil, or chemicals such as aluminum sulfate and sulfur can be spread on the soil surface and watered in. Overly acid soil can be sweetened with ground limestone or hydrated lime. Spread on the soil surface and water in. Improve heavy clay soil with humus, such as leaf compost or rotted manure and sand, to improve drainage. Adding humus to sandy soil will improve its ability to retain moisture. In areas of poor drainage, add a layer of gravel to the bottom of the planting hole or set the plant high.

Note that the soil should be "amended" according to directions for each species of plant. Amending the soil, or improving its organic content, was as important in Emily's day as in our own. Today, gardeners amend with plant-based composts and chemical fertilizers, as mentioned above; in the nineteenth century, soil was improved with animal manures. To maintain the high level of fertility necessary to guarantee abundant crops, "dressing" or manuring was performed each year in winter or early spring, as it is today. Manure was also added yearly to shrubs and flowerbeds. (In the fall of 1898, Lavinia was upset to discover that Susan Dickinson had directed her gardener to take all the "dressing" from under the Homestead barn to spread on her own garden at the Evergreens. The incident has sometimes been cited to illustrate Sue's tendency to selfishness.)

After cultivating the soil, rake over the surface carefully to level it. Let the area rest overnight or for several days to settle. After planting, water in well to rid the hole of air pockets and put the roots in contact with the soil. (At the Homestead, the well was the only source of water for all household and garden needs until water was finally brought in by pipes from Pelham in June 1880. In a letter to Elizabeth Holland in August 1881, Emily speaks of her birds following the hose for "a Crumb of Water" [L 721]. Because her Sweet Sultans did not flourish in the autumn of 1880, however, she blamed the "Pelham Water [that] shocked their stately tastes" [L 668].)

After watering, add 3 to 4 inches of mulch to conserve moisture and restrain weeds. Keep the area well weeded and water deeply if the season is dry, up to one inch a week.

During the growing season, groom plants to remove dead blossoms, foliage, and damaged stems. In late fall, clean up the planting areas by removing stalks and fallen leaves. After the first heavy frost, the beds can be mulched with salt hay or evergreen boughs to prevent small plants from heaving due to freezing and thawing of the ground.

Mail-order plants: Good mail-order nurseries generally include planting instructions with their plants. If in doubt, one can appeal to garden centers for plant care information. If mail-order plants can't be planted immediately, they can be held for a limited time. Remove them from the box and discard all packing materials. Be sure not to lose any identifying labels. Set in a sheltered, brightly lit spot but out of direct sunlight. Feel the top inch of soil in the pots. If it is dry to the touch, water immediately. Keep the plant moist until planting time but do not overwater because the roots will rot in soggy soil. Plant on an overcast day, or shelter newly planted stock with newspapers, burlap, or inverted cartons for a day or two.

Shrubs: Shrubs are sold bare-root, container-grown, or, if large, balled and burlapped (b&b). For large plants, dig a hole that is as deep as the root ball and twice as wide.

Bare-root shrubs are available in late fall, winter, and early spring when dormant, depending on where one is gardening. Soak the roots in tepid water for several hours, cut off any damaged or excessively long roots, and plant as follows: Dig a hole large enough to hold the roots spread out in all directions without crowding. Set the plant slightly higher than it had been growing and half fill the hole with soil. Adjust the positioning, then tamp down with the foot and water in slightly. Finish filling. Form a saucer around the trunk, about 12 to 18 inches in diameter, depending on the canopy of the plant. Water in slowly until the soil puddles. Mulch the plant but do not fertilize at this time. If it is not possible to plant immediately, protect the roots from drying out by covering them with moist soil, newspaper, or mulch. Or "heel in" by burying the roots in cool, moist soil, protected from the sun, for up to two weeks.

Container-grown plants: Container plants, including container-grown roses, can be planted at any time they are available as long as the ground is not frozen and no severe weather is predicted before they have time to become established. To release the plant from the container, moisten the soil in advance. Tap the container soundly on all sides. Run a knife deeply down inside the rim or, if the container is stubborn, cut it down the side. Score the root ball all around, including the bottom, to encourage the roots to reach out to their new home. If the plant is pot-bound, pull and untangle any encircling roots. (One should not be too gentle. Pot-bound plants can withstand tough treatment. Otherwise, the roots will continue to grow in circles and the plant will never adapt to its new environment.) If the plant is growing in a soil-less mix, knock off as much of it as possible. Spread the roots out carefully over the soil at the base of the planting hole. Set the plant in at the same depth it was used to while growing in the container or slightly higher, since it might sink. For the remaining instructions, see the last part of the section on "Shrubs" above.

The Conservatory

PLANTS AND SHRUBS GROWN IN EMILY'S CONSERVATORY

Emily Dickinson was successful in growing exotic plants in her conservatory because, in contrast to our modern houses, it was not centrally heated, well insulated, or tightly closed. The air inside remained cool, fresh, and damp. Today our challenge is to combat too much heat and dry air. Emily grew those plants that suited her New England conservatory, with its south-facing windows and cool to cold temperatures in winter. She generally chose plants with fragrance for her conservatory, although camellias and fuchsia were exceptions. She did not include cyclamen, orchids, or potted azaleas, popular choices at the time.

The plants she chose to grow do best in temperatures ranging from 50 to 60 degrees. Her challenge was to keep them from freezing in winter. During frigid nights, she may have moved the plants into a warmer region of the house or at least away from the windows to protect them from freezing. She may also have placed matting against the glass. Her success with camellias and gardenias would be difficult to duplicate today unless one has a similar glassed-in space such as an unheated porch.

Emily also grew less exotic plants in the conservatory. Her letter to the Norcross cousins in February 1863 mentions crocuses, a fuchsia, "primroses – like the little pattern sent in last winter's note – and heliotrope by the aprons full, the mountain colored one – . . . and gilliflowers, magenta, and few mignonette and sweet alyssum bountiful, and carnation buds" (L 279). (Gillyflowers were today's pinks or dianthus. By "little pattern sent," she is probably alluding to what seems to have been a continual exchange of seeds, cuttings, and even pressed flowers in certain colors or "patterns" between the Norcrosses and the Dickinsons.)

Her choice of containers would have been limited. Pottery or wooden containers or tubs, of simple design, would have been made in the vicinity by a local potter or carpenter. Today's choice is unlimited. Aesthetically, the size and shape of a container should be consistent with the size and shape of the plant or plants that it will hold. One should also choose a container that suits the growth habits of the plant, since the relationship between the volume and depth of the container and the spread of the root system is crucial to the health of the plant.

Emily's conservatory was not large, and some of the plants—oleanders, gardenias, camellias—would have taken up a large share of the floor space. Other plants were staged or set upon shelving at differing heights, the shortest in front with taller ones behind. Small plants were placed on white shelves arranged around the room. Bulbs could have been potted in the fall and stored under the shelving in the dark, waiting for spring when they would be brought into the light to bloom.

Camellias

Camellia japonica, the common camellia, is an evergreen shrub, native to East Asia. A member of the Tea family, it is cultivated for its showy blossoms. The camellia was named for Georg Joseph Kamell, a Bohemian missionary, who introduced it into Europe in 1739. A single red-flowered variety was introduced into America around 1798, followed by a white one, "Alba Plena," in 1800. Camellias were the most popular greenhouse flower in the North between 1825 and 1875, and growers in New York and New Jersey produced cut flowers for ladies' corsages and bouquets as well as gentlemen's lapels. In the South, it was discovered that camellias could be grown out-of-doors. First grown in conservatories as potted plants, camellias provided evergreen foliage and rich, dramatic flower color through the long winter.

Modern camellias are available in petal forms—single, semi-double, anemone, and rose forms—and in colors ranging from white to pink to red and various color patterns including speckled, striped, and picotee. Blossoms can be as much as 5 inches across. With careful pruning after bloom, camellias can be kept as compact, bushy specimens.

Camellia japonica is a plant that can be grown in the North in a cool greenhouse or on a barely heated sunporch in winter. Camellias prefer a constant nighttime temperature of 40 to 50 degrees with daytime temperatures of 68 degrees or less as buds are forming in the fall and developing into the winter. They need adequate moisture and should be misted often. Do not let the soil dry out. Pot in a mixture composed of two parts loam, one part packaged potting soil, and one part sand or perlite.

If indoor-grown camellias are set out in summer, mark the south-facing side of the pot before returning them indoors so as to set them facing the light in the same direction. The buds are sensitive to light and may drop off if they have to realign themselves. Again, do not let them dry out during the summer or they may drop their buds in the fall. Use an acid-based fertilizer—the kind used for rhododendrons and azaleas—each month while buds are setting. Mist frequently. To produce large blossoms, snap off all but one bud in each cluster. Watch for scale insects.

Outdoors, camellias have become a fixture in gardens from southern Virginia through the deep South. They thrive equally well in the mild climate of the Pacific northwest and Vancouver Island. They can become 20-foot-tall shrubs and can be trained as espaliers, standards, or bonsai. In mild climates (USDA Zones 7 to 9), camellias are easy to grow if their cultural needs are met. Provide a loose, well-drained, slightly acid soil (pH 4.0 to 5.5). Do not plant too deeply, as camellias are shallow-rooted plants and like to have their roots close to the surface. Plant them in a sheltered spot to protect them from drying winds and shade them from scorching sun, especially during the afternoon. Although camellias will tolerate temperatures down to 10 degrees, flower buds will be damaged at below-freezing temperatures. Good drainage is essential, with supplemental watering during dry spells. Camellias require constant moisture but do not survive in soil that is constantly wet. Mulch in winter with several inches of organic mulch, but keep it away from the main trunk of the plant. Keep mulch clean of dead blossoms and fallen leaves to discourage fungus diseases.

To push into new growth after flowering, treat camellias with ammonium sulfate (1 teaspoon to 1 gallon of water) as the plants are watered. Fertilize during the summer months with a cottonseed-based fertilizer, mixed especially for camellias. Apply in April, June, and August.

Daphnes

Daphnes are a temperamental group of plants, charming one with their delicious perfume and good looks, then up and dying without notice. *Daphne odora* (Fragrant or Winter Daphne), a native of China, is among the easier varieties to grow, being less fussy about soil conditions. It floats a delicious, warm, penetrating sweet perfume upon the air. An evergreen shrub, growing to 3 feet or more, it takes green-leaved and variegated forms. The flower buds may be pink to rosy purple, the flowers white to pink. *Daphne odora* blossoms in late winter or early spring, with flowers that can last a long time. It was first grown in warm, then cool greenhouses until growers discovered that it could perform out-of-doors in sheltered places in Zones 7 to

9. It does well in shade. *Daphne laureola* (Spurge Daphne), a daphne native to the British Isles and popular in the nineteenth century for its fragrance, has been used as a rootstock for *Daphne odora* and other evergreen daphnes.

Daphne odora prefers a moist, well-drained, acid (pH 4.5 to 5) soil and a layer of mulch. If daphnes are doing well in a selected site, it is best not to move them. In fact, do not even prune or disturb them in any way! An easier variety to grow in the Northeast, possibly, is the *Daphne caucasica*.

Fuchsia

Fuchsia magellanica, wildly popular in the Victorian period and probably the kind grown by Emily Dickinson, is a dwarf shrub that can grow outdoors in mild climates (Zones 8–10). In cooler climates it is grown under cover or used as a container plant outdoors in the summer. It thrives where nighttime temperatures are below 65 degrees. An upright or sometimes pendulous plant, fuchsia carries hanging, bell-shaped, single or double blossoms. The blossoms are spectacular and frequently two-colored, typically with flaring purple sepals and hanging scarlet petals with protruding stamen. Under sufficiently cool conditions, fuchsia can be kept growing and in bloom throughout the winter. Plant in soil that is equal parts loam, sand, and peat moss. It likes partial shade, ample water, and ample fresh air. Fertilize biweekly in fall and early winter.

Gardenias

Gardenia jasminoides (Cape jasmine) is an evergreen shrub prized for its fragrant, double white blossoms. It needs full sunlight for development of its dark green foliage and waxy flowers that appear most of the year. However, it should be shaded from strong summer sun. Normal household temperatures suit it during the day and night until flower buds form. Then a 5- to 10-degree drop at night (to 60–65 degrees) is important; otherwise, the flower buds may drop. For best results in flowering, use a rich but well-aerated potting mix of equal parts loam, sand, and peat moss or leaf mold. When the buds are setting, fertilize with a balanced houseplant fertilizer every two weeks. Use a fertilizer containing iron, since deficiency in iron causes yellow leaves. To maintain soil acidity (pH 5.0 to 6.0), on alternate weeks, water with a solution of 1 teaspoon ammonium sulfate mixed in 1 gallon of water. Provide ample fresh air.

Gardenias are notorious for sulking when moved from one environment to another. The leaves turn back at the tips, or the plant may completely defoliate. To avoid this predicament, provide a balanced supply of moisture and keep the soil constantly moist but not soggy. Mist the plant frequently. To increase humidity around the plant, place the pot on a saucer of pebbles that are partially covered with water.

Two varieties, *G. jasminoides veitchii,* introduced to the southern United States from China by way of England, and the dwarf Japanese *G. radicans floreplena,* both produce smaller flowers than the familiar florist's gardenia but are easier to cultivate as conservatory or house plants. Gardenias will grow out-of-doors in Zones 8 to 9, where they can become 2- to 6-foot shrubs, thriving under the same acid soil conditions as camellias.

Jasmine (also called Jessamine)

Jasmine *(Jasminum)* is among the world's most fragrant plants. For Emily Dickinson, it was third in her list of favorites:[5] "next dearest to Daphne – except Wild flowers – those are dearer" (L 513). Because of its trailing habit, jasmine makes a good hanging plant; it can also be trained on a stake, crossed wire arches, or a small trellis inserted in the pot. Or simply set the pot on a matching pot turned upside down to give it additional height, and let the stems tumble down. Place jasmine in a location that provides bright light, but when in bloom, keep out of direct sunlight. Jasmine needs good ventilation, but drafts should be avoided. After blooming, jasmine profits from as much sun as possible.

Martha Dickinson Bianchi remembered her aunt growing yellow jasmine. Carolina yellow jessamine (*Gelsemium sempervirens*) is a glossy vine native to our southern woodlands. Long cultivated within its natural range (mid-Florida to Texas and Virginia), it was introduced into England in 1840. It will remain dormant through the early winter and then produce its fragrant, funnel-shaped blossoms over a long period. It may have been the "inland buttercups" that Emily mentioned to Mrs. Edward Tuckerman in a letter of mid-April 1875 (L 437).

Perhaps also included in Emily's conservatory, and certainly more commonly grown today, is *Jasminum officinale grandiflora* (White Jasmine). This jasmine is a subtropical shrubby vine with dark green leaves and delicate, white, very fragrant, star-shaped blossoms. Judith Farr calls attention to the jasmine flower that Emily Dickinson sent to Samuel Bowles, Jr., and her accompanying poem declaring that an "Asterisk" stood against his father's name, whose immortality was "Secreted in a Star" (L 935). This may indeed be wordplay based on the fact that the blossoms of the white jasmine are star-shaped or like asterisks.

White jasmine will bloom successfully through the winter if given cool, moist air and plenty of light. It does not tolerate dry heat. If exposed to warm temperatures above 65 degrees, the plant will grow but not bloom. Set the plant outside for the summer. Jasmine needs 4 to 5 weeks of shortening days and cooling temperatures between 40 and 50 degrees to encourage the formation of flower buds, but bring the plant indoors before the first heavy frost. Prune out any dead wood but, to preserve newly formed buds, pinch back to shape only as necessary. Do not expose the plant to any artificial light after sundown as buds continue to mature. The plant will be ready to bloom again in early winter. Difficult to start from seed, jasmine is propagated from cuttings.

Oleander

Oleander (Nerium oleander) has become common in public gardens and as a hedge plant along highways in the South and far West. A good container or tub plant, it has long been a popular house plant. Indoors or outdoors, it should be used with caution since all parts of the plant are poisonous, including smoke from its wood should it be burned. Various varieties are in cultivation in different shades of red, single and double blossoms, or with striped flowers. Oleander will tolerate neglect and dark corners, but not frost. Keep the plant on the dry side in fall and early winter, then keep it evenly moist. To ripen buds and bring into bloom successfully, plants need to be kept warm and moist and fertilized every two weeks with "manure tea" over a long period beginning in early spring and into the summer. Promptly remove any shoots that appear at the base of the flowers. Outdoors (Zones 8 to 10) oleander will grow to 20 feet but can be kept to a manageable size by pruning, which should be done after blooming or in the fall. By sending the blossom from an oleander (known to be a tough plant) tied with black ribbon to a departing friend, Emily Dickinson may have been suggesting the endurance of their affection.

Pomegranates

Victorians considered the pomegranate *(Punica granatum)* symbolic of immortality. Large evergreen shrubs with shiny leaves native to the Mediterranean, they are very decorative, with colorful flowers and fruits. Summer-blooming, their coral to bright scarlet flowers are followed by rounded, leathery fruits with edible garnet-red seeds and yellowish pulps. (Ripe fruit would have been unlikely in Emily's Massachusetts.) In warm climates they can be grown as a decorative ornamental shrub against a warm wall. They like full sun, fertile and moist soil, and regular watering. There are dwarf forms, including *Punica granatum var. nana,* that make a charming container or tub plant, safe in a conservatory in winter, then moved out onto a terrace in summer.

BULBS GROWN IN THE CONSERVATORY

Emily Dickinson started seeds as well as bulbs in her cool bedroom and on her window sill and the east-facing dining room sills. Bulbs were also forced in her conservatory in soil. Some of the bulbs mentioned below and others in her garden—*Crocus vernus,* hyacinth, and *tazetta* narcissus—can be forced in water, although there is no indication that Emily tried forcing them in this way. She grew the following bulbs:

Amaryllis: also called "Jacobean lily," possibly the "rare scarlet lily" mentioned by her niece. This amaryllis may have been *Sprekelia formosissima* (also known as *Amaryllis formosissima*). It is native to Mexico. The striking lily-like flowers have petals that are divided into two groups—three that stand up, flaring backwards, and three petals that encircle the stamen at the base before reaching out and down. The foliage is daffodil-like. *Amaryllis formosissima* were mentioned by commercial florists at the beginning of the nineteenth century. They are recommended for pot culture in colder climates, as they are hardy only in Zones 8–10. They can be forced indoors or used as summer bulbs in the garden or in containers, grown in full sun in well-drained soil. They are not the more familiar modern "amaryllis" *(Hippeastrum* sp.) that come primarily from South Africa in a variety of colors and various flower forms.

Lily-of-the-valley *(Convallaria majalis):* These can be forced like any other hardy bulb. The "pips" can be bought pre-cooled from commercial sources and potted immediately upon receipt in a bowl of peat moss that is kept moist and placed in a cool, bright place. They will also grow in pebbles like narcissus bulbs. For a good show, plant a dozen pips in a 5- to 6-inch pot. Green tips will appear, and flowering will begin in about three weeks. If the foliage is kept green and growing, the pips can be transplanted to the garden as soon as weather permits after blooming. Select a semi-shady, moist location.

Paperwhite narcissus *(Narcissus tazetta):* This is a polyanthus or multi-bloom narcissus. Paperwhites are frequently forced in water, although those planted in potting soil will bloom longer. Chinese sacred lilies, Grand Soleil d'Or, and Ziva are among the modern varieties offered for indoor forcing. All are fragrant and carry several blossoms per stem. In warm climates (Zones 8–10), paperwhites can be successfully grown out-of-doors.

Oxalis *(Oxalis):* This is a clover-like plant whose flowers and leaves close up at night. The oxalis that Emily grew in her conservatory, *Oxalis versicolor,* is a tender bulb or tuber. With sufficient light, it can be brought to bloom indoors in winter. Oxalis are low, mounding plants, small in stature, with delicate clover-like leaves in various leaf-colors from green to deep purple. The blooms are a creamy white rimmed in pink. In summer Emily had oxalis dripping from hanging baskets, but they are equally charming set lower down in small containers.

In the fall, several oxalis tubers can be potted together, using small pots with well-drained, gritty potting soil (two parts clay, one part sand, one part humus). Plant the tubers barely 1 inch deep with the pointed ends up. Place the pots in a sunny window. Water well to start the growth cycle; thereafter, water only when the surface of the soil is dry to the touch. Leaflets and flower stems will appear within several weeks, and the first blossoms will appear three or four weeks later. The plants will continue to bloom heavily for several weeks. Fertilize every month while blooming. The leaves will remain green and decorative for several months longer. When the oxalis plants begin to look limp, with sprawling stems and drooping leaves, they are signaling that they are going dormant. Let them rest by withholding water for a few months. After this drying-out period, begin watering again and the cycle will recommence. Grow in the same manner as before. Repot when the multiplying bulbs become crowded.

Oxalis violacea, the common wood sorrel, grew wild in deep woods in the Amherst area.

PERENNIALS AND ANNUALS IN THE CONSERVATORY

Carnations *(Dianthus):* There are several types: carnations *(D. caryophyllus),* annual dianthus *(D. chinensis),* and perennial dianthus *(D. plumarius, D. gratianopolitanus),* as well as the biennial Sweet William *(D. barbatus).* The existence of numerous hybrids causes great confusion in the floral trade. Modern carnations are mainly grown for the commercial trade and do well under conservatory or greenhouse conditions. They are taller, need staking, and are less hardy. The shorter, hardier varieties are called dianthus or China pink, clove pink, cottage pink, border carnation, and cheddar pink. Dianthus differ from carnations in having markedly pinked or serrated petals. Many types of dianthus are deliciously fragrant, like spicy cloves. Emily undoubtedly grew both carnations and perennial dianthus, which she referred to as "gillyflowers." Annual stock was also called "gilliflower" or "stockgilly."

There is a modern hybrid called *Dianthus xallwoodii* that will do well indoors and is sweetly clove-scented. Plant it in a humus-rich, slightly alkaline soil. Dianthus will bloom over a long period in a cool, sunny window if temperatures remain between 50 and 60 degrees, with nighttime temperatures at the cooler end. Water when the potting soil surface is slightly dry to the touch. Removing spent blossoms (deadheading) regularly will encourage the plant to continue blooming. When they finish blooming indoors, keep potted dianthus plants in a sunny location with the coolest possible temperature. Keep the potting soil slightly moist, and fertilize every three weeks with a balanced houseplant fertilizer at half the recommended strength. In spring, after all danger of frost has passed, the plants may be transplanted to the garden.

Fresh plants can be started from division in early spring, from cuttings taken from vegetative shoots during early summer, or from seed (which may not run true to type). After the cuttings have rooted, three or more small plants can be potted up in a 4-inch pot for growing indoors.

Geraniums: Emily mentions growing geraniums both in the conservatory and in the garden. Those in the conservatory are more correctly called *Pelargonium* to distinguish them from the native geraniums or cranesbill *(Geranium maculatum)* that grew wild in lawns and nearby woodlands. It was originally believed that the "geranium," introduced to Europe in the seventeenth century from South Africa, was related to the hardy geraniums that grew wild in the northern hemisphere. Although they were reclassified and named *Pelargonium* in the eighteenth century, we continue to call them "geraniums." These include the popular florist and bedding geraniums, ivy-leafed geraniums, zonal geraniums, and scented-leaved geraniums. Emily grew scented-leaved geraniums indoors. They produce small blossoms in shades of pink or lavender but are grown mainly for their attractive, fragrant foliage. They can be grown in cool conservatories and require strong light and fresh air. Keep on the dry side until February, then fertilize and water more frequently. Pinch back as necessary until they are compact.

Heliotrope *(Heliotropum arborescens):* Heliotrope can be started from seed in late winter or early spring to bloom in summer. It is usually propagated from cuttings, since germination is very irregular and the plants are slow to bloom. Because not all flowers are fragrant, propagating from root cuttings of fragrant plants will ensure the uniquely fragrant flowers for which it is mainly grown. Heliotrope likes a rich, well-drained potting soil and moisture until well established. Then do not overwater. Emily Dickinson once wrote Mary Bowles, "I made a plant of a little bough of yellow Heliotrope which [your bouquet] bore me, and [I] call it 'Mary Bowles'" (L 212). Modern varieties are limited to whites and various "mountain colored one[s]" as Emily put it, or shades of blue and purple (L 279).

Mignonette *(Reseda odorata,* formerly *R. odonia):* Grown for its fragrance, mignonette has insignificant brownish-red or gray flowers. The small-flowered varieties are more fragrant than the large, and those grown in poor soil are also more fragrant. Fill a small pot with average garden soil or potting mix and scatter seeds lightly across the surface. Do not cover as they need light to germinate. A tender annual, mignonette will bloom about six weeks after sowing. It can be sown out-of-doors in early spring in sun or partial shade and will grow a foot tall.

Sweet alyssum (*Lobularia maritime* or *Alyssum maritimum*): Little bunches of tiny white flowers cover this low-growing plant, which is frequently used outdoors as an edger or ground cover. Its scent is like new-mown hay. Sow like mignonette (see above). An annual, it will self-seed in the garden.

Ferns

Emily Dickinson included sensitive fern *(Onoclea sensibilis)* in her herbarium and grew ferns—probably maidenhair ferns—in her conservatory. Ferns were among the first popular house plants. With their drooping fronds, they made a graceful show when raised up on pedestals or staged on shelving. Today we would use hanging baskets. In summer, fern fronds were used to fill the empty fireplaces, as were the fern-like fronds of asparagus gone to leaf in the vegetable garden.

Ferns require warmth, moderate to high humidity, and good light but not direct sunlight. Plant in a humus-rich soil or fibrous growing medium containing equal parts of loam and peat moss, leaf mold, or shredded fir bark and sand for good drainage. Ferns need a dormant period in winter from November through February, at which time they prefer a pale winter sunlight. Hold back on watering and maintain in a cool spot. When the fern is in active growth, fertilize with fish emulsion. If any yellow or brown fronds develop, cut them off at the soil line. Watch for scale which, if caught early, can be picked off. But do not confuse scale with the spores (seeds), small raised dots or lines that form in patterns on the underside of the fronds.

Best for indoor growing are the Boston fern *(Nephrolepsis exaltata),* coarse-leaved polypody *(Polypodium* sp.*)*, bird's nest *(Asplenium nidus)*, brake *(Pteris cretica)*, maidenhair *(Adiantum* sp.*)*, and rabbit's foot *(Davillia fejeesis)*.

Other Plants and Flowers

Both orchids and clematis are written about by Emily Dickinson.

Orchids: Though not fragrant, orchids were highly regarded by collectors for conservatories. They are best grown under warm, humid conditions, although *Paphiopedilum* spp., *Phalenopsis* spp., and some *Cymbidium* are adaptable to windowsill conditions. We know that Emily loved the yellow and pink cypripedium orchids that grew wild. These require moist acidic soil, rich in humus. Was she successful in growing orchids indoors? They are not mentioned; their lack of fragrance seems to have dissuaded her from trying.

Clematis: These began to enter the trade from Asia in the 1860s. *Clematis florida, C. Montana, C. lannuginosa, C. patens,* and *C. viticella* were all grown in England and used in breeding new hybrid varieties. There were native clematis such as Virgin's Bower *(C. virginiana)*, but they lacked horticultural merit. Climbing clematis today like their roots in shade and their heads in full sun, and a neutral to alkaline soil. Emily Dickinson's poem "'Tis Customary as we part" contains these lines: "Clematis – journeying far – / Presents me with a single Curl / Of her Electric Hair –" (F 628). Thomas H. Johnson notes in *Poems* (J 340) that the clematis was also known as "Traveler's Joy," and that this poem may have been "composed to accompany a gift of a clematis blossom for a departing friend." The "Curl" might refer to the fruiting bodies of the clematis—long, arching, and hairy—rather than to the flower itself.

CARING FOR PLANTS IN A CONSERVATORY

Light: Light is the most critical requirement. Lacking sufficient light, plants will grow slowly and become tall and spindly, and their leaves may be smaller. If insufficient light falls directly from above, plants tend to lean in the direction of other available light sources. Too much light results in desiccation and sun scald. Since plants are easier to maintain in good condition when their light requirements are met, today we add fluorescent lights or grow lights to supplement or replace natural light.

Water: It is difficult to avoid overwatering, especially in winter. Each plant should receive water according to its needs. Woody plants (camellia, gardenia, oleander) require more water than herbaceous plants, plants in active growth more than dormant ones, plants in warmer rooms more than those in cool ones. Plants do not want to dry out entirely. Plants should be watered sparingly when they are dormant, and only when necessary. If soil clings to the finger when the soil surface is touched, wait a day or two before watering. With practice, it is possible to learn by weight whether a plant needs watering. Small pots can be picked up. In the case of large, heavy containers, probe with an index finger several inches down into the soil to check for moisture. When watering, soak the pots, either by setting them in a pan of water until moisture shows on the soil surface or by using a scant trickle from a watering can or watering wand until excess water runs out of the bottom drainage holes. If possible, water before noon on days when the sun is shining, and use room-temperature water to avoid shocking the plants. Do not let the pot sit in water. Humidity can be increased by setting pots on trays of small pebbles and adding water up to the lower layers. Vapor will rise directly up and around the foliage. Fine mist spraying is another way to raise humidity levels.

Nutrients: Emily Dickinson probably started her plants in good potting soil, available from the garden. Large plants could have remained in the conservatory throughout their first winter without additional nutrition. A popular general potting mix at the time consisted of a mixture of well-rotted cow dung, fresh sound earth, rotten leaves, coarse sand, and ash, put through a screen to incorporate and even out all the ingredients. Today potting soils are readily available in bags at garden centers, and it is not necessary to prepare one's own mixture. For acid-loving camellias and gardenias, it is necessary to add aluminum sulfate or an acid-based fertilizer, which can be purchased at the garden center.

Repotting: Emily may have repotted plants each spring in fresh garden soil. For larger plants this is not necessary, unless the plant has become too big for the space it is occupying. Instead, each spring loosen the soil on the surface of the pots or tubs, remove the top inch or two, dress the plants with a compost or with clean garden soil, and follow up with a good watering. Should roots grow out of the bottom of the pot, the need for more frequent watering or a general loss of vigor are signs that a plant is pot-bound and needs repotting. Moisten the root ball slightly and run a long kitchen knife around the inside of the container to loosen the dirt. Lay the pot on its side and gently tap the plant out of its pot. Transplanting large specimens from heavy containers may require two people. Lay the container on its side on a tarp or piece of burlap, and with one person holding the foliage up off the floor, gently roll and urge the container off the root ball. In either case knock off most of the soil and prune back the roots by one-third to encourage new, vigorous roots to develop. Repot in fresh, well-draining potting soil. Prune back the top foliage to encourage new, low growth. Soon new shoots will develop. Fertilize weekly from April to August with a house plant fertilizer at half the recommended strength.

Insects: Some insects are easily spotted: aphids (variously colored, pear-shaped insects found clustered on succulent new growth), white flies (rapidly multiplying tiny flies that swarm up in clouds when disturbed), mealy bugs (slow-moving small insects covered with white fuzz), scale (hard or soft, brown or black bugs, often found along leaf veins), red spider mites (webs). Others are too small to be seen well without a magnifying glass. Watch for signs of insect damage: crumpled, deformed, or badly colored leaves, or leaves with chewed edges. Insects frequently hide on the underside of leaves or leave traces of a sticky residue called "honey dew" on leaves and on surfaces beneath the plants. Honey dew acts as a host to sooty mold.

Remove the most disfigured leaves, prune off any young shoots that appear damaged, and discard. Environmentally safe methods of insect control include hand-picking of unwanted insects and insect webs whenever possible, removing them with a cotton tip dipped in alcohol (scale), washing them off with a garden hose (aphids), or spraying with insecticidal soap and water. Use mechanical means such as commercial yellow sticky cardboard squares to attract white flies and aphids. Enlist friendly insects like ladybugs, lacewings, spiders, ground beetles, and crickets—especially in the garden—in the war against damaging bugs. When introducing a new plant into the group, quarantine it for the first week or so, watching for signs of insects or disease, in order not to contaminate the other plants. As a last resort, insecticides are available for indoor and outdoor use. Use only according to instructions, and make certain that the insecticide being used is compatible with the plant. Some plants, especially ferns, are easily burned by chemical sprays.

Fertilizing: Emily makes no mention of fertilizing her plants. She may have fed them with "manure tea," certainly readily available. In general, plants in active growth and planted in good basic potting soil need fertilizing every two weeks. Avoid fertilizing when a plant is dormant, if it appears wilted or diseased, or during periods of overcast, cloudy weather. Signs of insufficient nutrients include gradual yellowing of the leaves, often beginning at the outer edges and then spreading to the whole leaf. The cause may be worn-out soil, in which case fertilize the plant. Or the plant may simply have outgrown its pot and needs repotting.

Grooming: Groom plants at any time to remove spent blossoms, damaged leaves, or twigs. Pinch back to control and shape the plant and encourage branching. Winter-blooming plants such as camellias, gardenias, and jasmine set buds in late summer. Do not pinch them back after August 1. All plants that have summered outside should be brought indoors in the fall and no longer trimmed. Once a week, mist or shower plants in the kitchen sink to remove dust and debris. Aerate compact surface soil with a kitchen fork.

Summering plants out-of-doors: In late spring, after all danger of frost is passed, set plants out-of-doors. Information on the average date of the last frost in a particular area can be obtained from a local garden center or from the County Agricultural Agent, U.S. Department of Agriculture. When nighttime temperatures have stabilized and remain above 55 degrees, move plants out to a shady site such as a covered porch or under a tree canopy for protection from the wind and hot sun to let them harden gradually to their new environment. Gradually increase the amount of sunlight each day until the plant can tolerate a full day. This may take ten to twelve days. The plants can then be moved to their permanent summer site. To prevent insects from entering the bottom of the pot, stage pots on a plank raised slightly off the ground by bricks or place them on inverted pots of the same size or on saucers. It will be necessary to empty the saucers after rain to prevent root rot.

Move the plants back indoors before any danger of frost. Make sure they are healthy. Many insects like aphids and lacewing feed until the first hard freeze. Inspect the plants carefully along stems and undersides of leaves for pests, and spray them with a hard stream of water to dislodge insects or spray with insecticidal soap. It will be necessary to repeat the spraying in a few days to catch any late-hatching eggs. Reduce the frequency of watering and strength of fertilization during the winter months when plants are not actively growing.

Emily Dickinson was very alert to the seasonal needs of her plants, writing to Maria Whitney in autumn 1884, "The plants went into camp last night, their tender armor insufficient for the crafty nights" (L 948). In her inversion of the expected, "camp" was the house, not the garden.

MAINTAINING CONTAINER-GROWN
PLANTS IN THE GARDEN

Maintaining plants in containers out-of-doors creates additional challenges for the gardener. Careful siting is essential. Fluctuating temperatures, burning sun, and desiccating winds can destroy otherwise healthy plants. Fences, hedges, and trees can provide shelter from winds and protection from afternoon sun, which is hotter than the morning sun. Emily's *Daphne odora,* which was brought outside in the summer, was kept close to the house.

Planting containers: Make sure there is an adequate drainage hole in the bottom of the container. To further ensure good drainage in large containers, place several pot shards, a layer of crushed gravel, or packaging "peanuts" in the bottom and cover with a weed barrier or fine mesh screening to prevent soil from clogging the drainage material and insects from entering through the drainage holes. Excess water accumulating at the bottom of the container will exclude oxygen and promote root rot.

Fill the container with a good commercial potting mix, which can be purchased at a garden center. Do not overfill because this will lead to difficulty in watering. Allow room for a layer of mulch. When using new hard-baked pots, soak them in water for five or six hours before planting so that they won't draw moisture from the potting soil.

Watering: Watering is the trickiest part of container plant care because it depends on the temperature of the air and the material of which the pot is made. Large containers dry out more slowly than smaller ones. Porous containers will evaporate more moisture through the walls of the container than non-porous ones and will require more frequent watering. In hot weather, plants transpire more rapidly and soil dries out faster so that more frequent watering is necessary. Pots in more exposed positions dry out more rapidly, especially hanging pots. Do not let pots sit in water-filled saucers. During wet spells, turn saucers upside down under the pots so that rain water will drain away. Elevate large containers on clay feet or small pieces of flagstone. Mulching plants with 1 or 2 inches of a fine-textured mulch protects roots and conserves moisture.

Before watering, check the soil moisture with a finger. Touch an inch or so below the surface to determine whether the container plant needs watering. If so, water slowly and carefully until all the soil in the container is dampened and water runs out of the drainage holes in the bottom.

Fertilizing: Constant watering causes nutrients to leach out of containers. Fertilize plants biweekly with a balanced water-soluble fertilizer according to directions on the package. This can be done in conjunction with watering if the soil is slightly moist. Do not fertilize plants in dried-out containers; water thoroughly first and then wait a day to fertilize. Or, slow-release granular or pellitized fertilizer tablets can be mixed into manure and compost added to the soil medium at planting time. Slow-release fertilizers work best when there is a good soil mixture, a pH of 6.5 to 7.0, and warm soil temperatures. Toward the end of the growing season, as plants slow down, fertilize less frequently.

Plant care: Remove spent blossoms to encourage rebloom and keep the plants attractive. Do not hesitate to cut off branches that are too long, too ungainly, or damaged. Simply cut them back to a pair of leaves. Keep plants well watered and fed, since healthy plants will be more resistant to pests. Watch for insects and disease and treat promptly. Large insects can be picked off by hand, many smaller ones washed off with a blast from the hose. Improper watering and lack of good air circulation promote diseases and should be watched for. As a last resort, there are various chemical sprays to discourage bugs and diseases. Be sure to follow the instructions carefully.

❧

Emily Dickinson's conservatory housed many different plants in close proximity to one another. While creating a facsimile of her conservatory garden once, I could not help reflecting upon the skills she must have had—in floral preservation as well as arrangement—in order to cultivate her plants successfully. Susan Dickinson's obituary for Emily spoke of the "rare flowers filling her conservatory," flowers that were "ever abloom in frost or sunshine, so well she knew her chemistries." Thus Susan alluded to her sister-in-law's knowledge of all aspects of plant care, especially fertilization and maintenance of soil conditions. By saying there "entered nothing that could defile" the conservatory, she may have been thinking of Emily's knowledge of insect control and plant cohabitation, which was clearly equal to the demands of the most delicate flowers like the gardenia and the jasmine. Susan does not mention Emily's outdoor garden in the obituary, perhaps because it was better known to Amherst residents and also because she may have wished to focus on the superior techniques required by conservatory gardening.

In the early nineteenth century, the overall appearance or growth habit of a plant was rarely remarked upon and played little part in garden design, although close-up study of an individual flower was of great importance. Emily Dickinson's meticulous habits of observation were fruitfully exercised in poems about both individual flowers and large garden plots. Her poet's eye may certainly have contributed to her capabilities as a gardener—to the design and health of her gardens and to her choice of flowers that composed them. In Emily Dickinson's view, "Flowers had . . . Tongues" (L 746). Under her hand, they could address both reader and beholder.

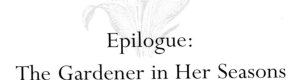

Epilogue:
The Gardener in Her Seasons

Second of March and the Crow and Snow high as the Spire, and scarlet expectations of things that never come, because forever here.

Emily Dickinson, Prose Fragment 43

IN EARLY 1862, those she called the "Hosts," the angels of imagination, visited Emily Dickinson so continually that she seems to have written constantly, despite the demands of her "Puritan garden" (L 685). During that winter, this "Recordless Company" of angelic muses gave her the perfect poem about death (F 303). She had already composed "Because I could not stop for Death —," a bitter yet exultant dream vision of death as a suitor who cheats her when she agrees to ride in his carriage, leaving her somewhere in empty space but unafraid (F 479). In 1862, when the mounting numbers of Civil War dead may have seemed to her "like the Flakes / When Gusts reverse the Snow," whirling pitifully in the winter dark, she thought more than ever about dying (F 480). There was a valiant way to attack this dreaded enemy who came like frost in the night to rob her of so many beloveds: She could write poems that would set against it several of her favorite natural symbols—sea, mountain, sun, and even the ancient snake from Genesis.

In one such poem, flowers again become for her the emblems of beauty and truth. Dickinson begins the poem with a meditation upon every gardener's enemy, freezing weather:

> The Frost of Death was on the Pane —
> "Secure your Flower," said he.
> Like Sailors fighting with a Leak
> We fought Mortality —
>
> Our passive Flower we held to Sea —
> To mountain — to the Sun —
> Yet even on his Scarlet shelf
> To crawl the Frost begun —
>
> We pried him back
> Ourselves we wedged
> Himself and her between —
> Yet easy as the narrow Snake
> He forked his way along
>
> Till all her helpless beauty bent
> And then our wrath begun —
> We hunted him to his Ravine
> We chased him to his Den —
>
> We hated Death and hated Life
> And nowhere was to go —
> Than Sea and continent there is
> A larger — it is Woe (F 1130)

This poem will enlighten anyone who wonders how Dickinson's flowers ranked among other cherished possessions or how much she may have esteemed them. The flower for which Death like a wild animal leaves his den represents "helpless" loveliness. Like a delicate woman in the nineteenth-century novels that often portrayed frail yet appealing heroines—Alcott's Beth March or Dickens's Dora Spenlow (each patterned upon a sister and sister-in-law who were pretty but sickly)—Dickinson's flower is "passive." The poet is not frivolous in implicitly comparing this flower (exhibited in a conservatory where the best is housed) to a maiden; rather, she thus emphasizes its pure uniqueness and equates it with the human spirit. One of her letters to Elizabeth Holland in the spring of 1866 told of "a woman [who] died last week, young and in hope but a little while – at the end of our garden. I thought since of the power of death . . . It is to us the Nile." The woman might have been a flower at the garden's edge—upright, vivid and fresh for a time, then abruptly blasted. To Dickinson, death was like "the Nile," the dark, mysterious river of ancient times, the "jealous brook" that claimed the lives of great men (L 318, 612). Her letter imagines the woman collapsing and expiring during a walk perhaps (although Dickinson sometimes creates narrative ellipses and may mean a neighbor dying in a nearby house). The association of women with precious flowers and both with death is for her as for other nineteenth-century artists—for example, Poe, Hawthorne, the John Everett Millais of *Ophelia* (1852) or the D. G. Rossetti of *Dante's Dream* (1856)—irresistible.

From the first quatrain of her poem, she resumes her earlier systematic imagery of the voyage of life in an imperiled boat, imagery that was probably inspired by Thomas Cole's *Voyage of Life* paintings, themselves based upon the ancient literary/painterly emblem of life as a sea voyage. She describes the flower's supporters as "Sailors fighting with a Leak," while the second quatrain of her poem imagines the gardeners' efforts to preserve the maiden/flower's health. They are "held to Sea / To mountain – to the Sun –," which recalls the prescribed vacations of the sick at watering places, mountains, or countryside and emphasizes the connection Dickinson characteristically makes between botanical and human.

This second quatrain also suggests the shifting stratagems of the worried plantsmen fighting "Mortality." The endangered flower is watered (sea), elevated (mountain), and exposed to enough "Sun." Perhaps Dickinson means that she shifted it about in the conservatory. Still, even on her sunniest shelf, Frost begins "To crawl" like a vicious snake or like the serpent that destroyed the First Garden. The gardeners' desperation is conveyed by the sense of strain in the words *"pried"* and "Ourselves we *wedged*" (emphases mine) in the third quatrain. Her reader envisions the efforts gardeners make to keep out cold, such as shawls wrapped around the flower, or newspapers or canvas. Mrs. Loudon's *Gardening for Ladies* (1840) devoted an entire fifth chapter to "Protecting from the Frost."

Writing to "my Jennie Humphrey" in October 1855, the twenty-five-year-old Emily, increasingly occupied with caring for her garden plots, speaks of being "just [in] from the frosts": "I have many a Bairn that cannot care for itself, so I must needs care *for it,* on such a night as this, and I've shrouded little forms and muffled little faces, till I almost feel maternal, and wear the anxious aspect that careful parents do" (L 180). Ten years earlier at only fifteen, her worries were the same while winter "wag[ged] on." She wrote Abiah Root that despite some "delightful weather" that made it seem "more like smiling May crowned with flowers than cold, arctic February wading through snowdrifts," she was concerned lest the birds would be "frozen up before their songs are finished" and rejoiced that her "plants look beautifully" and that "Old King Frost has not had the pleasure of snatching any of them in his cold embrace" (L 5). Later, in autumn of that year, she wrote Abiah a letter that revealed how deeply she cherished her flowers, how much she regretted losing them to winter, how closely they were associated with poetry in her imagination, and how profoundly she was affected, quite simply, by *endings:*

Have you any flowers now? I have had a beautiful flower-garden
this summer; but they are nearly gone now. It is very cold to-night,

*and I mean to pick the prettiest ones . . . and cheat Jack Frost of
so many of <u>the treasures</u> he calculates to rob . . . Won't it be a cap-
ital idea to put him at defiance, for once at least, if no more? I
would love to send you a bouquet . . . and you could press it and
write under it, The last flowers of summer. Wouldn't it be poetical[?]*
(L 8)

Frost is thus a powerful brigand in Dickinson's peculiar cosmos.
He bends the flower of her poem in "The Frost of Death" and robs it
of the ability to stand alone, a final stage in floral as in human endings.
Seeing the flower fail, its gardener-lovers are full of "wrath." They are
finally helpless to overpower the natural enemy of the living. They
cannot find and destroy Death in his "Ravine" or "Den" because "no-
where was to go": Death abides out of time and space, although his
onslaughts are miserably felt there. The gardener/poet is left with
"Woe" as the ground she must live on and tend. Ever since the Fall in
the first Garden, we have known that this space is much larger than
earth or sea.

Just as Dickinson adapted the biblical myth of the first Fall and
the "Expulsion from Eden" within her own "garden" of poems, so she
eagerly addressed the traditional nineteenth-century topic of the sea-
sons, those periods of the year that have classically described the de-
velopment of human life as well as nature's (L 552).[1] She was able to
envision every season and flower at will. Writing to Abiah Root in
1845, she explained that as she set about composing her letter she
had "no flowers before me as you had [when writing me] to in-
spire you. But then you know I can imagine myself inspired by them
and perhaps that will do as well" (L 7). (Here, her flowers become
her Muse.) On many occasions, she envisioned summer or spring, In-
dian summer or even winter inspiring her as she wrote. Each season
had its singular ability to stimulate and direct her fancy. At the same
time, so distinctly did the special features of each season live in her
thoughts that her own life with *its* "seasons" seemed an articulation of

the universal mystery of time and eternity. Some poems reveal that the unique qualities of the seasons were "forever here" in the mind that knew them so well (Prose Fragment 43). She could humorously describe herself as confounded by what seemed either a mistake of nature or of her own poet's nature that desired to experience all the "mighty show / To which without a Ticket go / The nations and the Days —" (F 1678)—and all at once:

> The ones that disappeared are back
> The Phebe and the crow
> Precisely as in March is heard
> The curtness of the Jay —
> Be this an Autumn or a Spring
> My wisdom loses way
> One side of me the nuts are ripe
> The other side is May (F 1697).

Winter might have been expected to provoke Dickinson's extreme dislike since it killed her colorful annuals, buried her brilliant perennials, and was all too often the setting of the deaths of friends. If we exempt childbirth, which killed Susan Dickinson's sister Mary, Emily's loved ones were carried off most often by tuberculosis or "la grippe" or by what George Washington died of, strep throat: pulmonary diseases associated most often then with cold. Dickinson's letters about winter often bring the news of illness, whether of her plants, herself, or her family or friends. In the winter of 1862, for instance, she sent a note to Frances Norcross, trying to relieve Fanny's mind about the health of her Amherst cousins: "Poor Vinnie has been very sick," she explains, "and so have we all, and I feared one day our little [cousins] would see us no more, but God was not so hard . . . We have had fatal weather—thermometer two below zero all day . . . Summer was always dear, but such a kiss as she'll get from me if I ever see her again, will make her cry . . ." (L 254). Because her conception of the four seasons was intricately related to her vision of death and immortality, winter sometimes oppressed Emily Dickinson despite her knowledge that it would pass. When she complains in her letter to Fanny that the weather has been "fatal," it is as though she were speaking of plants rather than human beings, who do not always find winter cold "fatal." But her flowers *were* people to her, while at the same time her friends seemed—in that age of often primitive medical techniques—as susceptible to illness as an aster is to aphids or a rose, to black spot; the adjective "fatal" seemed to her morbidly, terrifyingly, universally apt.

For all its destructive powers, however, winter was Dickinson's frequent subject. Sometimes she engaged it as a symbol of misery and with shrinking dismay or aversion as a bitter source of lack of faith in the beauty of all plenitude, everlasting life, and divine mercy:

> My Summer – is despoiled –
> Because there was a Winter – once –
> And all the Cattle – starved –
> And so there was a Deluge –
> And swept the World away – (F 532)

Because she was an aesthete, however, this inhabitant of the grim New England landscape was susceptible to all kinds of beauty, including that of chill winter, though it might have appeared final as the "Deluge" to Noah. "Winter under cultivation," she judged, "Is as arable as Spring" (F 1720). The seasons inspired her to frame such aphorisms, which were both sound and arresting. So, times of emptiness, ruin, or decay, she says, can become seasons of fulfillment provided we use them to cultivate the gardens of our souls. Such a philosophy might have suggested itself when Dickinson inspected her conservatory, where refulgent bloom within triumphed over sleet without because—quite simply—she would have it so. She never fails to remark the gorgeousness of her "Pearl Jail," the elegant tracery of rime on her father's hemlocks and pines, or the fragrant softness of the snow

shawling down around the garden's naked shrubs and rose bushes
(L 487).

In the winter of 1873, Dickinson wrote a peerless quatrain about
"February, that Month of fleetest sweetness" (L 971). It will always
transcend paraphrase, the poem of one for whom plants and flowers
are quintessentially emblematic:

> White as an Indian Pipe
> Red as a Cardinal Flower
> Fabulous as a Moon at Noon
> February Hour – (F 1193)

Did Dickinson mean that winter's shimmering snows resemble the
ghostly Indian pipes of early spring, both seasons being fused in one
vision of the immaculate? Did she mean that fires in February blaze
with a cardinal flower's scarlet? Writing to Elizabeth Holland in
March 1866, she had spoken of her "heart [as] red as February" since
for some reason—the crimson of the sundown reflected upon snow in
deep winter? the color associated with Saint Valentine's Day? the
ruddy interiors of tight-closed buds?—February seemed red to her
(L 315). Like March, it brought her "scarlet expectations": heartfelt
hopes for spring and a reawakened garden. ("Expectations," of course,
were always "scarlet" to Emily Dickinson. It was in their nature to be.
In her intensity, she recognized that blessings to come—like spring—
were "forever here," if one consulted the imagination.)

Even as she relished paradox as a poet, Emily Dickinson the gar-
dener knew that winter is requisite to the flora of the northeast. Ever
since she was sixteen, tending "a large stand of plants" all winter long,
she had always craved to look upon the "visages" of "Sun and Summer"
and to see spring come to the garden each year (L 9, 487). We re-
member her words to her fellow gardener T. W. Higginson in 1877:
"When Flowers annually died and I was a child, I used to read Dr
Hitchcock's Book on the Flowers of North America. This comforted
their Absence – assuring me they lived" (L 488). Two writers in par-

ticular have claimed that Dickinson had a sickness called "seasonal affective disorder," which causes depression, apathy, and inactivity in the sufferer deprived of sunlight.[2] But while Dickinson certainly preferred "Mighty Summer" with its "'legions' of daisies" to winter cold, she writes about days when "the Grass is Glass" as eloquently and energetically as if snow and ice were themselves species of spectral bloom (L 381, 207, 381). The "winter red" and the "dazzling Winter Nights"—even those that "wreck . . . the budding Gardens"—excite her fancy, if not her love, and some of her best poems are composed when the weather prevents her from gardening out of doors (L 365, 901). Then, too, winter never keeps her from picturing soothing, more cordial seasons. She implies, in fact, that winter cold may shock the imagination into a reverie of sunshine and ease:

> Conjecturing a Climate
> Of unsuspended Suns –
> Adds poignancy to Winter –
> The shivering Fancy turns
>
> To a fictitious Country
> To palliate a Cold –
> Not obviated of Degree –
> Nor eased – of Latitude – (F 551)

Indeed, in her maturity Emily Dickinson seems to have decided that winter—only apparently barren—provided time to replenish the "Mine" of imagination that is too often distracted from its exercise by social tasks, and especially by the actual seductions of spring and summer in a blooming rather than an imaginary or dormant garden (L 908). Among the Dickinson manuscripts is this winter poem:

> Winter is good –
> his Hoar Delights
> Italic flavor yield –
> To Intellects

inebriate
With Summer,
or the World —

Generic as a
Quarry
And hearty — as
a Rose —
Invited with
Asperity
But welcome
when he goes. (F 1374)

This poem's important words—*quarry, rose, asperity*—are empha-
sized by their improvisational arrangement (as reproduced above) in
Emily Dickinson's manuscript book. The poem distinguishes how
summer affects an intellect, inebriated as with alcohol or worldly
pleasures, from the "italic"—that is, italicized or emphatic—character
of winter. Winter shakes/wakes one up; it is restorative. Using the
word *generic,* which alludes to a biological genus like a plant, Dickin-
son writes that, as a genus, winter is a quarry, a rich source. She does
not say of *what* it is a source, although the word *quarry,* like *mine,*
she usually employs for imagination. Someone who did not work
with plants and flowers might not make such an association, for gar-
deners realize that without snow and frost, without dying and mold-
ering in the soil, perennials cannot produce new growth. A "green"
or warm winter is much feared by them. Just so, without the death
and burial of their bodies, human beings (Christianity teaches) cannot
attain everlasting life. As Ecclesiastes 3:2 ordains—skeptic or no, Em-
ily was able to quote Ecclesiastes with startling fluency—the seasonal
life of the garden is emblematic of human life which has its own sea-
sons, its times "to plant . . . and . . . to pluck up that which is
planted."

Ordinarily Dickinson characterizes the plush, deep-cup roses of

35. Otis A. Bullard, portrait of the Dickinson children (1840): Emily (holding an open book and a rose), Austin, and Lavinia.

her garden as fragile; in this poem, however, she envisions winter as a "hearty" fiery red rose. So often associated with June, passion, and weddings, the rose as a symbol of winter may explore a paradox typical of her: At the heart of love is death, and so winter must pass like one of the transitory roses she was painted holding as a child [Fig. 35].

That winter is "welcome / when he goes," moreover, makes another implicit contradiction. For sometimes, after all, Emily Dickinson could not help regarding winter as an infectious malady, and she would write warmly of "that sweet Physician, an approaching spring" (L 807). As she tells her neighboring Aunt Katie Sweetser, a gardener praised for both her sweet sultans and her conservatory, Emily's garden always vanished "with beautiful reluctance, like an evening star —" (L 668). To her, it was the planet Venus, intimately associated with love and joy.

Not unlike the painters she admired—Cole, Van Dyck, Titian, Domenichino, and the Victorian favorite Guido Reni, whom she names, and (hypothesizing from the subject matter and wording of certain poems) Turner, Durand, Gifford, Church, and Heade—Emily Dickinson was greatly moved by light. In accord with the Impressionists to whom Mabel Loomis Todd early compared her, she was given to noticing the quality and shadings of light as they discriminate, reveal, hallow, and enchant. "A Light exists in Spring," she could write of that rescuing season, "Not present on the Year / At any other period —" (F 962). One of her most imaginative fantasies describes the arrival in her village of dawn, spring's counterpart:

> The Fingers of the Light
> Tapped soft opon the Town
> With "I am great and cannot wait
> So therefore let me in."
>
> "You're soon," the Town replied,
> "My Faces are asleep
> But swear, and I will let you by
> You will not wake them up."
>
> The easy Guest complied
> But once within the Town

The transport of His Countenance
Awakened Maid and Man

The Neighbor in the Pool
Opon His Hip elate
Made loud obeisance, and the Gnat
Held up His Cup for Light (F 1015)

A painterly poem with mythic overtones whereby "Light" as a pow-
erful magical figure addresses a persona called "Town," this narrative
is a Dickinsonian version of that miracle of Genesis, the *fiat lux*. The
poem might be about both nature and art or nature and language/
imagination; for light is essential to man and woman but also neces-
sary to the well-being of the smallest creatures and insects like the
frog and the gnat, beautified here through personification and by be-
ing captured in characteristic attitudes—the loudly croaking, squat-
ting frog and the black fly or gnat, ever attracted to daylight in whose
course he will find sustenance. If the natural world needs illumina-
tion, so, too, does the artist whose strokes of paint, like light's
"fingers," compose his picture.

Spring suggested illumination, actual and symbolic, to Emily
Dickinson. When she wrote of March, it was as a rival artist whose
exploits she misses and cannot herself duplicate, for the ordinal col-
ors belong to him alone: "All those Hills you left for me to Hue – /
There was no Purple suitable – / You took it all with you –"
(F 1320). Here again is the important word "purple" with all its impli-
cations of dignity, rank, brilliance, and sanctity. Arriving between
brutal winter and benign spring, March excited her. In that spacious
magic country created by her reclusive genius wherein hills are popu-
lated with shadows like men and women, and "East" and "West" are
giants that carry the sun in and out of a door called "Day," spring
was the potent elixir. She describes it in housewifely images: "Put
up my Heart thy Hoary work / And take a Rosy Chair –." And
she encounters it with ecstatic jubilation: "I cannot meet the Spring –

unmoved – / I feel the old desire –" (F 1319, 1122). Winter was "Hoary," spring "Rosy," because of their respective colorations: the gray-white of hoar-frost in winter, the rosiness of spring's sticky red buds on tree, bush, and flower. The desire that Dickinson expresses for spring is, with few exceptions, matchless.

As a result, perhaps, it is tinged with fear. Since spring reawakens the garden she has tended—the garden that is a major poetic subject— she worries lest it might someday fail to arrive:

> When it is May, if May return,
> Had nobody a pang
> Lest in a Face so beautiful
> He might not look again? (F 1042)

Spring had other private meanings for Emily Dickinson, who confided to Elizabeth Holland, "It sometimes seems as if special Months gave and took away – August has brought the most to me – April – robbed me most – in incessant instances" (L 775). Again she wrote Mrs. Holland: "Love has but one Date – 'The first of April' 'Today, Yesterday, and Forever' –" (L 801). Charles Wadsworth, sympathizing with the South during the Civil War, was forced to leave the Arch Street Presbyterian Church of Philadelphia for San Francisco in April 1862. He died on April 1, twenty years later. Dickinson's letter with its allusion to the gift of flowers and its two quotations from Tennyson (the first, as Thomas Johnson tells us, from "In Memoriam" and the second, from "Love and Duty") might be thought to identify Wadsworth conclusively as "Master." Yet Dickinson often consecrated exceptionally loving, seemingly exclusive tributes to friends with whom she was not precisely "*in* love." Intensity of phrase, like intensity of emotion, was necessary to her. That Wadsworth visited Emily in August 1880 and may have done so earlier in the summer of 1861 also appears to support his candidacy for the role of the "Master" until one recalls that Samuel Bowles sailed for England on April 5, 1862. Dickinson's note to Mary Bowles alluding to Samuel's absence is so full of desire and woe that she might have been recording Bowles's death: "When the Best is gone – I know that other things are not of consequence – The Heart wants what it wants . . . Not to see what we love, is very terrible" (L 262).

As the season in which the resurrection of her flowers took place— daffodils, lilies-of-the-valley, peonies, crocuses—and yet a time that also brought her sorrow, spring could certainly be described as an "inundation" that "enlarges every Soul –" (F 1423). To Dickinson spring was sacramental. Its "inundation"—spring rains—constituted a baptism and a direct revelation of the sanctifying power of the deity. Her garden in spring made God manifest to her:

> Spring is the Period
> Express from God –
> Among the other seasons
> Himself abide
>
> But during March and April
> None stir abroad
> Without a cordial interview
> With God – (F 948)

Such a poem reveals that what faith in God Emily Dickinson could profess was shaped in part by the experience of gardening since after 1860, "abroad" meant her father's acres primarily. For her, all seasons are divinely imbued, but spring is direct proof of God's existence and good will. If flowers give messages to human beings, the resurrection of the flowers each spring permits them a fond "interview" with the Creator.

More than one hundred years before Dickinson was born, another Massachusetts writer who also frequented "secret places of my own in the woods" and "retired spot[s]" where he could contemplate the divine in nature had described the soul as "like . . . a garden of God." Jonathan Edwards, the Puritan minister and poet, meditated eloquently in his *Personal Narrative* on the effect of conversion to faith upon the Christian soul as "like such a little white flower as we see in the spring of the year; low and humble on the ground, opening its bosom to receive the pleasant beams of the sun's glory; rejoicing as it were in a calm rapture; diffusing around a sweet fragrancy." To Edwards, the behavior of such small white flowers as Dickinson's preferred anemone suggested "loveliness, . . . humility, brokenness of heart, and poverty of spirit." They served him as virtuous exemplars: "there was nothing that I so earnestly longed for [as their qualities]." Ultimately, the sweetness of low-standing spring blooms convinced him of the sweet "loveliness and beauty of Jesus Christ." (One wonders whether John Ruskin, with his belief in the artistic superiority of small flowers, read Jonathan Edwards.) Emily Dickinson does not, like Edwards, relate such flowers to the Second Person of the Trinity who bade the faithful to "receive the kingdom of God as a little child." But certainly in Dickinson's case as in Edwards's, spring kindled "inward burnings of [the] heart" and, like him, she ventured to suppose that the resurrection of the flowers might presuppose her own.

It is probably no coincidence that, speaking of herself as "a Puritan," Emily Dickinson also alludes to her "Puritan Garden" (L 866, 685). That she wrote the phrase after a winter snowfall cannot fully explain it. No one who knew Dickinson well, moreover, would have associated her ardent sensibility with the sterner dogmas of Puritanism. What she meant by "Puritan" seems simply to have been *pure,* white. Thus, she asked Mrs. James S. Cooper, "will you . . . accept a View of *my* House, which Nature painted White, without consulting me – but Nature is 'old-fashioned,' perhaps a Puritan –" (L 706). Dickinson's conception of whiteness, similar to that of Edwards, is not confined to the look of snow but embraces the idea of *inner purity.* Gardens could encourage one in holiness:

> The good Will of a Flower
> The Man who would possess

> Must first present Certificate
> Of minted Holiness (F 954).

Spring could readily be associated with the fresh, pure, and godly, but what of summer? Dickinson's vision of summer was curiously complex. It could summarize the consummate rapture of fruition, the triumph of the blossoming soul or blooming garden:

> My Garden – like the Beach –
> Denotes there be – a Sea –
> That's Summer –
> Such as These – the Pearls
> She fetches – such as Me (F 469)

This poem, like many others, may have been sent accompanied by flowers, her garden's "Pearls." In the poem "*One life* of so much consequence!" (F 248), Susan Dickinson seems almost certainly to be the Pearl akin to the "pearl of great price" to which Dickinson's preferred gospel of Matthew (13:46) compares the soul itself. In the word *pearl* spiritual meanings frequently vibrate for her. That her garden contained flowers like pearls emphasized the flowers' sanctifying properties. The sea itself, like the "East," could be a multivalent symbol meaning eternity or misery or passion or the wide sky in which the earth spins, hapless. Associated with summer here, the sea becomes unthreatening, however—a large and simple jewel box observed casually, with joy. A short poem such as "My Garden – like the Beach –" can have an unfinished quality, as if the flowers in an accompanying box or package were meant to complete it. In merit, in structure, such poems are not to be compared with frequently anthologized lyrics such as "The Soul has Bandaged moments –" (F 360) or "Of Bronze – and Blaze –" (F 319). They are poem-notes of greater or less literary value. Yet Dickinson frequently regarded them as complements to the flowers and the reverse, implying an association between her two vocations, poet and gardener.

In one of Dickinson's most pictorial poems about summer, she describes "a Butterfly / As Lady from her Door" emerging from a cocoon to carry itself like a colorful parasol above a hay field until sundown. The butterfly, unlike farmers haying in the meadows, "stray[s] abroad / On miscellaneous Enterprise," "Repairing Everywhere − / Without Design" as if "In purposeless Circumference." Using her freighted adjective, Dickinson calls this "a *Tropic* show" (emphasis mine). In contrast to the bees "that worked" or the flowers "that zealous blew," the butterfly and other "Parties − Phantom as Herself −" constitute an "Audience of Idleness" for the workers. Perhaps Dickinson was aware that the butterfly is a traditional icon of the soul in Western art; in any event, a certain Emersonian rectitude inhabits her poem ("purposeless," "Without Design") yet is countered by the speaker's appreciation of the butterfly's deliciously lazy ease. Its nonchalance, "The Clovers − understood −." The reader is put in mind of the conflict between the need for labor and the quest for pleasure—a conflict that charges the Dickinson psyche. At the end, those who work and those who play disappear together. Indeed, the afternoon itself disappears as if it were no more than a butterfly, while the speaker observes:

> Till Sundown crept − a steady Tide −
> And Men that made the Hay −
> And Afternoon − and Butterfly −
> Extinguished − in the Sea − (F 610)

This sketch of the summer day is not without a certain darkness. The vast glimmer of afternoon gives way to sundown, in whose "steady Tide" everything that formerly met the poet's sight is "Extinguished." These words, which evoke eighteenth-century hymns like Isaac Watts's "O God, our help in ages past" (1712) with its declaration that time bears its sons ineluctably away on the tide of eternity, add a somber cast to this otherwise buoyant, light-filled picture. Yet we infer not so much the butterfly's annihilation as its absolute union with nature. It is passively "extinguished," yet it actively "extin-guish[es]" itself in the fullness of its day, its life. Although its light is snuffed out—not a positive conceit, certainly, for the Dickinson who hoped for "the Extension of Consciousness, after Death"—its disap-pearance in the sea of eternity is also, like the laborers', an easy, inev-itable passage into another sphere (L 650).

Different from other seasons, summer for Dickinson can mean sensuous fulfillment, a release from the stern requirements of reason and analysis. She "reckon[s]" it with poets, the sun, and "the Heaven of God" as being of most value, and if poets rank first, she explains, it is because imagination allows "Their Summer [to last] a solid Year —" (F 533). Nevertheless, because one of Dickinson's signal attributes is *fear* of completion, of satisfaction (of blossoming?), it is a tribute to her breadth of spirit and to the faith in continuance that gardening gave her that she wrote so convincingly about summer's opulence. In a poem composed around 1859, summer appears as a magical season, attended by sacramental powers both intimidating and "transporting." Yet her poem concludes with a quatrain—perhaps too slight a set of lines after the power of her earlier stanzas—that suggests a desire to modify the drama of what summer's vistas inveigle her to imagine: "Caravan[s] of Red." This enchanting poem makes one realize how formidable and instinctive was her attraction to all that she called "tropic":

> A something in a summer's Day
> As slow her flambeaux burn away
> Which solemnizes me.
>
> A something in a summer's noon —
> A depth — an Azure — a perfume —
> Transcending extasy.
>
> And still within a summer's night
> A something so transporting bright

> I clap my hands to see —
>
> . . .
>
> Still rears the East her amber Flag —
> Guides still the sun along the Crag
> His Caravan of Red —
>
> So looking on — the night — the morn
> Conclude the wonder gay —
> And I meet, coming thro' the dews
> Another summer's Day! (F 104)

Images like "flambeaux," "Crag," and "Caravan of Red," the presence of the "East" and of the "amber Flag" that once announced sunrise and still maintains the daylight, inflect the sybaritic Oriental motifs that frequently color Dickinson's response to beauty and romance. At noon, at night, the summer holds aloft her torches made of sun or moonlight; the sky is perfumed; the poet-observer is "solemnize[d]" as if by sacred ritual. "Wonder gay" in the final quatrain may seem too awkward and inefficient a summary of the quasi-religious splendors that Dickinson records, but she concedes from the first her inability to describe such splendors: it is "A something" that affects her. Certainly, however, this early poem written almost entirely and musically in the tercet form (unusual for her) seeks to portray Emily Dickinson as the initiate of a religion of nature.

In that religion, summer is both goddess and article of faith:

> Summer — we all have seen —
> A few of us — believed —
> A few — the more aspiring
> Unquestionably loved —

"The greatest of these is charity," says Saint Paul, comparing faith, hope, and charity; in the lines above, Dickinson, too, exalts love above belief. Summer, however, resembles God the Father as Dickinson irritably conceived of him, with his failures to show sympathy to

Moses, Adam, and herself. "Summer does not care" for human beings; rather, "She goes her spacious way" (F 1413).

Although they were often regarded as her children or playmates, Emily Dickinson does not usually accuse flowers and plants of disappointing her. Only by their absence or death do these charges, like departed lovers, give her pain. Summer, however, who figures in her writing as a woman, can indeed betray her sharply (like the beloved woman, probably Susan Dickinson, for and about whom she wrote a cycle of poems that include "Now I knew I lost her —" [F 1274]). Having established what seems a fond connection with the gardener-speaker, summer can abruptly abandon her. This is possible because summer as a goddess and the speaker as the human inhabitant of a cold cottage surrounded by frost are "Estranged, however intimate" they once were. Summer's is the sort of feline betrayal Dickinson hates, and only when they are fast in summer's thrall do her flowers also betray her: "A Summer's soft assemblies go / To their entrancing end / Unknown — for all the times we met —." That summer is sly and indifferent as she snubs the speaker who has served her so long, that her "assemblies" of flowers long tended by the speaker do not disclose where they are going, are afflictions which prompt her cry: "What a dissembling Friend —" (F 1340). By exaggerating all that summer's leave-taking causes her to feel, and by using diction suitable to a breach in human relations, Dickinson is able to write about the experience with an irony that does not eradicate sentiment.

Like summer, Susan Dickinson, so closely associated in her sister-in-law's lyrics and letters with volcanoes, the East, India, Italy, Egypt, vibrant emotions, and torrid scenes, is frequently imagined as entrancing. For summer and Susan, Emily Dickinson fashions a kinetic language. They both represent nature at her most beguiling, and thus in variants of the same poem they are unknown to ordinary folk. The first version in the three-volume *Poems* considers external Nature:

> Nature is a stranger yet;
> The ones that cite her most

Have never passed her haunted house,
Nor simplified her ghost.

To pity those that know her not
Is helped by the regret
That those who know her, know her less
The nearer her they get (F 1433a)

In the variant meant for Susan (F 1433c), Dickinson substitutes "Susan" for "nature," "scaled" for "passed," and "compromised" for "simplified." "Scaled" expresses Dickinson's conception of her sister-in-law: that she had more stature, was more powerful, tempestuous, and somehow more *grand* than Emily. Susan was "Goliah" (Goliath) to her who, like "David" with his slingshot, "took [her] Power" or art "in [her] hand / And went against the World" (F 660). Like summer, Susan is desirable and desired, in part because her "ghost" or spirit cannot be "compromised," cannot be deprived of its rich fullness. Mourning the early deaths of her mother and sister, Susan exhibited wellsprings of emotion in girlhood that impressed the young and sensitive Emily Dickinson. Ever afterward, Susan appeared to Emily as a natural force such as summer's: blooming, surprising. Yet, ironically, like that "man of noon . . . *mightier* than the morning," that fantastic prospective husband whom Dickinson fears in a famous letter to Susan, hot summers can burn and destroy just as does "the mighty sun" of masculine love (L 93). Thus, Susan and summer, the burning sun, passion and marriage are strikingly conflated because each is, after all, dangerous yet attractive.

Finally, in "The Birds reported from the South —," Dickinson explains that she and summer "dwel[l]" together by "Contract," their remarkable relationship having been forged by the fact of death; for the poet has long been "a Mourner" while summer, too, laments "Her Dead," her annuals that appear for a season and depart, never to return (F 780). For all their acquired intimacy, summer remains a "miracle" and her mysteries, sacramental, like those of spring (F 374). Even in an early poem, Emily Dickinson was not afraid to implore the everlasting company of summer in a prayer that any gardener confronted with denuded plots would understand:

> Summer – Sister – Seraph!
> Let us go with thee! (F 22)

And yet it was not for summer's "Consummated Bloom" but for "the happy Sorrow of Autumn" that Dickinson reserved her most wistful yet impassioned descriptions (F 822, L 945). In this she had much in common with such landscape artists as her favorite Thomas Cole, who engendered a school of autumn painters that focused on the mournful placidity or savage brilliance of autumn's changing colors. The art historians Robin Asleson and Barbara Moore observe in *Dialogue with Nature* that there are many "American" characteristics in the landscape painting *Autumn on the Hudson* by Thomas Doughty, such as "vastness" and "rawness," but that "most American of all" is Doughty's selection of the season itself, with its vibrant reds and yellows unfamiliar within the European landscape tradition of Claude Lorrain.[3] (In fact, such vivid colors were altogether foreign to the European landscape itself. The painter Jasper Cropsey presented some American autumn leaves to Queen Victoria in order to persuade her of the veracity of the flaming hues of his *Autumn—on the Hudson River*.)[4] Autumn—in particular, that period of unexpected warmth preceding winter called "Indian summer"[5]—inspired many Hudson River School paintings and several of Emily Dickinson's poems. It was perhaps the season most fascinating to her as a person and as an American artist. Uniting summer and fall in a creative continuum, it represented the death of the year with an uncanny spiritual light that suggested life to come. The artifices of Indian summer—its vibrant colorations, its harmonies that were always the same and yet new every year—seem to have suggested to her the powers of art.

Alfred Habegger writes that "flowers helped [Emily Dickinson] articulate the seasons of [the human] spirit"; that, to her, "seasons came to be emblems of the phases of psychic existence."[6] This was largely true, yet Dickinson's response to the seasons as to her flowers was distinctly personal, apparently immediate, and allowed for comparisons and erosions of boundaries among them. She enjoyed contrasting autumn, summer, and the false or tricky Indian summer. It ought to be no surprise that the latter, which revives the garden and cheers the gardener just before cold sets in, reminded her that she had always judged "finer is a going / Than a remaining Face" (F 1457) and that "To disappear enhances" (F 1239). Indian summer, the fleeting "June" that sometimes arrives *after* the corn is cut, when people are picking pumpkins and are unprepared for it, put her in mind of heaven: the harvest home of the soul that may come at any moment. Her autumn poems are full of a grave enchantment, a melancholy that, like the season itself, is founded on a perception of the beauty of last things.

As a poet of nature, Dickinson usually prefers to observe it in motion: the iridescent wheel of the hummingbird riding among the flowers, trees swinging their boughs like tassels, thunder clouds striking against one another to make lightning, snow being driven by the wind, even the coursing of the sap through the branch in spring. In one poem, the autumn that brings about the death of the year suggests the storm of war:

> The name – of it – is 'Autumn' –
> The hue – of it – is Blood –
> An Artery – opon the Hill –
> A Vein – along the Road –
>
> Great Globules – in the Alleys –
> And Oh, the Shower of Stain –
> When Winds – upset the Basin –
> And spill the Scarlet Rain –

Nature's afflictions during autumn were as grisly and visceral to Dickinson as the general devastation caused by the Civil War, for here she chooses to envision the beautiful crimson and gold of autumn leaves as wounds, indiscriminately severed veins and arteries, the havoc and change ("Winds – upset the Basin –") wrought by battle. As if in acknowledgment of gothic excess, however, she ends this poem on a peaceful note when autumn becomes a rainbow following the storm and "eddies like a Rose – away – / Opon Vermillion Wheels –" (F 465) that suggest spring.

One of her most famous poems about autumn begins by calling it "Antiquest felt at Noon –," a "spectral Canticle" in which the crickets "Pathetic from the Grass" celebrate an "unobtrusive Mass" (F 895). The speaker observes that "a Druidic Difference / Enhances Nature now –," although its "Grace" is "gradual" and the fires of August that produce it are "low." This lapse of summer into autumn "Enlarg[es] Loneliness," Dickinson writes, and the reader realizes once again how profound was the effect of nature's ways upon her, and that however merry she could be, her fundamental emotion was one of wistfulness, even desolation. Having once written "A loss of something ever felt I –," having characterized herself as "the only Prince cast out," "still softly searching / For my Delinquent Palaces," she appealed to her plants and flowers as trustworthy company while, "homeless at home," she quested "For the Site of the Kingdom of Heaven" (F 1063, 1072). Without her garden, her "homelessness"—an exaggeration, to be sure—seemed to her more pronounced.

In medieval symbology, the garden was a metaphor of the soul; so it is for Emily Dickinson. At the advance of autumn she prays: "Grant me, Oh Lord, a sunny mind – / Thy windy will to bear!" (F 123) and imagines Indian summer as the final sacred rite of nature (F 122):

These are the days when Birds come back –
A very few – a Bird or two –
To take a backward look.

These are the days when skies resume
The old – old sophistries of June –
A blue and gold mistake.

Oh fraud that cannot cheat the Bee.
Almost thy plausibility
Induces my belief,

Till ranks of seeds their witness bear –
And softly thro' the altered air
Hurries a timid leaf.

Naming herself "The Wayward Nun – beneath the Hill –" (F 745) in a poem famous for its use of the Roman Catholic imagery she may have learned from Maggie Maher and her other Irish servants, Emily Dickinson prayed in her enclosed gardens—one, a conservatory, the other, hedge-surrounded—to the divinity that made nature holy. Although she regarded spring and summer as sacramental, it was Indian summer, the season of miracles creating June in October, that prompted her to invoke the imagery of transubstantiation in the Mass:

Oh sacrament of summer days,
Oh Last Communion in the Haze –
Permit a child to join –

Thy sacred emblems to partake –
Thy consecrated bread to take
And thine immortal wine! (F 1 2 2)

Dickinson's oft-used slant rhymes are well suited to an expression of confusion, disorder, or dismay. Some of these musical tercets, however, rhyme fully ("days"/"Haze," "partake"/"take") to suggest the harmony of the Communion rite as the speaker perceives it. Here, the Christian injunction to "be as a child" in approaching the Lord is fulfilled, yet according to nature's rite rather than the Christian one.[7] Indian summer resembles a work of art, a painting, as well as a sacrament in that it is plausible enough to "induce . . . belief" in its subject: summer. Moreover, it is not lustrous fakery but is like a Eucharist wherein, according to Roman Catholic teaching, Christ's body and blood are actually present under the appearances of bread and wine.

In two poems written later than this one of 1859, her meditations upon autumn cause Dickinson to make important observations about life and life eternal. The first poem was composed in 1877 and declares:

> Summer has two Beginnings —
> Beginning once in June —
> Beginning in October
> Affectingly again —
>
> Without, perhaps, the Riot
> But graphicer for Grace — (F 1457)

While she sojourned with the Norcross cousins in their Cambridge boarding house, taking treatment for anterior uveitis—the painful eye complaint that caused her to shrink from bright light even in winter— Emily wrote to Susan Dickinson, "I knew it was 'November,' but then there is a June when Corn is cut, whose option is within" (L 292). Her letter is dated "June 1864." Like so many of Dickinson's letters, this one is privately allusive. Its author means she is aware that she is now enduring a time of exile and trouble, a November, but that Indian summer is always a possible choice or "option" as a season for the spirit "within." One can choose (take the option to) *imagine* a summer that will support and delight at any season. This second June may lack summer's "Riot" of color and scent, but it is nevertheless full of a more graphic or schematic "Grace" as boughs and branches are stripped to reveal their essential structures. Indian summer is both color and form in motion, and its message is Dickinsonian: failure can promote success; departure assures return; in deprivation lies fulfillment.

One of the intentions of this book is to pay tribute to what Harold Bloom enthusiastically calls Emily Dickinson's "intricate intellect" and "literary originality."[8] (It is often an incidental aim of many studies of the poet.) In writing of the seasons, Dickinson demonstrated both the complexity of her mind and its unique temper. Although the Dickinson library contained a marked copy of James Thomson's *The Seasons* (1817) and Emily might have been moved by his traditional associations of winter with death and suffering, spring with love and light, her own approach to the months was clearly hers and triumphed over the calendar. Phrases from her poems and letters remark on June's loveliness that renders "swamps" pink (F 31). But she writes no poems about the sixth month of the year. Rather—and with typically innovative daring—she reminds us of June while writing a poem about autumn:

> There is a June when Corn is cut
> And Roses in the Seed –
> A Summer briefer than the first
> But tenderer indeed
>
> As should a Face supposed the Grave's
> Emerge a single Noon
> In the Vermillion that it wore
> Affect us, and return –
>
> Two Seasons, it is said, exist –
> The Summer of the Just,
> And this of our's, diversified
> With Prospect – and with Frost –
>
> May not our Second with it's First
> So infinite compare
> That We but recollect the one
> The other to prefer? (F 811b)

Like other Dickinson poems, this one begins with a stately and serious biblical cadence reminiscent of Ecclesiastes' discrimination of the appropriate times for each human activity. A "June when Corn is cut" cannot exist in reality since the harvest takes place in autumn. Roses are "in the seed" in fall, not June. Therefore, the authority implicit in "There is a . . ." is summoned to distinguish a symbolic rather than actual June, a "June" that is really Indian summer, "briefer" and "tenderer" than burning July, for example. To describe it hauntingly, Dickinson provides the splendidly ghastly intrusion of a living ghost who appears in "vermilion," the bright red color of mercuric sulfide— or of autumn leaves—to "affect" us and then disappear. As summer's ghost, Indian summer is miraculous.

In an earlier poem, she had written of "Midsummer" as "A full, and perfect time" when some she mourned went to heaven or "leaned into Perfectness – / Through Haze of Burial –" (F 822). In "There is a June," Indian summer causes her to think elegiacally once more. She contrasts this life, "this [summer] of our's"—an Indian or make-believe summer in which the "Prospect" of beauty is challenged by frost— with the afterlife, the "Summer of the Just" in heaven. Her poem ends with a prayer that we will enjoy in paradise a second late summer and a harvesting that will be "infinite" compared with earlier summers spent here on earth. Although this poem is about Indian summer, an artificial June, it prompts the reader to remember the beauties of the actual June, harbinger of the perfection of heaven. In that way, the garden in its several seasons disciplines her to consider the possibility of immortality.

It can be dangerous, of course, to speak of Emily Dickinson's use of religious themes and imagery in poems like "There is a June" lest she be considered a religious poet in the style of John Donne or George Herbert, who believed rather than hoped to believe in the Christian mysteries. When their minister informed an anxious Edward Dickinson that "Emily was sound," he probably meant that her knowledge of Congregationalist dogma was thorough, not that she was convinced of it. Her letters provide pictures of the author seated on a garden step while her family sang hymns in the neighboring church, images of a nervous or indignant Emily fleeing up the church aisle after an annoying sermon or daydreaming during communion. We cannot entertain the notion that she was consistently enraptured by the divine, like those Renaissance priests called "metaphysical" whose poetic techniques have so much in common with her own.[9] "Sermons on unbelief ever did attract me," she informed Sue (L 176). Hers was neither a settled nor a confident nor an ecstatic faith. Compared with her stout belief in certain persons—and in her muse—it was not precisely "faith" at all.

Nevertheless, it is important to remember that Dickinson appealed to the idea of God throughout her life with manifest hope and desire. In 1864, imagining herself a flower, she declared,

> But, Blossom, were I,
>
> . . .
>
> Content of fading
> Is enough for me –
> Fade I unto Divinity – (F 888)

She gave credence to "The Fact that Earth is Heaven –" (F 1435), and yet she longed to envision herself united with her dead in a heaven unlimited by time and season. Such thoughts were hardly original, of course; they were the staples and commonplaces of Victorian art, fascinated as it so richly was by mourning and by the transmutation of sex as death. In Dickinson, however, with her "achieved strangeness" and her "unmatched" originality, as Bloom puts it, the ideas of God and heaven were subjected to rigorous examination by a brain that rarely allowed itself a sentimental comfort:

> We can but follow to the Sun –
> As oft as He go down
> He leave Ourselves a Sphere behind –
> 'Tis mostly – following –
>
> We go no further with the Dust
> Than to the Earthen Door –

And then the Panels are reversed –
And we behold – no more (F 845)

In this fiercely economical poem, the extent of a day and the extent
of a life are fused. "'Tis mostly following" is Dickinson's description
of life itself. Her speaker is "a Sphere behind" the setting sun; she can-
not see where it goes when it sets behind the rim of the earth. She
is also separated by the sphere of her own condition from the "Dust"
that was once a living person; she can follow the latter only to his
grave, his "Earthen Door." The "Panels" of the coffin, once closed, hin-
der sight. For Dickinson, the darkness of the grave made it impossible
to do more than hope that "following" her loved ones or that expect-
ing another morning would result in union with them on mornings
to come.

❧

Emily Dickinson might have chosen an aesthetic avocation other than
gardening. It is significant, for example, that although she sketched a
little—Susan Dickinson once planned to illustrate a collection of Em-
ily's poems with the poet's drawings[10]—she never painted, like the
poet Celia Thaxter. Nor did she follow fashion and paint flowers on
china. She never wrote about *how* to garden, as did Gertrude Jekyll
or Vita Sackville-West. She did very little floral embroidery, that seri-
ous pastime of artistic women that produced works of real complex-
ity as well as refinement. Such feminine accomplishments were highly
praised in the nineteenth century (although needlework as a course of
instruction began to decline in the 1840s, with the rise of extended
academic education for girls). It is not enough to point out that gar-
dening was sacred to her from childhood; not enough to mention that
her mother, sister, and aunts were devoted gardeners, in order to ex-
plain why Emily Dickinson gave so much of her life to gardening
rather than to another pursuit.

That her gardening—like writing poetry—was the manifestation of profound and even occasionally rebellious desire, we learn from Dickinson's correspondence. An innocent reader might encounter with surprise her letter to Louise and Frances Norcross, written in October 1863. It begins "Nothing has happened but loneliness" and continues with another brave but sad confidence that she probably expected such avid gardeners to receive with sympathy: "I got down before father this morning, and spent a few moments profitably with the South Sea rose. Father detecting me, advised wiser employment, and read at devotions the chapter of the gentleman with one talent. I think he thought my conscience would adjust the gender" (L 285). The "South Sea rose" was undoubtedly her *Camellia japonica,* the fashionable flower of American conservatories after 1825. It was associated with the "Spice Isles" of Emily Dickinson's enraptured note of early March 1866 to the Hollands, praising its scent (L 315), but it had been made famous by Alexandre Dumas *fils* in *La Dame aux Camélias* (1855). The subtitle of that work, well known in the United States, was *"Le Demi-Monde."* Since Edward Dickinson was said to have built the conservatory in order that Emily might garden even in winter, it might seem strange that "detecting" her working "profitably" over her camellias—no doubt misting or fertilizing them—he stopped her, sought to awaken her "conscience," and then reminded her of her "one talent": for baking, probably, not writing. Perhaps, as a recently committed Christian, her father considered Emily's devotion to her flowers disproportionate, irreligious. Perhaps the sober lawyer imagined that tending her camellias might warp his daughter's rational good sense and infect her with the taint of worldly vanity and the *demi-monde.* Certainly the delicate, opulent camellias, unlike the inhabitants of her "Puritan Garden," did not immediately suggest fortitude and industry (L 685). This vignette shows that Emily Dickinson's passion for gardening, like her passion for writing poetry, was not altogether encouraged at home; it had to be indulged in some instances early in the morning or even secretly, privately.

When we recall her poem about the "June when corn is cut," however, we understand the gravity of her commitment. When Dickinson named Indian summer "June" in that poem, she was exhibiting her belief in the continuum of being. In the cycle of her flowers' birth, death, and resurrection, she found hope and symbolic proof of the promise of eternal life. (Since she called death "the Nile," she must have remembered that the Nile was a symbol of fertility to the Egyptians, whose dead sailed into immortality on its waters [L 318].) Gardening endowed Emily Dickinson with another world of living forms

36. Rear door of the Homestead, with path to the garden beyond.

to know, tend, and love. It rendered her, however reclusive, a member of the larger company of mid-Victorian women. It gave her themes, narrative tropes, and an elaborate and rich language that related her to other artists. By leaving the door of her house to enter the garden [Fig. 36], she encountered another theater for action and experience in which she could learn both success and failure, exultation and disappointment.

But the garden also allowed her to "follow" to the "Earthen Door." That is, it brought her as close as possible to earth, to nature in all its radical power and beauty, thus nullifying and discovering another name for the terrible grave. To art, Emily Dickinson owed her identity. But perhaps only her experience of the garden could truly tempt her to believe in the reality of "perennial bloom" and a "Certain June," or that in eternity "No Desert Noon," "No fear of frost to come" (F 230) would ever exist to trouble her.

Appendix

Flowers and Plants Grown by Emily Dickinson

From evidence furnished by her letters and from the testimony of others like her niece, Martha Dickinson Bianchi, Emily Dickinson is thought to have grown or, in the case of woodland plants like the clover or dandelion, occasionally displayed the flowers listed below in her garden and/or conservatory:

Amaryllis	Daffodil
Anemone	Dahlia
Arbutus	Daisy
Aster	Dandelion
Baby's breath	Daphne odora
Balsam	Delphinium
Bartsia	Dianthus
Bleeding heart	Fern
Buttercup	Forget-me-not
Camellia	Foxglove
Campanula	Fritillaria
Chrysanthemum	Fuchsia
Clematis	Gardenia
Clover	Gentian
Columbine	Geranium (Cranesbill)
Cowslip	Harebell
Crocus	Heliotrope

Hollyhock
Honeysuckle
Hyacinth
Iris
Jasmine
Jockey club
Lady's slipper orchid
Lilac
Lilies (Daylily,
Oriental lily, Pond lily)
Lily-of-the-valley
Lobelia
Marigold
Mignonette
Mock orange
Narcissus
Oleander
Peony
Phlox

Pomegranate
Primrose
Rhododendron
Rhodora
Rose (Old or Bourbon rose,
Damask, China or Tea rose,
Sweet briar rose, Calico
rose, Harrison's Yellow,
and others)
Salvia
Snapdragon
Star-of-Bethlehem
Sweet alyssum
Sweet pea
Sweet Sultan
Trillium
Verbena
Violet
Zinnia

Abbreviations

F   F followed by a number refers to poem numbers in *The Poems of Emily Dickinson,* Reading Edition, ed. R. W. Franklin (Cambridge, Mass.: The Belknap Press of Harvard University Press, 1999)

J   *The Poems of Emily Dickinson,* 3 vols., ed. Thomas H. Johnson (Cambridge, Mass.: Harvard University Press, 1955)

L   L followed by a number refers to letter numbers in *The Letters of Emily Dickinson,* ed. Thomas H. Johnson (Cambridge, Mass.: The Belknap Press of Harvard University Press, 1958)

Leyda   Jay Leyda, *The Years and Hours of Emily Dickinson,* 2 vols. (New Haven: Yale University Press, 1960)

Sewall, *Life*   Richard B. Sewall, *The Life of Emily Dickinson* (Cambridge, Mass.: Harvard University Press, 1994; originally published, New York: Farrar, Straus and Giroux, 1974)

Notes

Introduction

1. Cf. Sewall, *Life,* 217–218. Mabel Loomis Todd, Austin Dickinson's mistress from 1883 to 1885, and ED's first editor, wrote to her parents when she first came to live in Amherst: "I must tell you about the *character* of Amherst. It is a lady whom the people call the *Myth.* She is a sister of Mr. Dickinson, & seems to be the climax of all the family oddity." Later, Mabel wrote in her journal, "[Austin's] sister Emily is called in Amherst 'the myth.' She has not been out of her house in fifteen years."

2. See my account in *The Passion of Emily Dickinson* (Cambridge, Mass.: Harvard University Press, 1992), 28–31. Richard Sewall in *Life* (passim) discusses the variously proposed "lovers" of ED, arguing that Samuel Bowles best corresponds to the description of "Master," the mysterious addressee of Dickinson's three most enigmatic love letters. Nevertheless, some writers propose other candidates. Cf. Chapter 1, note 31 below. In *Emily Dickinson Face to Face* (Boston: Houghton Mifflin, 1932), 51–53, ED's niece Martha Dickinson Bianchi strongly defends the family story that "the man [Emily loved] was the [married] clergyman of Philadelphia whom she met on her way back home" to Amherst from a Washington trip in 1854, but she does not cite Charles Wadsworth by name.

3. See Sewall, *Life,* 153.

4. See Martha Dickinson Bianchi, "Emily Dickinson's Garden," *Emily Dickinson International Society Bulletin,* vol. 2, no. 2 (Nov./Dec. 1990), 2.

5. See "'A Little Taste, Time, and Means'": Dickinson and Flowers" in Domhnall Mitchell's *Emily Dickinson: Monarch of Perception* (Amherst: University of Massachusetts Press, 2000), 112–177. This study examines Dickinson according to the currently fashionable critical categories of politics, race, and gender, and argues that the poet's interest in gardens was largely a function of her wish to be viewed as "a 'lady'" engaged in "a prestigious activity" (132). Regarding her exchange of flowers with friends as the feminine activity of "gifting" (although she engaged in it with male intimates like Samuel Bowles for whom, as for Dickinson, horticulture had scientific, emotional, and aesthetic importance), Mitchell emphasizes gardening as one of ED's aristocratic activities, performed to emphasize Edward Dickinson's "class status"—Betsy Erkkila's phrase in "Book Review," *The Emily Dickinson Journal,* vol. X, no. 2, 72 (Johns Hopkins University Press, 2001). Mitchell's study receives fuller attention in my Chapters 2 and 3.

6. See Farr, *Passion,* 9–11, for the full text.

7. See Guy Leighton, "The Emily Dickinson Homestead," in *The Emily Dickinson Homestead: A Historical Study of Its Setting with Recommendations for Preservation and Restoration.* M.A. Thesis, Department of Landscape Architecture and Regional Planning, University of Massachusetts, Amherst, 1978, 35–36.

8. In *Emily Dickinson's Fascicles: Method and Meaning* (University Park, Pa.: Pennsylvania State University Press, 1995), Dorothy Huff Oberhaus regards "flower" as a "trope" for the word "poem," declaring that in some instances the poet "blurs the distinction between both herself and her poems" (180) and herself and her flowers.

9. For example, "There came a Day – at Summer's full –" (F 325).

10. Cf. *The Poems of Emily Dickinson,* Variorum Edition, ed. R. W. Franklin (Cambridge, Mass.: The Belknap Press of Harvard University Press, 1998), I, 110.

11. Cf. Joanna Yin, "Garden, as Subject" in Jane Donahue Eberwein, ed., *An Emily Dickinson Encyclopedia* (Westport, Conn.: Greenwood Press, 1998), 122–123.

12. See Marisa Anne Pagnattaro, "Emily Dickinson's Erotic Persona: Unfettered by Convention," *The Emily Dickinson Journal,* vol. V, no. 2 (1996), 35, and K. Linnea Takacs, "Emily Dickinson: The Sensual Observer," in *Dickinson Studies* (1968–1993) [publ. privately by Frederick L. Morey], 1992, 35.

1. Gardening in Eden

1. "rare and strange": Untitled reminiscence of ED, quoted in Willis J. Buckingham, ed., *Emily Dickinson's Reception in the 1890s* (Pittsburgh: University of Pittsburgh Press, 1989), 350. "a flower herself": Emily Fowler Ford, untitled reminiscence in *Letters of Emily Dickinson*, 2 vols., ed. Mabel Loomis Todd (Boston: Roberts Brothers, 1894). Quoted in Buckingham, ibid., 348. Ford recalls excursions with ED as girls to Mount Norwottock, five miles from Amherst, "where we found the climbing fern, and came home laden with pink and white trilliums, and . . . yellow lady's slippers. She knew the wood-lore of the region round about, and could name the haunts and the habits of every wild or garden growth with her reach."

2. But he also declared "her verses" "like poetry plucked up by the roots" because of its "defian[ce] of form, measure, rhyme, and even grammar." "An Open Portfolio," *Christian Union*, 42, Sept. 25, 1890, reprinted in Buckingham, *Emily Dickinson's Reception*, 8. Many of ED's early reviewers compared her poems to flowers, either orchids or wildflowers.

3. Ford, quoted in Buckingham, *Emily Dickinson's Reception*, 350.

4. Sewall, *Life*, II, 377.

5. Ibid.

6. Leyda, II, 239.

7. Cf. Buckingham, *Emily Dickinson's Reception*, 27. In a German essay on Dickinson's *Poems* (1890), the writer commented, "[The book's] gray-green cover was stamped in gilt with the drawing of an Indian Pipe, a strangely delicate plant that grows from rotted tree roots and sends forth stems, blossoms, and leaves—all pale as death. This flower of stillness, shadows, and secrecy was the poet's favorite." See Buckingham, ibid., 532. Mabel Todd recalled deciding to paint Indian pipes for Emily Dickinson, calling them "those weird but perfect flowers of shade and silence," while again and again the "silver Indian pipe, half fungus, half flower," with its preference for shade, was linked with the reclusive poet. Mabel Loomis Todd, "Emily Dickinson's Letters," *Bachelor of Arts* I, May 1895, quoted in Buckingham, ibid., 439. Some nineteenth-century critics identified the flower, however, as a lily or fleur-de-lis.

8. Thomas Wentworth Higginson, "An Open Portfolio," quoted in Buckingham, *Emily Dickinson's Reception*, 4.

9. From the account of Edward's funeral in *The Springfield Republican*,

June 20, 1874, quoted in Millicent Todd Bingham, *Emily Dickinson's Home: Letters of Edward Dickinson and His Family* (New York: Harper and Brothers, 1955), 473.

10. Elizabeth Smith Brownstein, *If This House Could Talk* (New York: Simon and Schuster, 1999), 170—171.

11. In an unpublished letter in the Houghton Library Dickinson Collection, Susan writes, "I went past your village home [and] revelled in the forsythias. How stunning they are [like] the ramparts of the New Jerusalem!" Like Emily—perhaps influenced by her—Susan sometimes made extravagant comparisons founded on the Bible (as in this case) or Shakespeare. In *Emily Dickinson Face to Face* (Boston: Houghton Mifflin, 1932), 96, Martha Dickinson Bianchi writes warmly of her mother's affection for flowers, one of Susan's attractions for Austin, who wrote in 1850 before their marriage, "All the livelong day I have written under the soul-inspiring beauty and sense-intoxicating perfumes [of your flowers]." Again like Emily, her taste was for wildflowers: "One of Susan's choicest pleasures was to gather wild flowers [*sic*] for the church. . . . Not only the familiar roadside bloom . . . but the rarer shades of lupine, the lady's slipper, the shy rhodora, the azalea of the swamps, and the vivid red lilies [*hemerocallis flava?*]" (ibid., 155).

12. From a courtship letter to Emily Norcross, written two months before their wedding, and quoted in Sewall, *Life*, I, 47.

13. Quoted in May Brawley Hill, *Grandmother's Garden: The Old-Fashioned American Garden, 1865—1915* (New York: Harry N. Abrams, 1995), 27.

14. Martha Dickinson Bianchi, "Emily Dickinson's Garden," *Emily Dickinson International Society Bulletin*, vol. 2, no. 2 (Nov./Dec. 1990), 1.

15. Ibid., 2.

16. With typical self-importance, Lyman called it "that charming second home of mine in Amherst." Cf. Richard B. Sewall, *The Lyman Letters* (Amherst: University of Massachusetts Press, 1965), 1.

17. See Sewall, *Lyman Letters*, 65: "But she is rather morbid and unnatural—." Sewall comments that Lyman's next sentence, "Vinnie's kisses were very very sweet," reveals the source of his displeasure with Emily: she was "platonic" and did not fit Joseph's "concept of the romanticized ideal."

18. Ibid., 69.

19. Ibid. The "Newman girls," Clara and her sister, were Edward Dickinson's wards and lived with Susan and Austin Dickinson for several years dur-

ing their late childhood and adolescence. Clara's understanding of Emily Dickinson seems to have been remarkable, as is shown by one memoir: "The world would not call her's an eventful life. *Her events* were the coming of the first bird;—the bursting of a chrysalis;—the detection of the fascinating spring fuzz of green in the air—the wondering opening on the new world of every little flower. . . . Her *Tragedies*—the wild storm;—the bruising of a plant; . . . the falsity of a friend . . ." Cf. Sewall, *Life*, II, 269.

20. To Mrs. Edward Tuckerman, also a gardener, ED wrote in mid-April 1875, "I send you inland buttercups as out-door flowers are still at sea" (L 437). Dickinson transplanted certain field flowers to pots in the conservatory, where she kept them alive during the winter. Buttercups may have been among them, although Louise Carter hypothesizes that "inland buttercups" may mean yellow jasmine blossoms. (The jasmine or "poet's jessamine" given to ED by Samuel Bowles would have been white, but Martha Dickinson Bianchi claimed she also grew the yellow jasmine.) Envisioning her own funeral, ED wrote in 1884 to Elizabeth Holland, "When it shall come my turn [to be buried], I want a Buttercup – Doubtless the Grass will give me one, for does she not revere the Whims of her flitting Children?" (L 901).

21. Leyda, II, 469. Sent to Mrs. Mariette Thompson Jameson, a neighbor, on April 24, 1886, about one month before ED died. These geraniums were probably the old sweet-scented kind, recommended by Joseph Breck of Boston in his *New Book of Flowers* (1866) for "parlour culture" (along with camellias, salvias, and begonias).

22. Leyda, II, 322.

23. Ibid., II, 457.

24. See Judith Farr, *The Passion of Emily Dickinson* (Cambridge, Mass.: Harvard University Press, 1992), especially chapters 2 and 5, and Farr, "Emily Dickinson and the Visual Arts," in *The Emily Dickinson Handbook,* ed. Gudrun Grabher, Roland Hagenbüchle, and Cristanne Miller (Amherst: University of Massachusetts Press, 1998), 61–92. In 1859, ED sent Susan Dickinson a note scribbled on a page from the *New England Primer* which said: "My 'position'! Cole. P.S. Lest you misapprehend, the unfortunate insect upon the left is Myself, while the Reptile upon the *right* is my more immediate friends, and connections. As ever, Cole" (L 214). She obviously associated Cole with nature painting and the myth of Eden, elaborated in such of his works as *Expulsion from the Garden of Eden* (1827–28).

25. Hill, *Grandmother's Garden*, 18.

26. See Ann Leighton, *American Gardens of the Nineteenth Century* (Amherst: University of Massachusetts Press, 1987), 222.

27. Ibid.

28. Cf. *American Art 1700–1960*, ed. John W. McCoubrey (Englewood Cliffs, N.J.: Prentice-Hall, 1965), 112.

29. In his biography *My Wars Are Laid Away in Books: The Life of Emily Dickinson* (New York: Random House, 2001), Alfred Habegger adopts the view of Norbert Hirschhorn, M.D., and Polly Longsworth that ED's eye complaint was "anterior uveitis," "what used to be called rheumatic iritis" (485). His discussion (pp. 485–493) of the pain, physical and psychological, that it caused ED is well worth reading.

30. Cf. Buckingham, *Emily Dickinson's Reception*, 3.

31. A number of scholars regard Bowles as the man ED loved during the "Master" years. See Jean McClure Mudge, *Emily Dickinson and the Image of Home* (Amherst: University of Massachusetts Press, 1975); Ruth Miller, *The Poetry of Emily Dickinson* (Middletown, Conn.: Wesleyan University Press, 1968); David Higgins, *Portrait of Emily Dickinson* (New Brunswick, N.J.: Rutgers University Press, 1967); Sewall, *Life;* and Farr, *Passion.* Her fondness for Otis Lord is described in Millicent Todd Bingham's *Emily Dickinson, A Revelation* (New York: Harper, 1954). According to Bingham, Austin Dickinson "said that at different times Emily had been devoted to several men. He maintain[ed] that she had been several times in love, in her own way." See Bingham, *Emily Dickinson's Home,* 374. Martha Dickinson Bianchi—sometimes in error about details of her aunt's life and correspondence and known to have altered facts and dates—claimed that her mother designated Charles Wadsworth, a Philadelphia minister, as "Master" (*Emily Dickinson Face to Face,* 52). Wadsworth's son was angered by the assertion, as Alfred Habegger reveals in *My Wars Are Laid Away in Books,* 574. A few other scholars support Wadsworth: Vivian R. Pollak, *Dickinson: The Anxiety of Gender* (Ithaca: Cornell University Press, 1984); William Robert Sherwood, *Circumference and Circumstance: Stages in the Mind and Art of Emily Dickinson* (New York: Columbia University Press, 1968), and Polly Longsworth in an essay contained in Liebling, Benfey, and Longsworth, *The Dickinsons of Amherst* (Hanover, N.H.: University Press of New England, 2001). Habegger is in favor of some minister, possibly though not necessarily Wadsworth.

Some feminist scholars, especially Martha Nell Smith, regard Susan

Dickinson as both "Master" and the subject of certain Dickinson poems considered to be homoerotic. See *Rowing in Eden: Rereading Emily Dickinson* (Austin: University of Texas Press, 1992), passim, where Smith advances the thesis that ED and her sister-in-law Susan were engaged in a "powerfully sensual relationship" (129) and that "their emotional ties can be characterized as lesbian" (150). In *Open Me Carefully: Emily Dickinson's Intimate Letters to Susan Huntington Dickinson* (Ashfield, Mass.: Paris Press, 1998), an edition of what the editors call the two women's "correspondence" but which consists of ED's letters to Susan with two brief exceptions, Smith and her co-editor Ellen Louise Hart go further, ambiguously claiming that Susan and Emily "lived and screened their passion" (xviii) and that, because ED sent her 250 poems, Susan must have been ED's writing master, chief critic, "imagination," and muse. Although Smith characterizes Susan as "devoutly religious from late teens through adulthood," she has no difficulty in imagining her leading a furtive adulterous life with her husband and his sister, based on such "evidence" as Martha Dickinson Bianchi's recollections in *Emily Dickinson Face to Face* of Susan and Emily's private meetings in the "Northwest Passage" of the Homestead (Smith, "Susan Dickinson," in *The Emily Dickinson Encyclopedia,* 81). Smith and Hart tie their assumptions about a sensual relationship to their theories about Susan's verse and Emily's poetry, which they regard as interrelated. But Susan's verses, now reproduced on the Emily Dickinson site on the Internet (*http://jeffersonvillage.virginia.edu/dickinson/*) are so effete, so badly written, as to make the idea that she "co-authored" ED's poems and served as ED's "mentor" defy belief (*Rowing in Eden,* 3, and passim). Susan's flower poem "Of June and her belongings," which ruminates on "daisies white / And violets blue / And butter cups / With hearts so true," is embarrassing evidence of the difference between her performance as a writer and ED's.

32. George S. Merriam, *The Life and Times of Samuel Bowles* (New York: Century, 1885), II, 59.

33. He writes again for *The Emily Dickinson Journal,* vol. XI, no. 2, 2002 (Baltimore: Johns Hopkins University Press), that Bowles met the Austin Dickinsons when he visited Amherst to see the new haying equipment shown on the Cowles's "large North Amherst farm" (2). Here Habegger enlarges his brief argument in *My Wars* by saying that "Dickinson may not have met Bowles on 30 June 1858 but she was probably aware of the occasion" (2–3) and offers as proof Letter 193 that alludes to "men . . . mowing the second

Hay," a remark that could be merely seasonal, counting on Bowles's knowledge of the rhythms of country life. He concludes that his thesis "shows how important it is to get chronology right" (3). But he does not explain the intimate tones of Letter 189. Letter 193 might be part of a frequent correspondence. (The Bowles family destroyed many letters from ED.)

34. Habegger, *My Wars Are Laid Away in Books,* 352.

35. Habegger, whose biography of ED strives to imperil a number of long-established views of Dickinson's life, proposes that this poem beginning "If it had no pencil" was intended for *Mary* Bowles. The fifth line, "If it had no word," might suit the poem to the silent if not taciturn Mary, but "Mr. Sam" also failed to write when ED longed to hear from him. ED's relationship with Mary was dutifully affectionate, more respectful than playful. Not Mary but Sam is known to have called her "Daisy," like the poem's addressee. Habegger's view of Bowles over-emphasizes his illnesses, accuses Bowles of a frantic personal recklessness that ill consorts with his successful life as editor, abolitionist, trustee, and reformer, de-emphasizes his attractiveness and religious serenity, ignores the tenderness so many people attributed to him, and mysteriously alludes to his "temptations to infidelity, *rarely yielded to*" (emphasis mine) (378). Bowles never became ED's "former friend" as Habegger claims (521), for only four years elapsed between his special appearance at her father's funeral and Bowles's death. Habegger's argument for a minister as "Master" fails to consider the consistent image patterns ED chose when addressing both Bowles and "Master," but Habegger spends limited time with the language of his subject in her poems and letters.

36. Habegger, *My Wars Are Laid Away in Books,* 332.

37. Cf. Farr, *Passion,* 27–28.

38. Cf. Sewall, *Life,* 469.

39. Merriam, *Life and Times of Samuel Bowles,* II, 59.

40. R. W. Franklin, ed., *The Poems of Emily Dickinson,* Variorum Edition (Cambridge, Mass.: The Belknap Press of Harvard University Press, 1998), II, 1015. The Dickinsons retained the manuscript, written in pencil. The presence of *Mary* Bowles on this occasion may have determined his behavior.

41. In *The Passion of Emily Dickinson,* I argue that Bowles was probably "Master," while in my novel *I Never Came to You in White,* I declare in an Afterword that the Muse was Dickinson's true beloved. The two points of view are not meant to be opposed, for although ED loved several persons deeply and recorded this in verse, her life was essentially dedicated to those

"Hosts" or angels of art who visit her in the poem "Alone, I cannot be —" (F 303).

42. See Johnson, *Letters,* II, 609n.

43. The Crown Imperial, called by the French botanist Carolus Clusius the "Persian lily," is especially associated with arrogance, pride, and social climbing (all of which were attributed to Susan Dickinson by contemporaries). In Turkish legend, the Crown Imperial once grew in Paradise, bearing its petals upright. Because all the other flowers admired it, it became conceited, whereupon God punished it so that it hung its flowers downward in shame.

44. Cf. "The Narrative of Sue" in Farr, *The Passion of Emily Dickinson,* 100–177, and "Emily Dickinson's 'Engulfing' Play: *Antony and Cleopatra,*" *Tulsa Studies in Women's Literature,* 9 (Fall 1990), 231–250 and passim.

45. Quoted in Sewall, *Life,* 88.

46. This letter is contained in the Dickinson-Todd Collection, Yale University Library.

47. Bingham, *Emily Dickinson, A Revelation,* 3.

48. Some feminist critics, preferring to inscribe Emily Dickinson as lesbian, have especially resisted the Lord connection.

49. Bingham, *Emily Dickinson, A Revelation,* 45.

50. Leyda, II, 475.

51. But a contemporary watercolor, "reputedly of Emily Dickinson," in *The Dickinsons of Amherst* (127) renders the poet incontestably homely, with none of the "beauties" ascribed to her by Emily Ford and others.

52. Yet the ninety-year-old dressmaker, "Miss Marian," reported (wrongly) that the poet had black hair rather than auburn. Cf. Leyda, II, 480.

53. Emily Ford, "Untitled reminiscence," in Buckingham, *Emily Dickinson's Reception,* 350.

54. Leyda, II, 475; 151.

55. Bianchi, *Emily Dickinson Face to Face,* 46.

56. Leyda, II, 273.

57. Two essays by Judith Walsh, published in *The Magazine Antiques,* October and November 1999, describe the "Language of Flowers" in detail and chart the various meanings of flowers in the nineteenth century as I present them here. These quotations from Elizabeth Wirt appear in the October issue, 521, 522.

58. ED's botanical education was the fruit of Edward Hitchcock's profound influence. This author of both the *Religious Lectures,* which taught

the truth of the Resurrection, and *Catalogue of Plants Growing Without Cultivation in the Vicinity of Amherst College* was responsible for the curriculum Dickinson followed at Mary Lyon's Seminary, and his essay "The Resurrections of Spring" finds echoes in her mature poems about the seasons. At his funeral, the elegist observed grandly, "We often hear of the language of flowers. There is much of fancy in the details, but the idea is based on a profound truth. There *is* a language of flowers . . . and it is the language of God." Cf. Sewall, *Life,* 355.

59. Sarah Josepha Hale, *Flora's Interpreter; or, The American Book of Flowers and Sentiments,* quoted in Walsh, "The Language of Flowers in Nineteenth Century American Painting," *The Magazine Antiques,* October 1999, 521.

60. Elizabeth A. Petrino, *Emily Dickinson and Her Contemporaries: Women's Verse in America 1820–1885* (Hanover, N.H.: University Press of New England, 1998), 137. It is Petrino's contention that "Dickinson's habit of presenting flowers with poems falls within the context of the language of flowers, which constructed a nonverbal system of communication based on a series of codes" (7). She compares and contrasts ED's apparent understanding of this "language" with the writer Frances Osgood's, finding ED's richer. Reading a few of the same poems like "I tend my flowers for thee –," she judges them more full of obvious "sexual innuendo" (145) than I do.

61. Thomas Wentworth Higginson, "Emily Dickinson," in *The Magnificent Activist: The Writings of Thomas Wentworth Higginson,* ed. Howard N. Meyer (New York: Perseus Press, 2000), 545.

62. See Leighton, *American Gardens of the Nineteenth Century,* 86.

63. Cf. Leyda, II, 478.

64. Sharon Paiva Stephan's sensitive study *One Woman's Work: The Visual Art of Celia Laighton Thaxter* (Portsmouth, N.H.: P. E. Randall, 2001) presents a portrait of this other poet-gardener who fascinates by her many personal and artistic differences from ED. Friend and hostess to T. W. Higginson and a contributor of poems to the *Atlantic Monthly, Harper's, Scribner's,* and other magazines, Thaxter became a wife and mother in her early teens, kept the famous salon/hotel Appledore House on the Isle of Shoals, and earned the acclaim of Mark Twain and William Dean Howells for the beautifully designed, lyrical accounts of her life there, especially *An Island Garden* (1894). She resembled ED in her cultivation of old-fashioned flowers, in regarding flowers as her intimates and gardening as a high aesthetic endeavor. She also exhibited similar excitement in imagining her world: "I want to

paint everything I see." In contrast to ED, however, poetry became inadequate to Thaxter as an expression of her vision of life; finally she "turned her emphasis from the verbal to the visual arts," excelling at flower arrangement and painting flowers on china (Stephan, *One Woman's Work,* 77). Her line "The sunrise never failed us yet" shows the same ardor for natural miracles that one meets in ED, and the same faith in the healing powers of nature. But Thaxter's voice is late nineteenth century without ED's original, even revolutionary accents.

2. The Woodland Garden

1. See Mary Elizabeth Kromer Bernhard, "Lost and Found: Emily Dickinson's Unknown Daguerreotypist," *The New England Quarterly,* vol. 72 (December 1999), 594–601.

In April 2000, Professor Philip Gura purchased a 3⅞" by 5½" albumen photograph, mounted originally on photographer's board, that depicts a serious and delicate-looking woman, elegantly attired and wearing a lorgnette, who is seated in a chair of Gothic design. Her eyes, nose, mouth, and pale complexion are very like those of Emily Dickinson in the 1847 daguerreotype. Written in pencil on the back of the photograph are the words "Emily Dickinson/Died/rec[eived?]/1886." This photograph seems far more likely to represent the poet than does the picture discovered by Herman Abromson in Greenwich Village and reproduced a few years later in Sewall's *Life* (1974). Nevertheless, neither the Gura photograph nor Abromson's picture of a black-eyed, gypsy-like woman in earrings has been authenticated.

2. See Farr, *The Passion of Emily Dickinson,* 17–21, and the illustrations on pp. 18 and 19 of that book showing ED and a woman named Margaret Aurelia Dewing, also depicted in 1847 in an identical pose.

3. May Brawley Hill, *Grandmother's Garden: The Old-Fashioned American Garden, 1865–1915* (New York: Harry N. Abrams, 1995), 21.

4. In Susan Tolman's "Mt. Holyoke Journal" (quoted in Leyda, I, 134) the entry for January 1, 1848, speaks of the students' "excitement" "for some days" at sitting for their "miniatures" at the office of an itinerant daguerreotypist established "just across the way" from the school. It was formerly assumed that ED was among them.

5. Ruskin's art criticism was having an extraordinary effect upon American writers and painters just as Emily Dickinson was beginning her creative

life. See Judith Farr, "Emily Dickinson and the Visual Arts," 70–71 and passim in *The Emily Dickinson Handbook*. Volume III of Ruskin's *Modern Painters* discusses subjects that greatly interested her, for example, the sublimity of art and the idea of eternity. Among the Dickinson books is a copy of the third edition of Ruskin's *The True and the Beautiful in Nature, Art, Morals, and Religion* (New York: John Wiley, 1860). These volumes, now at the Houghton Library, Harvard University, were read by both the Austin Dickinson family and ED. For decades, the light double markings in pencil at some passages have been thought to be ED's, in part because the marked passages seem so clearly to reflect her own ideas and concerns. Although there is no mark in this copy of Ruskin, it shows signs of use and opens easily to the chapters on "Mountains." On well-worn page 75, a passage reads, "It fell within the purpose of the Great Builder to give, in the highest peaks of mountains, examples of form more strange and majestic than any which could be obtained by structures so beneficently adapted to the welfare of the human race."

Mountains were emblems of aspiration and permanence for Thomas Cole and the Hudson River School. ED wrote twenty-three poems that directly concern mountains; she lived in sight of neighboring Mount Tom and in daily communion with sunrise and sundown as they colored the Pelham hills. See "Bloom opon the Mountain stated —" (F 787) wherein she unites the idea of flowers with the emblem of the mountain in a moving, dynamic sunset poem.

6. From the obituary written by Susan Dickinson. See the Introduction, p. 5.

7. See Hill, *Grandmother's Garden*, 43–161, and, in particular, William H. Gerdts, "Through a Glass Brightly: The American Pre-Raphaelites and Their Still Lifes and Nature Studies," in Linda S. Ferber and William H. Gerdts, *The New Path: Ruskin and the American Pre-Raphaelites* (New York: The Brooklyn Museum and Schocken Books, 1985), 39–77.

8. Gerdts, *The New Path*, 62. The "casual wayside growth" had such pronounced spiritual and Christian connotations during the Romantic period that one finds wildflowers like the dandelion, cornflower, or anemone praised alongside the rose or lily in highly devotional contexts. For example, the Roman Catholic saint Thérèse of Lisieux (1873–1897) developed a language of nature in her devotional poems and autobiography, *L'Histoire d'une Âme*. In that language, the humblest field flowers were equal to the most refined. "If

all flowers were roses," she wrote, "nature would lose her springtime beauty and the fields would no longer be decked out with little wild flowers . . . [God] willed to create great souls comparable to lilies and roses, but He has created smaller ones and these must be content to be daisies and violets." The fact that Thérèse disliked hothouse flowers perhaps reveals the penetration to the continent of Ruskin's prohibitions against formality.

9. There was no "Pool" on the Homestead grounds. ED probably meant the small pond in which she grew pond lilies. The phrase is reminiscent of Thoreau's description of "The Ponds" in *Walden* (1845): transparent, surrounded by wildflowers, and "continually receiving new life and motion from above." Being "rippled by the wind" and visited by water bugs, streaked by dashes of light, troubled by perch, and made musical by raindrops, Thoreau's favorite pond is filled with what ED calls "noise," and he—like she—clearly finds it superior to the man-made music furnished by the pianos of Salem or Boston.

10. Cf. Sewall, *Life,* 407n.

11. See Hill, *Grandmother's Garden,* 29.

12. Cf. Martha Dickinson Bianchi, "Emily Dickinson's Garden," *Emily Dickinson International Society Bulletin,* vol. 2, no. 2 (Nov./Dec. 1990), 2.

13. Using *Hortus,* Bernard McMahon's *American Gardener's Calendar,* and Favretti's *Landscapes and Gardens for Historic Buildings,* Louise Carter provides the botanical identifications of these plants: wild cucumber / *Echinocystis lobata;* coltsfoot / *Galax urdeolata;* stargrass / *Aletris;* climbing fumitory / *Andlumia fungosa;* Sol's or Solomon's Seal / *Polygonatum biflorum;* scouring rush / *Equisetum hyemale;* pigweed / *Amarathanthus hybridus;* bellflower / *Campanula;* passion flower / *Passiflora;* plantain-leaved everlasting / possibly *Anaphalis margararitacea;* candle larkspur / *Delphinium;* whorled loose-strife / *Lysimachia;* rough bedstraw / *Galium;* robin-run-away (or "false violet") / *Dalibardia repens;* butterfly flower / *Asclepias tuberosa;* love-in-a-mist / *Nigella damacena;* bastard pennyroyal / *Trichostema dichotomum;* Dutchman's breeches / *Dicentra culcullaria;* common lousewort / possibly false foxglove or *Aureolaria pedicularia;* hog peanut / *Amphicarpaea bracteata;* mad-dog skullcap / possibly bog plant, *Alima plantago-aquatica;* turtlehead / *Chelone glabra;* Grass of Parnassus / *Parnassus glauca.*

14. Memoir of a Dickinson neighbor, Harriet Thompson Jameson, after ED's funeral. See Leyda, II, 476.

15. See Martha Nell Smith and Ellen Louise Hart, eds., *Open Me Carefully: Emily Dickinson's Intimate Letters to Susan Huntington Dickinson* (Ashfield, Mass.: Paris Press, 1998), 261.

16. Convincingly, Smith and Hart suggest that what they call "Dickinson's letter-poem" beginning "That any Flower should be so base as to stab my Susan" constitutes her reaction to Mabel Todd's affair with Austin Dickinson. The note, which Johnson numbers 911, continues, "Choose Flowers that have no Fang, Dear – Pang is the Past of Peace –." Mabel would thus be the "Flower" whose thorns/fangs stab/betray Susan. Too portentous a note not to be coded, perhaps, it does seem to employ the mid-Victorian flower language wherein a beautiful woman (Mabel was known as a "stunner") is a rose.

17. This letter, discovered after Johnson finished his edition of the *Letters,* is reproduced in *Open Me Carefully* as letter 28, p. 73. Smith and Hart declare that ED "uses the symbols of the rose and the lily to represent Susan and herself," but it is the rustic dandelion with which ED identifies herself in this letter. Polly Longsworth thinks the letter is intended for another friend, "Susan Phelps of nearby Hadley" (*The Dickinsons of Amherst*, 40).

18. See Theodore E. Stebbins, Jr., *Martin Johnson Heade* (Boston: Museum of Fine Arts, 1999), 110.

19. See the chapter "A Passion for Flowers" in Jack Kramer, *Women of Flowers: A Tribute to Victorian Women Illustrators* (New York: Stewart, Tabori, and Chang, 1996), 30–31.

20. Ibid., 31.

21. Leyda, I, 248.

22. This strain appears in the verse of other nineteenth-century women. Thus, Lucy Larcom (1824–1893), a popular poet of the Civil War period and a laborer in the Lowell, Massachusetts textile mills, wrote the poem "Flowers of the Fallow," praising "these plants that you call weeds" (sedge, hardhack, mullein, yarrow) which grow everywhere. Such plants she considered blessed for their humility and constancy. In her works they became types of women who are brave despite advancing age and faded looks.

23. Cf. Paula Bennett, *Emily Dickinson, Woman Poet* (Iowa City: University of Iowa Press, 1990), 102, 103.

24. In a collection of his own and his deceased first wife Mary Thacher Higginson's poems entitled *The Afternoon Landscape* (1889), T. W. Higginson

published "Beneath the Violets," an elegy for their little daughter. It imagines the frail child buried beneath violets. Like ED, Higginson does not avoid linking violets with remembered anguish, but his lines are morbidly sentimental and his speaker too easily dismisses his own sorrow. Comfort is achieved through the conceit of death as sleep, popular in Victorian sculptures and daguerreotypes of dead children: "Safe 'neath the violets / Rests the baby form; / Every leaf that springtime sets / Shields it from the storm. / Peace to all vain regrets / Mid this sunshine warm . . . / While safe 'neath the violets / Sleep the violet eyes." Were violets not so prized for their sweetness, Higginson might not have been able to get away with the absurd and willful "safe," even in the 1880s.

25. Domhnall Mitchell, "A Little Taste, Time, and Means: Dickinson and Flowers," in *Emily Dickinson: Monarch of Perception* (Amherst: University of Massachusetts Press, 2000). The quotations here and on the next several pages are found on pp. 120, 112, 121, 118, and 124. Mitchell's essay, in which ED's upper-middle-class place in society is linked to her love for flowers—a preference for "the decorative and uncommon rather than the utilitarian," "an atmosphere of mysticism, taste, and exclusivity"—may be in part inspired by such remarks as Martha Dickinson Bianchi's, that her aunt would "tolerate none of the usual variety of mongrel houseplants" (121). Actually, the conservatory impartially displayed transplanted meadow and field flowers that overwintered there with her exotics and tropical flowers.

26. Betsy Erkkila, "Emily Dickinson and Class," *American Literary History*, 4 (1992), 1–27, 22.

27. Ann Leighton, *American Gardens of the Nineteenth Century* (Amherst: University of Massachusetts Press, 1987), 42, 101.

28. Ibid., 90.

29. The Dickinson-Todd Archive at Yale contains a letter (dated 1883) from Austin Dickinson to Mabel Todd, explaining that at last he was tinkering with a lawn mower to cut the Homestead grass for Lavinia.

30. Alfred Habegger, *My Wars Are Laid Away in Books* (New York: Random House, 2001), 363.

31. Like other critics, Mitchell sometimes attacks Dickinson's character because he misunderstands her idiom and her language. Writing about her important poem "Essential Oils –are wrung" (F 772), he recognizes that it describes how poetry is made: by means of hard labor and with inspiration. But

he calls Dickinson "breathtakingly arrogant" in assuming that her poem, or "rose," will survive while what she calls "the General Rose"—which Mitchell interprets as "the mass of ephemeral texts produced casually for the market"—will decay (124). ED means, however, to contrast the "rose" pressed into perfume with "the General Rose," that is to say, all living roses. "Essential Oils" is not about herself precisely but about the perfect artifact: the perfect poem that surpasses nature's perfect rose. It does not contrast her with other poets but continues the Dickinsonian debate about which is more valuable: nature or art.

32. ED has not usually been accused by earlier biographers of manifesting "arrogance and narcissism" (Habegger, *My Wars*, 245), of being a "snake" (231) who wrote "seething letters" (236) and "crazy compositions" (231), or a person with "claws" (545) who regarded even children of the lower classes with condescension. Quite the contrary. Most who knew her well found ED tenderhearted, sensible, and especially kind to children from all neighborhoods. A letter of Otis Lord to Lavinia provides one typical impression: "[Emily's] last note gave me a good deal of uneasiness, *for knowing how entirely unselfish she is* . . . ., I fear that she has been more ill, than she has told me" (emphasis mine). Cf. Sewall, *Life*, 657.

33. Rebecca Patterson, *Emily Dickinson's Imagery* (Amherst: University of Massachusetts Press, 1979), 48.

34. See Bianchi, "Emily Dickinson's Garden," 2.

35. Cf. Susan A. Roth, *Complete Guide to Flower Gardening* (Des Moines, Iowa: Meredith Books, 1995), 245.

36. In "Susan and Emily Dickinson: Their Lives, Their Letters" (*The Cambridge Companion to Emily Dickinson*, ed. Wendy Martin [Cambridge: Cambridge University Press, 2002], 70), Martha Nell Smith claims that it was Susan Dickinson who fashioned ED's white flannel burial robe and arranged the flowers at her throat. ED's cousin, Clara Newman Turner, said that *she* had made ED's "little white wrap . . . little dreaming I was weaving her shawl" (cf. Sewall, *Life*, 273). Most accounts of ED's illness and death record Lavinia's constant nursing, not Susan's, although it is generally accepted that Susan dressed ED's body for burial. There is no evidence for Smith's assertion that the "cypripedium and violets" symbolized "faithfulness" and the heliotropes "devotion" on the part(s) of Susan and Emily. According to T. W. Higginson, the heliotrope symbolized ED's love for Judge Lord, as Lavinia (adorning her sister's body) described it.

3. The Enclosed Garden

1. See Willis J. Buckingham, *Emily Dickinson's Reception in the 1890s* (Pittsburgh: University of Pittsburgh Press, 1989), 257–258.

2. See Alfred Habegger, *My Wars Are Laid Away in Books* (New York: Random House, 2001), 243.

3. Ibid., 410.

4. See Nancy Milford, *Savage Beauty: The Life of Edna St. Vincent Millay* (New York: Random House, 2001), xiv.

5. When Martha Dickinson Bianchi brought out *Poems by Emily Dickinson* (1937), the book jacket featured gardenias. More than half a century later, the jacket of R. W. Franklin's "Reading Edition" of *Poems* (Harvard University Press, 1999) shows white flowers, probably miniature roses. *Open Me Carefully* (1998), edited by Ellen Louise Hart and Martha Nell Smith, a controversial edition of Dickinson's "intimate" letters to Susan Dickinson, displays the bin of a Calla lily on the cover. (Since a Calla lily's bin resembles an ear, the editors clearly mean to insinuate the reader into a private, even secretive world.) The cover of Paula Bennett's *Emily Dickinson, Woman Poet* bears a white morning glory, and Elizabeth A. Petrino's *Emily Dickinson and Her Contemporaries,* a rose. Many other examples of floral covers on books by or about Dickinson make it clear that editors regard flowers as one of her essential subject matters, actual or symbolic.

6. See "The Courtship of Winslow Homer" in *Winslow Homer,* ed. Nicolai Cikovski, Jr., and Franklin Kelly (Washington, D.C., and New Haven, Conn.: National Gallery of Art and Yale University Press, 1995), 71.

7. See Vivian R. Pollak, ed., *A Poet's Parents: The Courtship Letters of Emily Norcross and Edward Dickinson* (Chapel Hill, N.C.: University of North Carolina Press, 1988), 210.

8. In alluding to the jasmine, Dickinson herself uses the Tennysonian spelling "jessamines."

9. Katherine Emma Manthorne, *Tropical Renaissance: Northern American Artists Exploring Latin America, 1839–1879* (Washington, D.C.: Smithsonian Institution Press, 1989), 10. Manthorne provides an excellent overview of the use of the word "Eden" in nineteenth-century texts and observes, "Th[e] association of the landscape of the American Tropics with an edenic garden was expressed verbally and visually by nearly every northern artist who traveled there in this period" (11).

10. Heade's decision to live in Boston for two years (1861–1863) caused him to be favorably reviewed in Boston newspapers received by the Dickinsons long after he had ceased to live there.

11. "Wild nights" is an example of the poems debated about by textual critics. Martha Nell Smith calls attention to the difference between its presentation as three quatrains in editions of Dickinson's verse since 1891 and its lineation in fascicle 11, the poet's private handwritten copy. There, the word "tonight" is set off at the beginning of the line following "moor," evidence to Smith of Dickinson's "breathless sexuality" (*Rowing in Eden: Rereading Emily Dickinson* [Austin: University of Texas Press, 1992], 65). Smith reads Dickinson's intention as emphatic: *tonight* as exclamation/demand. But reading the set-off "tonight" as a panting exclamation seems too crude in the case of a poem whose distinction rests in the speaker's subtle, witty control of its erotic voice.

12. The boat as symbol of the soul is to be found in the Renaissance emblem tradition. This tradition explains the steady destruction of Cole's boat (representative of the soul of his voyager) in the *Voyage of Life*. Pamela J. Belanger in *Inventing Acadia: Artists and Tourists at Mount Desert* (East Greenwich, R.I.: University Press of New England, 1999) traces the ubiquity and prominence of scenes of vessels wrecked or tossing on stormy seas in American art of the 1830s to 1870s. It was a genre of distinct spiritual significance.

13. "Parlor-Plants and Flowers in Winter" in *Plain and Pleasant Talk about Fruit, Flowers, and Farming* (New York, 1859) quoted Henry Ward Beecher: "The thermometer [of the parlor] should never be permitted to rise above sixty degrees or sixty-five degrees; nor at night to sink below forty degrees. . . . [T]he chill of a temperature below forty degrees will often be as mischievous to tender plants as frost itself." A proper degree of evening coolness was as difficult to achieve in the Victorian period as the correct degree of daytime warmth. (I met this quotation in Domnhall Mitchell, *Emily Dickinson: Monarch of Perception* [Amherst: University of Massachusetts Press, 2000], 322 n.19.) ED writes Maria Whitney in September 1884, "The plants went into camp last night, their tender armor insufficient for the crafty nights" (L 948). "Camp" may have been the shelter of the conservatory.

14. See White Flower Farm Catalogue, Fall 2001 (Litchfield, Conn.), 20–23.

15. See Leyda, II, 30. Mrs. Jackson, then Helen Hunt, wrote to her sister Ann: "[last night] we walked down to Prof. Hitchcock's to see a night bloom-

ing cereus—the first I ever saw; it is surely the solemnity & poetry of blossoming." Hitchcock's textbooks were used by Emily Dickinson; he probably influenced her attraction to tropical flowers.

16. See Leyda, II, 269.

17. Martha Dickinson Bianchi, *Emily Dickinson Face to Face* (Boston: Houghton Mifflin, 1932), 136.

18. Ibid.

4. The "Garden in the Brain"

1. MacGregor Jenkins, *Emily Dickinson, Friend and Neighbor* (Boston: Little, Brown, 1930), 9.

2. Ibid., 91.

3. Penelope Hobhouse, *Plants in Garden History* (London: Pavilion Books, 1992), 224, 225. This "new reading matter took every advantage of the scientific botany introduced by Linnaeus and expanded by [Antoine de Jussieu's] *Genera Plantarum Secundum Ordines Naturalis Disposita,* which arranged plants according to natural affinities rather than sexual distinctions."

4. Sharman Apt Russell, *Anatomy of a Rose: Exploring the Secret Life of Flowers* (Cambridge, Mass.: Perseus, 2001), 4.

5. Michael Pollan, *The Botany of Desire, A Plant's-Eye View of the World* (New York: Random House, 2001), 77.

6. Russell, *Anatomy of a Rose,* 70.

7. Ibid., 70–71.

8. Ibid., 71.

9. Mary Loeffelholz, "Corollas of Autumn: Reading Franklin's Dickinson," *The Emily Dickinson Journal,* vol. 8, no. 2 (1999), 61.

10. Ibid., 63.

11. Elizabeth A. Petrino (*Emily Dickinson and Her Contemporaries* [Hanover, N.H.: University Press of New England, 1998]) calls attention to Dickinson's "If she had been the Mistletoe / And I had been the Rose" (Johnson's poem 44), a poem-message sent to Samuel Bowles in 1858, saying that ED's rejection of the rose suggests that she "rejects the decorative function common for women" (146). Certainly Dickinson appears to prefer the contradictory role of "Druid," with its implications of magical power. Druids were also sun-worshippers. Bowles is often described as her "Sun," so she may be paying him a subtle compliment by calling herself a Druid.

12. Pollan, *Botany of Desire*, 70, 77.

13. Russell, *Anatomy of a Rose*, 49.

14. Alfred Habegger, *My Wars Are Laid Away in Books* (New York: Random House, 2001), 439.

15. In her essay entitled "'Neighbor – and friend – and Bridegroom –': William Smith Clark as Emily Dickinson's Master Figure" (*The Emily Dickinson Journal*, vol 9, no. 2, [2002], 48–85), Ruth Owen Jones proposes that Professor Clark, who taught botany at Amherst College and was co-founder with Edward Dickinson of the Massachusetts Agricultural College, inspired "I tend my flowers for thee –" and, indeed, all the "Master" literature. Born in 1826, Clark died two months before ED in 1886. Jones demonstrates that Clark's life and the poet's had much in common: friends like Samuel Bowles, "cousins" like Maria Whitney, and in particular that passion for flowers cherished by "Emily's Master figure." Jones's assertion that this passion was "unusual for a man in the 1860s" (53), like another claim—"The only other men besides Prof. Clark that [ED] knew who adored flowers were . . . Professor Tuckerman, and T. W. Higginson" [55]—mars a valuable essay since Samuel Bowles was famous for loving flowers, as did many Victorian men. (See my Chapter 1. Jones herself reveals that Clark's male students enthusiastically organized an Amherst Floriculture Society, and in this they had much company in most Victorian towns.) Professor Clark possessed beauty, personal magnetism, and intellectuality, but not "Master"'s spirituality and his propensity to illness. Nor was ED known to maintain a correspondence with him as she did with Bowles, Wadsworth, Lord, and the other "Master" candidates. Though unconvincing on its primary grounds, Jones's essay is valuable for addressing the issue of botanical knowledge in mid-Victorian Amherst and in the Dickinson family. For example, she tells us that Clark grew "*Victoria regia* water lilies at his Massachusetts Agricultural College's Durfee Plant Houses, ornate greenhouses modeled after London's Kew Gardens" (72).

16. Barton Levi St. Armand, *Emily Dickinson and Her Culture: The Soul's Society* (Cambridge: Cambridge University Press, 1984), 278.

17. See St. Armand, *Emily Dickinson and Her Culture,* where he writes perceptively about ED's fascination with the sunset: "If dawn followed . . . then resurrection and redemption were secure: if it did not, there was only the eternal abyss and limbo of those who mourned without hope" (278). For ED, the arrival of spring after winter was similarly important. If spring came,

there was eternal life; if it did not, there was only everlasting winter—and death.

18. Habegger, *My Wars Are Laid Away in Books,* 622.

5. Gardening with Emily Dickinson

1. Martha Dickinson Bianchi, "Emily Dickinson's Garden," *Emily Dickinson International Society Bulletin,* vol. 2, no. 2, (Nov./Dec. 1990), 4.

2. Ibid., 2.

3. See *Letters of Emily Dickinson,* ed. Mabel Loomis Todd (1894), quoted in Willis J. Buckingham, *Emily Dickinson's Reception in the 1890s* (Pittsburgh: University of Pittsburgh Press, 1989), 346.

4. Guy Leighton, *The Emily Dickinson Homestead: A Historical Study of Its Setting with Recommendations for Preservation and Restoration.* M.A. Thesis, Department of Landscape Architecture and Regional Planning, University of Massachusetts, Amherst, 1978, 24, 25, 43.

5. Emily Dickinson represented her favorite flowers differently at different times. It was even possible for her to omit an obvious favorite (like the gentian or the Indian pipe) when ranking her flowers. She wrote no poem for the *Daphne odora,* although one of her letters—sent just before her death—called it "as beautiful as Delight can make [it]" (L 1037). Yet surely the violet, like the gentian, aroused her affection quite as much and over a longer period of time than the daphne, while the Indian pipe provoked summary praise, seeming to her "the preferred flower of life" (L 769). It seems clear, however, that Dickinson loved wildflowers best, judging from her protestations to that effect from girlhood until her final hours, when the ("sweet") arbutus figured in her memories (L 1038).

Epilogue: The Gardener in Her Seasons

1. ED wrote to Mrs. Thomas Field around 1878, "Expulsion from Eden grows indistinct in the presence of flowers so blissful, and with no disrespect to Genesis, Paradise remains" (L 552). The phrase "expulsion from Eden" probably derives from the title of a well-known painting by Thomas Cole, *Expulsion from the Garden of Eden.* The theory that "Paradise remains" in the pure American landscape was the theme of Cole's "Essay on American Scen-

ery" (1836). It is entirely possible that Orra White, Dickinson's instructor in linear and perspective drawing at Mary Lyon's, might have introduced her to the works of this poet-painter so beloved in New England in the 1840s.

2. John F. McDermott and Nancy Andreasen, psychiatrists. See *The Washington Post,* May 14, 2001, A7.

3. See Robin Asleson and Barbara Moore, *Dialogue with Nature: Landscape and Literature in Nineteenth-Century America* (Washington, D.C.: The Corcoran Gallery of Art, 1985), 27.

4. Andrew Wilton, "The Sublime in the Old World and the New," in *American Sublime: Landscape Painting in the United States, 1820–1880,* ed. Andrew Wilton and Tim Barringer (Princeton, N.J.: Princeton University Press, 2002), 25.

5. According to the Oxford English Dictionary, a time of "calm, dry, mild weather, with hazy atmosphere" that occurs either in late October or in November. Use of the adjective "Indian" has been variously attributed: to the Indians' belief in the southwestern god Cautantowwit, to their attacks on white settlements just before winter, to the underhand trickery associated with "Indian" warfare, to the colors of both autumn and Indian dress.

6. Alfred Habegger, *My Wars Are Laid Away in Books* (New York: Random House, 2001), 156, 161.

7. In her fine essay, "Emily Dickinson and the Calvinist Sacramental Tradition," *ESQ,* vol. 33 (2nd quarter 1987), Jane Donahue Eberwein writes that "the 'unobtrusive Mass' [Dickinson] intuits [in this poem] seems to be a requiem that confers peace on its participants by affirming a cosmic order that both accepts and transcends death" (76).

8. Harold Bloom, *The Western Canon* (New York: Harcourt Brace, 1994), 295.

9. See Judith [Banzer] Farr, "'Compound Manner': Emily Dickinson and the Metaphysical Poets" (1961), in *On Dickinson: The Best From "American Literature,"*ed. Edwin H. Cady and Louis J. Budd (Durham, N.C.: Duke University Press, 1990), passim, for an analysis of the resemblance in vision and technique of ED's poems to those of John Donne, George Herbert, and Henry Vaughan, for a discussion of her exposure to metaphysical verse in the *Springfield Republican,* and for a description of what were probably ED's pencil markings—light, double, different from Susan Dickinson's coarse underlinings—in metaphysical texts of the Dickinson collection, Houghton Library.

10. Martha Nell Smith and Ellen Louise Hart remind their readers that Susan may have failed to edit ED's poems because she desired to "showcase the entire range of Emily's writings: letters, humorous writings, illustrations." *Open Me Carefully,* ed. Hart and Smith (Ashfield, Mass.: Paris Press, 1998), xvi. Susan's heartbreak over the death of her eight-year-old son in 1883 and her wretchedness during Austin's affair with Mabel Todd resulted in a loss of the strength and serenity which might certainly have been necessary to so formidable an undertaking.

ACKNOWLEDGMENTS

I would like to offer cordial thanks to the many curators, special collections and research librarians, museum and permissions registrars who assisted my quest for the rights to reproduce texts and illustrations that appear in this book. For the Dickinson texts and images of the Dickinson family, friends, and grounds, my thanks to Leslie A. Morris, Curator of Manuscripts at Houghton Library, Harvard University, and Susan Halpert of her staff; to Tevis Kimball, Curator of Special Collections at the Jones Library, Amherst, Massachusetts, with special appreciation of her search for information among unlikely sources; to Cynthia Dickinson, Curator of The Dickinson Museum in Amherst, especially for information about the Dickinson garden in the nineteenth century; and to Daria D'Arienzo, Curator of Special Collections in the Amherst College Library.

I express my gratitude also to the following individuals and institutions who gave permissions for and information about other images in the book: Dorothy Davila and Michelle Lamuniere of the Harvard University Art Museums; Linda Lott, Research and Rare Book Librarian at Dumbarton Oaks Studies in Landscape Architecture, Harvard University; Hope Mayo, Curator of Printing and Graphic Arts at Houghton Library, and Thomas Ford of her staff; Jonathan Lightfoot of the Museum of Fine Arts, Boston; Danelle Moon, Reference Manager of Manuscripts and Archives at the library of my alma mater, Yale University (whom I thank in particular for her swiftness and the merciful price assigned the manuscript and photograph I wished to reproduce); the permissions staff of the National Gallery of Art, Washington, D.C., and of the Brooklyn Museum of Art; Roberta Zonghi, Keeper of Rare Books and Manuscripts at the Boston Public Library; the permissions staff of the Cooper-Hewitt, National Design Museum, Smithsonian Institution; Cathy Frye, Assistant Editor, National Museum of Women in the Arts; Julie Zeftel of the Photograph Library of the Metropolitan Museum of Art, New York City; Mel Ellis, Director of Operations of the New Britain Museum of Art, New Britain, Connecticut; the permissions staff of the Colby College Museum of Art, Waterville, Maine; Elizabeth E. Fuller, Librarian, the Rosenbach Museum and Library, Philadelphia; and Christopher Webster of the Tate Gallery, London.

I am grateful to Mark Brown, Curator of the Martha Dickinson Bianchi Collection at Brown University Library, for his response to my questions about gardening texts in that archive.

Two of the illustrations in this book—the "Rear door of the Homestead" and "Lithograph view of Main Street, Amherst"—I first encountered in Polly Longsworth's *The World of Emily Dickinson* (New York, 1990).

To work with the superb staff of Harvard University Press is a great pleasure. Margaretta Fulton, General Editor for the Humanities, gave me wise counsel and tactful support as well as real practical aid in achieving the right to reproduce a crucial painting. My thanks go also to her capable assistant, Alex Morgan. Mary Ellen Geer, Senior Editor and herself a writer, prepared the manuscript with the special care, precision, and sensitivity I now associate with her. Marianne Perlak, Art Director, and an imaginative gardener, devoted her distinctive artistic skill to the book's design.

The book's title was established by the late, loved Edward Carter II, husband of Louise. When we announced our intention to collaborate on a study of the "the gardens of Emily Dickinson," Ted said quietly, "You should call it that." I wish he had lived to see his title plain!

To my husband, George F. Farr, Jr., who during the forty years of our marriage (and my writing life) has so often been asked to "Read this!" and "Tell me what you think!" I offer the "Gratitude [that] bears / When Obelisk decays." For his expert advice and sympathy, for his patient interest in my interest in the poet, and for those generous occasions when my eye and ear have been informed by his own, thanks will always be needed and will always be inadequate.

Finally: A strange thing occurred in the course of producing this book. When Dickinson's poems were first published in 1890, Roberts Brothers of Boston chose a picture of white Indian pipes, painted by one of her first editors, Mabel Loomis Todd—Emily called them "the preferred flower[s] of life"—to appear on the book jacket. These ghostly growths that the poet habitually culled from land beyond the Homestead are rare and were becoming so, even in her day. But suddenly an especially silvery cluster of Indian pipes sprang up and began to flourish in the shadow of Mary Ellen Geer's house as she was editing the manuscript of this book. "A tribute to you from Emily," I joked. But after all, "There are more things in heaven and earth . . ."

Index of Poems Cited

Index

plants/flowers as gifts, 23, 36, 42, 44–47, 50, 52, 104, 150, 161, 198, 231–232, 238–239, 244, 307n20; roses, 234–237; sending plants/ flowers as gifts, 3, 5–8, 26, 46, 54–55, 60, 96, 175–177, 249, 312n60; shrubs, 234–239, 243–251; and wildflowers, 20–21, 41, 53, 59, 84, 93–94, 99, 105, 125, 132, 136–137, 230, 323n5

IMPORTANT RELATIONSHIPS: with Austin Dickinson (brother), 55–56; with Charles Wadsworth, 2, 34, 37, 41, 199, 277, 308n31; with Edward Dickinson (father), 5, 19–20, 55–56, 148, 295; with Emily Norcross Dickinson (mother), 4, 53, 136; with Lavinia Dickinson (sister), 49–50, 318n36; with Otis Lord, 34, 41, 56–60; with Samuel Bowles, 2, 34–42, 44–47, 49, 57, 119, 152, 197–198, 277–278, 308n31, 310nn35,41; with Susan Dickinson (sister-in-law), 34, 41, 50, 52–54, 57–58, 76, 102–104, 119, 172, 280, 284–285, 303n31, 318n36; with Thomas Wentworth Higginson, 13–14, 32–33, 41, 63–66, 70–72, 179

POEMS. *See* Index of Poems Cited

POETRY COLLECTIONS: *Poems* (1890), 2, 14–15, 102, 131–132, 142, 178, 194, 305n7; *Poems, Second Series* (1891), 15; *Poems, Third Series* (1896), 11, 15

Dickinson, Emily Norcross (mother), 10, 15, 83; death, 136, 149, 170; illness, 7, 38; interest in flowers, 3–4, 6, 17–19, 53, 218–219, 223,

229, 235, 294; marriage, 17–18, 149–150

Dickinson, Gilbert (nephew), 170, 325n10

Dickinson, Lavinia ("Vinnie") (sister), 2, 10, 27, 50, 70–71, 129, 169, 219, 269, 274, 317n29, 318n32; courted by Joseph Lyman, 21, 306n19; domestic activities, 49, 125; and ED's death, 59–60, 136–137, 227, 318n36; and ED's poems, 14; interest in flowers, 3, 17, 23–24, 72, 90, 109, 120, 123–125, 215, 217–218, 221–223, 241, 294

Dickinson, Martha. *See* Bianchi, Martha Dickinson

Dickinson, Samuel Fowler (grandfather), 15, 18–19

Dickinson, Susan Gilbert (sister-in-law), 2, 13, 30, 50, 62, 67, 91, 95, 127–129, 153, 173, 192–193, 215, 269, 290, 293, 306n19, 307n24, 316n17, 324n9; and ED's death, 318n36; ED's love for, 50, 52–54, 57–58, 76, 102–104, 119, 172, 280, 284–285; ED's obituary by, 5–6, 45, 263; and ED's poems, 5–6, 14, 207, 325n10; interest in flowers, 17, 54, 123, 223, 241, 306n11; marriage, 41, 54, 101, 306nn11,16, 325n10; as "Master," 34, 308n31; and Samuel Bowles, 36–38, 40–41, 44, 54, 160–161, 200; writings by, 3, 5–6, 294

Diseases, plant, 141, 225–226, 238, 262, 270

Disraeli, Benjamin: *Endymion,* 103

Domenichino (Domenico Zampieri), 275

Donne, John, 292, 324n9

Dickinson poems are reprinted by permission of the publishers and the Trustees of Amherst College from the following volumes: *The Poems of Emily Dickinson: Variorum Edition,* ed. Ralph W. Franklin (Cambridge, Mass.: The Belknap Press of Harvard University Press), copyright © 1998 by the President and Fellows of Harvard College; *The Poems of Emily Dickinson: Reading Edition,* ed. Ralph W. Franklin (Cambridge, Mass.: The Belknap Press of Harvard University Press), copyright © 1998, 1999 by the President and Fellows of Harvard College; *The Poems of Emily Dickinson,* ed. Thomas H. Johnson (Cambridge, Mass.: The Belknap Press of Harvard University Press), copyright © 1951, 1955, 1979, 1983 by the President and Fellows of Harvard College; Dickinson letters are reprinted by permission of the publisher from *The Letters of Emily Dickinson,* ed. Thomas H. Johnson (Cambridge, Mass.: The Belknap Press of Harvard University Press), copyright © 1958, 1986 by the President and Fellows of Harvard College.

Publication of this book has been supported through the generous provisions of the Maurice and Lula Bradley Smith Memorial Fund.

Library of Congress Cataloging-in-Publication Data

Farr, Judith.
The gardens of Emily Dickinson / Judith Farr with Louise Carter.
p.   cm.
Includes bibliographical references (p.) and index.
ISBN 0-674-01293-3 (alk. paper)
1. Dickinson, Emily, 1830–1886—Knowledge—Gardening.
2. Dickinson, Emily, 1830–1886—Knowledge—Botany.
3. Gardening—Massachusetts—Amherst.
4. Gardens in literature.   5. Flowers in literature.
6. Botany in literature.
I. Carter, Louise.   II. Title.

PS1541.Z5F265   2004   2003056973
811'.4—dc22